EMBATTLED ISLAND

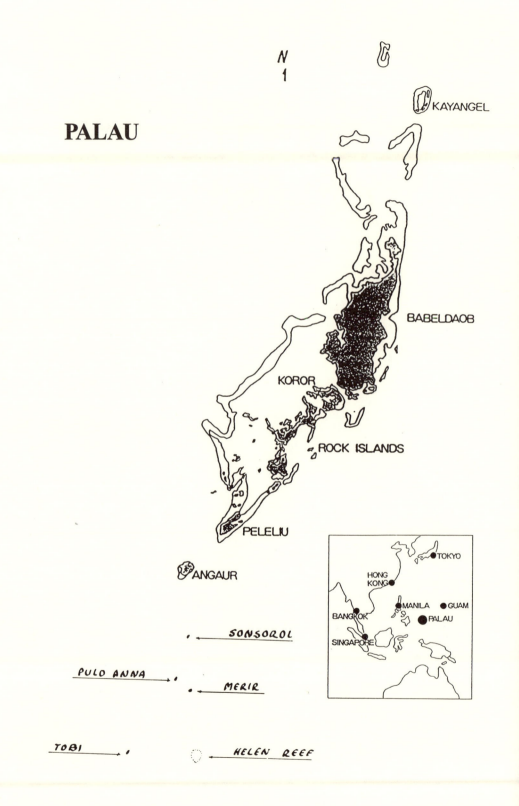

PALAU

EMBATTLED ISLAND

Palau's Struggle for Independence

Arnold H. Leibowitz

PRAEGER

**Westport, Connecticut
London**

Library of Congress Cataloging-in-Publication Data

Leibowitz, Arnold H.
    Embattled island : Palau's struggle for independence / Arnold H.
Leibowitz.
        p.   cm.
    Includes bibliographical references and index.
    ISBN 0–275–95390–4 (alk. paper)
    1. Palau—History—Autonomy and independence movements.   2. Palau—
Foreign relations—United States.   3. United States—Foreign
relations—Palau.   I.   Title.
DU780.L45   1996
996.6—dc20   95–30700

British Library Cataloguing in Publication Data is available.

Library of Congress Catalog Card Number: 95–30700
ISBN: 0–275–95390–4

First published in 1996

Praeger Publishers, 88 Post Road West, Westport, CT 06881
An imprint of Greenwood Publishing Group, Inc.

Printed in the United States of America

The paper used in this book complies with the
Permanent Paper Standard issued by the National
Information Standards Organization (Z39.48–1984).

10 9 8 7 6 5 4 3 2 1

To Sandy, with much love

Contents

Acknowledgments

During the course of writing this book, I tried to talk to as many people as possible who were involved in the ratification of the Palau Compact and especially the politics of the Salii administration, both in Washington and in Palau. I think it fair to say that although not all people talked to me and not all were equally forthcoming, I was able to talk to persons on all sides of the issue and discuss their attitudes at great length. To all of these people who very kindly cooperated in the effort to write this book, I acknowledge not only their friendship but also their support for establishing a full record of that trying time. I received a number of documents from the executive branch, the Congress, and the General Accounting Office that were not previously available to the public. Many officials in Palau and in the United States were kind enough to review drafts of sections of the book.

In addition to these officials, I want to acknowledge scholarly support, especially that of a number of people who reviewed the book in draft and advised me at some length on Palauan customs and issues that I might not have known. I want to thank, especially, Mary McCutcheon, Professor of Anthropology and Sociology at George Mason University and the leading Palauan anthropologist; Dirk Ballendorf, Professor of History and Micronesian Studies at the University of Guam and the first director of the Peace Corps in Palau; and George Milner, former deputy director of the Office of Territories in the Department of the Interior. They reviewed the manuscript both to ensure historical accuracy and to enlarge my understanding of the dynamics of the executive branch-Palau relationship.

A number of friends reviewed the book in manuscript for clarity and correctness and I am very thankful for their support. In this connection, I want to especially thank Martin Kohn and Mary Conabee, who had the fortitude to review the manuscript more than once. Special thanks goes to my daughter, Wendy, who reviewed the book with the kind of painstaking thoroughness that only a professional editor and relative can give. The book has gained enormously from the care and loving concern she lavished on the book. Finally, Hilda Vanover, my secretary, was kind enough to make the many changes and keep track of the enormous number of documents over the three years this book was in composition, and it is a pleasure to publicly recognize this.

Preface

I had not intended to write this book. During the dramatic events of 1987 and 1988, I had considered writing a book on Palau and its people and had begun to take extensive notes. But in the succeeding months, I questioned whether it was appropriate to talk in depth about a former client and, therefore, put the project aside and decided to go no further. In 1989, and then more frequently in 1990 and 1991, a series of advocacy pieces appeared—speeches, monographs, and books—which seemed to me, intentionally or not, to do an injustice both to President Salii and to the people of Palau. Palau also began to change. It seemed important to include this broader perspective.

This is one of the very few, detailed, contemporary histories of a Pacific nation-state. I hope there will be others. Small states require their own histories just as large nations do.

This is, as well, the first detailed history of the U.S. decolonization process. Imperialism is painful. The process of withdrawal turns out to be painful as well, and in Palau it was very painful.

Ernest Hemingway once advised a writer "to tell it true." I have been impressed at the different reactions to my own efforts to tell this story. In the States and Washington, where advocacy was very strong, it appears to still be present. Many people either will not talk to you or will talk to you only very guardedly. By late 1991, I decided to revisit Palau and talk to all I could about the Compact then and now. In Palau, where there was so much more to lose, and, indeed, where so much has been lost already, reluctance to talk was not the case. People, regardless of their views in the past or even at present, were more than ready to talk to me and discuss very openly their vision of what the facts were and what the situation is.

That persuaded me. In Palau, knowledge is an intimate thing. There is a Palauan saying: "Some knowledge, like the coconut juice, goes from darkness to darkness." If the Palauan people were prepared to light that darkness, then I felt my obligation not only to Lazarus Salii but to the people of Palau to tell the full tale.

In only a few points in the book, as far as I know, have I been strongly condemnatory. I focused on those instances where I believed government officials did not play by the rules and, insofar as that occurred, endangered democracy. There is no excuse for that, and I don't accept it whether they did so in favor of the Compact or against it.

In other respects, I have tried to follow Hemingway's admonition; I have tried "to tell it true."

Introduction

If you fly west from Washington, D.C., staying north of the equator, and fly past Los Angeles, past Hawaii, past Guam——nineteen hours in the air——about two hours before you would reach the Philippines, you will be above the Republic of Palau, the newest independent nation in the world. Palau is comprised of a group of more than a hundred tropical islands in the southwest corner of Micronesia, holding slightly less than 16,000 people. It was until recently the last remaining part of the U.S. Trust Territory, the last trusteeship in the world.

From afar, from the air, the islands of Palau are the most beautiful islands in Micronesia, particularly the Rock Islands——the tiny, umbrella-shaped limestone islands——providing secluded beaches amid clear tranquil channels, and, when covered with thick jungle growth as most are, mystery and unexplored frontiers as well.

On the ground only a few houses are visible amidst the tropical foliage. Penetrating the privacy of these houses is difficult, but if you could have done so prior to Independence Day, October 1, 1994, you would have observed a fierce, ongoing struggle for power. The struggle was complex, embracing the elected and traditional leadership of this small republic, three committees of the U.S. Congress, the Departments of State, Defense and Interior, and a variety of antimilitary, antinuclear groups from Japan, Australia, Europe and the U.S.

This book tells the story of a small island nation's struggle for independence.

Pronunciation of Palauan Names

Palauan names look very formidable, but because many letters are silent, the names are much simpler to pronounce than to spell. Thus, in the Palauan language, the *g* that follows the *n* is silent, as in Ngiraked (pronounced near-a-ged). The same is true of the *ch* and the *t* that precedes the *m* so that the name Tmetuchl is pronounced muh-tool.

The double *ii* is pronounced as a long *e* as in Salii (pronounced soll-ee), Rengiil (pronounced wren-eel), or Remeliik (pronounced rem-e-leek). The *uhe* diphthong is pronounced as a *w* as in Uherbelau (pronounced wer-be-lau).

In two-syllable names, the accent is on the second syllable; in the case of names of three syllables, the accent is on the first syllable.

List of Key Officials

U.S. Congressional Officials

Beirne, Jim. Senior Counsel of the Senate Energy and Natural Resources Committee, aide to Senator McClure.

de Lugo, Ron. U.S. Congressman and Chairman of the Subcommittee on Insular and International Affairs of the Committee on Interior and Insular Affairs.

Farrow, Jeffrey. Staff Director, House Subcommittee on Insular and International Affairs of the Interior and Insular Affairs Committee; aide to Congressman de Lugo.

Johnston, Bennett. U.S. Senator. Chairman of the Senate Energy and Natural Parks Committee.

Lagomarsino, Robert. U.S. Congressman. Ranking Minority member of the de Lugo Committee.

McClure, James. U.S. Senator. Ranking minority member on the Senate Energy and Natural Parks Committee.

Miller, George. U.S. Congressman. Successor to Congressman Morris Udall as Chairman of the House Committee on Interior and Insular Affairs.

Mukaihata, Gail. Staff member, House Subcommittee on Insular and International Affairs of the Interior and Insular Affairs Committee; aide to Farrow.

Roth, Stanley. Staff Director, House Asia and Pacific Affairs Subcommittee of the House Committee on Foreign Affairs.

Solarz, Stephen. U.S. Congressman. Chairman of the House Asia and Pacific Affairs Subcommittee of the House Committee on Foreign Affairs.

Stayman, Al. Staff member of the Senate Energy and Natural Resources Committee and aide to Senator Johnston. Subsequently appointed as Deputy Assistant Secretary of the Office of Territories and International Affairs, U.S. Dept. of the Interior.

Udall, Morris. U.S. Congressman. Chairman of the House Committee on Interior and Insular Affairs.

U.S. Executive Branch Officials

Berg, James. Director, Office of Freely Associated State Affairs, Department of State.

Hills, Howard. General Counsel, Office of Freely Associated State Affairs, Department of State.

McCoy, Janet. High Commissioner of the Trust Territory of the Pacific Islands.

Sanjuan, Pedro. Assistant Secretary of the Department of the Interior for Territorial and Insular Affairs.

Zeder, Fred. President Reagan's Personal Representative for Micronesian Status Negotiations, Department of State.

Palau Executive Branch Officials

Basilius, Bonifacio. Aide to President Salii.

Etpison, Ngiratkel. Third President of Palau, January 1989 to January 1993.

Isaac, Philip. Attorney General under Presidents Salii and Remengesau.

Mirando, Michael. Stateside attorney, Aide to President Salii.

Nakamura, Kuniwo. Fourth elected President of Palau, January 1993 thru Independence Day, October 1, 1994.

Ngiraked, John. Minister of State under President Salii.

Oiterong, Alfonso. Vice President of Palau under Remeliik; head of IPSECO Task Force.

Remeliik, Haruo. First elected President of Palau from January 1, 1981, to June 30, 1985.

Remengesau, Thomas. Vice President under President Salii.

Remengesau, Thomas, Jr. Vice President under President Nakamura.

Rengiil, Wilhelm. Minister of Natural Resources under President Salii.

Salii, Lazarus. Second elected President of Palau 1985-1988.

Uherbelau, Victor. Counsel to President Remeliik, Minister of State under President Nakamura.

Willter, Haruo. Minister of Finance, director of Washington office, close aide to President Salii.

Palau OEK Officials

Koshiba, Joshua. President of Palau Senate.

Olikong, Santos. Speaker of the Palau House of Delegates (1985-88); strong opponent of the Compact.

Salii, Carlos. Speaker of the Palau House of Delegates (1981-85); brother of President Lazarus Salii.

Palau Judicial Officials

Hefner, Robert. Northern Marianas Judge, sitting specially in Palau.

King, Edward. Chief Judge, Federated States of Micronesia Supreme Court, sitting specially in Palau.

Nakamura, Mamoru. Chief Justice, Palau Supreme Court.

Ngiraklsong, Arthur. Member, Palau Supreme Court.

O'Brien, Frederick. Member, Palau Supreme Court.

Sutton, Loren. Member, Palau Supreme Court.

IPSECO Officials

Mochrie, Gordon. Managing Director and principal shareholder of IPSECO.

Syrett, Stephen. Vice President, Morgan, Grenfell & Co., in charge of IPSECO negotiations.

Palau - Others

Basilius, Polycarp. Prominent businessman and supporter of President Salii.

Gibbons, Yutaka. High Chief Ibedul.

Heinrick, Sulial. Alleged conspirator in the slaying of President Remeliik.

Maidesil, Mistycal. Key prosecution witness in Remeliik assassination case.

Ngiraikelau, Namiko. Second key prosecution witness in Remeliik assassination case.

Ramarii, Patrick. Self-confessed killer of President Remeliik.

Smith, Patrick. Counsel to High Chief Ibedul Yutaka Gibbons.

Tmetuchl, Melwert; Tewid, Leslie; and Sabino, Anghenio. Alleged assassins of President Remeliik. Convicted by trial court; acquitted for lack of evidence by Palau Supreme Court.

Tmetuchl, Roman. Chairman of Palau Political Status Commission. Runner-up in 1980, 1984, and 1988 presidential elections.

Toribiong, Johnson. Attorney in Palau, counsel to Roman Tmetuchl, and runner-up in 1992 presidential election.

Chronology of Events in Palau

September 30, 1579. Sir Francis Drake's *Golden Hind* sights Palau on its round-the-world journey. Brief contact with Palau.

December 11, 1710. Captain Francisco de Padilla and the *Sentissima Trinidad* make contact with Palau.

February 15, 1712. Captain Don Bernardo commanding the *Santo Domingo* lands at northern tip of Babeldaob.

August 10, 1783. Captain Wilson's *Antelope* runs aground near Ulong Island.

1788. Publication of George Keate's account of the *Pelew Islands*, the first published account of local customs and politics.

1832. American whaler, *Mentor*, wrecked at Ngeruangel reef.

1840-1900. A number of Western commercial trading vessels stop at Palau: Andrew Cheyne (1863-1866, 1881), Edward Woodin (1861-1863), Alfred Tetens (1862-1868), David O'Keefe (1871-1885).

1885. Pope Leo XII accepts Spain's claim to Palau.

1885-1899. Palau under sovereignty of Spain.

1891. Capuchin missionaries establish first permanent Catholic mission.

1899-1914. German administration of Palau.

1900. Population of Palau between 3,000 and 4,000, down from estimated precontact population of 25,000 to 50,000.

1914. Japanese armed forces occupy Koror and Angaur on behalf of the Allied Powers.

1920-1945. Japanese administration of Palau.

1921. League of Nations awards Emperor of Japan a Class C mandate over German Micronesia, including Palau.

1944. United States invades Palau Islands. Brutal battles of Angaur and Peleliu.

1947. United States becomes the administering authority of the Trust Territory of the Pacific Islands, including Palau.

1965. The first Congress of Micronesia. Roman Tmetuchl, John O. Ngiraked, and Lazarus Salii elected as Palau representatives.

1966.   The Congress of Micronesia (COM) petitions President Lyndon B. Johnson to establish a Micronesian Status Commission.

1967.   The COM establishes the Future Political Status Commission (FPSC). Lazarus Salii of Palau selected as chairman.

October 1969.   FPSC decides upon free association as the preferred status for Micronesia. Negotiations with the United States begins.

1970.   United States presents a plan under which Micronesia would become a permanent territory, or commonwealth, of the United States.   Micronesians reject plan.

1971.   U.S. creates Office of Micronesia Status Negotiations and establishes an inter-agency task force on Micronesian status.

April 1972.   The Marianas breaks away from the other districts and begins separate status negotiations with the United States.

July 1972.   COM demands negotiations on option of independence.   United States is unwilling.

April 1975.   Palau Political Status Commission created to begin separate negotiations with the United States, with Roman Tmetuchl leading the movement in Palau. Lazarus Salii, the chief Micronesian negotiator and the father of free association, opposes the Palau separate negotiation.

April 1978.   United States and Micronesia sign the Hilo Principles, recognizing the unilateral right to opt out.

July 1979.   Palau adopts Constitution with nuclear substances ban.   Nuclear substances ban can be suspended only by 75 percent affirmative vote.

January 1, 1981.   President Haruo Remeliik sworn in as first elected president of Palau.

January 1981.   Reagan administration conducts formal review of the initialed Compact.

September 1981.   President Remeliik signs $32 million preliminary contract with UK contractor, IPSECO, to build 16 megawatt power station in Palau.

October 1981.   United States agrees to Compact as initialled.

January 1982.   Palau, led by Ambassador Salii, moves to reopen the Compact.

August 26, 1982.   United States and Palau sign Compact of Free Association (COFA) and nine subsidiary agreements.

February 10, 1983.   First COFA plebiscite.   Vote is 62 percent in favor of COFA, but insufficient majority to waive Palau's nuclear ban.

June 8, 1983.   Loan agreements signed for IPSECO power plant deal.

September 1984.   Second COFA plebiscite.   COFA receives 66 percent.

March 2, 1985.   Palau defaults on first IPSECO payment.

June 30, 1985.   President Haruo I. Remeliik is assassinated.

August 28, 1985.   Salii elected president in special election.

December 6, 1985.   Melwert Tmetuchl, Leslie Tewid, and Anghenio Sabino arrested in connection with the assassination of President Remeliik.

December 17, 1985.   Morgan, Grenfell and other banks sue Palau for $32 million in New York court in connection with IPSECO.

February 21, 1986.   Third COFA plebiscite.   COFA receives 72 percent.

February 24 thru March 6, 1986.   Trial of alleged Remeliik assassins results in conviction.   Sentenced to 25 to 35 years.

September 17, 1986. Palau court rules (*Gibbons v. Salii*) that 75 percent is needed on revised Compact.

November 14, 1986. COFA approved by U.S. Congress under P.L. 99-658.

December 2, 1986. Fourth COFA plebiscite. COFA receives 66 percent.

June 30, 1987. Fifth COFA plebiscite. COFA receives 67 percent.

July 1987. Plaintiffs file lawsuit to stop vote on Constitutional Amendment; *Merep v. Salii* court denies injunction.

July 1, 1987. Nine hundred government workers furloughed.

July 14, 1987. Constitutional Amendment passed by OEK.

July 16, 1987. The Palau Supreme Court reverses the convictions of alleged killers of Remeliik. Orders acquittal.

August 4, 1987. Vote on constitutional amendment. Fourteen of sixteen states approve by majority vote.

August 21, 1987. Sixth COFA plebiscite. COFA receives 73 percent.

August 28, 1987. Salii, Ibedul, and plaintiffs settle *Merep v. Salii*.

August 31, 1987. Women reinstitute lawsuit *Ngirmang v. Salii*.

September 7, 1987. Bedor Bins is murdered.

September 8, 1987. *Ngirmang* case is withdrawn.

November 1987. IPSECO payments to Lazarus Salii and other Palauan leaders are revealed.

November 1987. Territories Subcommittee requests GAO Report.

November 1987. Territories Subcommittee retains special consultant, Thomas Dunmire, to investigate.

December 17, 1987. House Foreign Affairs Subcommittee holds hearings on Palau.

January 1988. Dunmire submits report. Territories Subcommittee suppresses Dunmire report.

January 1988. Senate Committee on Energy holds hearings on Palau. Women in opposition to Compact testify.

March 3, 1988. House Foreign Affairs Subcommittee approves Palau Compact.

March 28, 1988. U.S. Senate passes Palau Compact.

March 31, 1988. Women reinstitute lawsuit. *Ngirmang* case renamed *Fritz v. Salii*.

April 10, 1988. International Commission of Jurists issues its report.

August 20, 1988. Salii commits suicide.

August 29, 1988. *Fritz v. Salii* decided. Constitutional amendment invalid.

November 1988. Ngiratkel Etpison elected president.

August 1989. H.R.175 passes with Special Prosecutor included.

August 18, 1989. GAO issues its report on Palau.

February 6, 1990. Seventh COFA plebiscite. COFA receives 59.8 percent.

November 1990. State Department suggests unilateral termination of Palau trusteeship.

July 1991. David Webster is appointed special interim prosecutor in Palau.

March 2, 1992. Special Prosecutor issues arrest warrants for killers of Bedor Bins.

March 20, 1992. Prominent politician John O. Ngiraked, his wife, and two others are arrested in connection with the assassination of President Remeliik. Patrick Ramarii is self-confessed killer.

June 22, 1992. Alleged killers of Bedor Bins acquitted.

September 18, 1992. U.S. Interior Department fires Webster as prosecutor, citing an undisclosed previous suspension from the Florida Bar Association.

November 1992.   Constitutional Amendment passed to permit ratification of Compact by majority vote.

January 14, 1993.   John O. Ngiraked's trial begins, with former U.S. Assistant Attorney Jerry D. Massie as prosecutor.

April 29, 1993. Judges find Ngiraked and his wife Emorita Kerradel guilty of aiding and abetting first degree murder. A third codefendant is acquitted.

November 9, 1993. Compact ratified with a 68 percent approval vote.

September 6-9, 1994.   National Museum of Palau convenes an international conference on "The War in Palau: Fifty Years of Change."

September 11-15, 1994.   Commemoration of fiftieth anniversary of the battle of Peleliu.

October 1, 1994. Palau celebrates its independence.

1

The Suicide of President Salii; The Strange Funeral

On August 20, 1988, the president of Palau killed himself with one shot to the head. At hearing the news, Palauans could not believe that their president, Lazarus Salii, had committed suicide. Salii's predecessor, Haruo Remeliik, the first President of Palau, had been assassinated three years before. The possibility of murder was real. Suicide was not consistent with Salii's character. He had been known as a fighter, a determined leader who, even if events went against him, continued to plan and struggle. Moreover, the timing was wrong. A major political rally was scheduled for the very next day, Sunday. There, Salii was to have announced his candidacy and be formally nominated for reelection. His longtime secretary, Joyce Isechal, had delivered the nominating petitions to him at his home just the night before. She had brought some letters as well. He gave them back to her. "These can wait 'til Monday. We'll work on them then," he said.

Salii's minister of state, John O. Ngiraked, had talked to him on the telephone the day before his death. Ngiraked was in Los Angeles organizing Palauans living outside Palau to vote in the election. These Palauan statesiders had provided the margin of victory for Salii in 1985. They would be needed again. Ngiraked had called to protest once more the timing of the rally. He wanted Salii to delay the announcement of his candidacy for reelection to permit representatives of the off-island Palauans to arrive in Palau and be present at the convention. And Ngiraked was ambitious; he wanted to be at the rally himself. But President Salii had refused, claiming his party, Ta Belau (One United Palau), was pressing for his announcement.

Nonetheless, the facts were incontrovertible. The revolver Salii had requested from his bodyguard four months earlier was found on the floor by his chair. The front door to his home was dead-bolted from the inside. Salii's wife, maid, and chauffeur were eating lunch in the back of the house in full view of the side door. No intruder could have entered the house, killed the president, and fled unseen.

After the coroner's report, when the facts of Salii's death became clear, the talk changed from "Was it suicide?" to "Why suicide?" Had something occurred on Saturday to change his mood so drastically as to crush his general determination and destroy his plans for the Sunday rally?

Palau's Washington representative, Haruo Willter, a longtime confidant of Salii's, had returned to Palau early Saturday morning. He had immediately telephoned the president and then driven over to see him. For about two hours they drove together. Salii liked to discuss serious matters while driving; the car was secure from eavesdroppers, and driving relaxed him. They discussed the Compact, ever the Compact, the unratified agreement between the United States and Palau on which Salii had staked his entire career and his presidency. Where his predecessor had failed, he would succeed over the opposition of Greenpeace in the United States, the antinuclear movements in Japan, the Palau judges, and the local chieftains in Palau. But in the U.S. Congress, the House Subcommittee on Territories had blocked Salii's efforts to ratify the Compact. The subcommittee would not budge. Salii had not expected that. Would they come around? Willter thought they would not. What did they want? Did they want him? Willter had asked Congressman Ron de Lugo, chairman of the subcommittee, and his aide, Jeffrey Farrow, that very question. "No, our concern is only with the people of Palau." But Willter did not believe them. Willter did not sugarcoat his message to Salii. "They want you out of office." After their long, painful talk, Willter dropped Salii off at his home. It was midmorning. For a few hours more Palau's world would remain unchanged.

The date of Salii's funeral, like his suicide, was surrounded by controversy. Ngiraked argued for at least a week's delay to permit dignitaries from outside Palau to attend. But Tina Salii, Salii's widow, did not wish the burial postponed. Vice President Thomas Remengesau, desirous of stability, did not want to delay his accession to the presidency.

It rained on Friday morning, the morning of the funeral. I had been retained by Salii almost two years before to represent Palau before the courts of Palau and in Washington to obtain ratification of the Compact. After I received the stunning news of his death, I immediately flew to Palau to attend the funeral. On the way to the Catholic church service, Ngiraked told me the Palauan proverb: "When a great man dies, the heavens weep." I doubted the Palauans had such a saying. Ngiraked, extremely sophisticated and eager to impress an outsider, was quite capable of inventing such romance at short notice.

The white stucco church was decorated outside with religious murals painted along the side and above the main portal, the murals somewhat faded by now. Inside, a few solid red and yellow window panes suggested stained glass. We sat on metal folding chairs. There were no hymnals or

Bibles for the congregants. Bishop Martin Neylon, the presiding bishop of the Marshalls and Carolines, conducted the service. He was assisted by two Micronesian priests and another aged, white priest, a Spanish Basque named Fr. Juan, from Angaur, Salii's home island. Fr. Juan's presence was a remarkable vestige of nineteenth century Spanish control over Palau.

Sunday best in Palau usually was only a small step removed from everyday clothes, but some special effort was being made by the women to dress more formally today. The men generally wore black pants and a rayon, untucked Aloha shirt, and the women, a lightweight dress. The practice of dressing in white for church—still the fashion in Polynesia—was never introduced in Palau. We had arrived early, and I spent the minutes before the ceremony berating myself for wearing a light beige suit. The U.S. representatives were solemnly dressed in black suits. Jim Berg, head of the Office of Freely Associated State Affairs (OFASA) in the State Department, and Fred Zeder, Berg's predecessor, who now headed George Bush's fund-raising effort, had negotiated with Salii as far back as the early seventies, when Salii headed the Joint Commission on Political Status for all of Micronesia. Fortunately for me, Rear Admiral Thomas Johnson and his aides were in dress whites. The admiral, head of the U.S. Naval Command at Guam, had been a frequent golfing partner of Salii. Janet McCoy was also present. She was the director of the Territorial Office in the Department of the Interior and former high commissioner of the Trust Territory, and had known Salii since the late seventies when he worked as chief of planning in the Trust Territory office in Saipan. Berg, Zeder, Johnson, and McCoy came not only to represent the administration; they came to grieve as friends.

Gail Mukaihata, a tall, striking Asian-American, represented the House Interior and Insular Affairs Committee. Her relatively low rank offended Salii's supporters, although others accepted the gesture as the best that could be done given the terrible relations between Palau and the House Committee on Interior and Insular Affairs. Congressman Morris Udall, who chaired the committee, was suffering from Parkinson's disease and was probably too sick to come.

Congressman Ron de Lugo, chairman of the House Subcommittee on Territories, and Jeffrey Farrow, his staff director, had waged an open battle against ratification of the Compact, the agreement between Palau and the United States effectively granting Palau independence in exchange for military base rights. They had also supported an unremitting public relations campaign against Salii that had damaged him in the States and in Palau as well. De Lugo and Farrow may have stayed away out of a legitimate fear for their safety.

The choir began to sing in Palauan, the songs quite beautiful—some melodies standard to the Catholic mass, others distinctively Micronesian. The family entered, walking alongside the coffin, and the poignancy of the moment, lost in the logistics of the comings and goings of the crowd, returned with a sudden rush. Two odd notes were struck during the day's activities: the small number of people in attendance and the impersonal tone of the funeral ceremony. Although newspaper accounts described an overflowing throng in the church, in fact the service was not crowded. There were many empty seats along the sides and a few in the center.

The service itself was surprisingly cold. The bishop, who had known Salii for many years, spoke of redemption, forgiveness, and resurrection. But whether it was the controversy surrounding Salii's life or the controversy surrounding his death, the bishop consciously delivered a restrained, standard service. There was no eulogy. Salii's name was not mentioned.

This pattern repeated itself elsewhere. At the airport there was no indication President Salii had died, not even a single picture framed in black crepe paper. At the Palau Pacific Resort, the Japanese-owned, luxury tourist hotel in Koror, which was keenly attuned to Palauan sensitivities, there was no change from the normal tourist routine.

After the church service, the officially printed "Programme for the State Funeral of the Late President Lazarus E. Salii" called for a convocation in the Senate Hall of the Palau legislature, an institution that bore the splendid name in Palauan of the House of Whispered Decisions, the Olbiil Era Kelulau, or the OEK. The Senate Hall was decorated in purple, the Catholic color of mourning, at the behest of Mrs. Salii. The seating at the convocation was much more formal than at the church service, and dress was more formal as well. All wore jackets and most were clad in dark suits. On the dais sat Sylvester Alonz, a representative of the OEK; the Ibedul, the young, traditional leader of Palau; the new President, Remengesau; and Ms. McCoy. Attendees were shown to their seats: nonPalauans sat to the left, Palauan dignitaries in the center, and the mourners, including Salii's family, his wife, Tina, and their four children—three daughters and a teenage son—to the right.

The casket, half-opened, draped in flowers, dominated the center of the room. Death did not become Salii. The bullet had crushed his skull and the reconstruction left his face more angular than it was in life, his face losing its babylike chubbiness. There was an innocent charm in Salii that death had taken from him. I remembered how pleasantly surprised he was when I asked to have a picture taken with him. In life, his chunky body never seemed at rest and his dark, round face changed rapidly, displaying the passions within him. His style was quite different from the expressionless "cool" style of many Palauans. I expected him even now, as he lay in state, to somehow rise up and direct the gathering.

The chief justice, Mamoru Nakamura, who had sat behind me in church with his wife, had been placed on the dais. He looked somewhat uncomfortable at being on such public display. I looked for the other native Palauan judge, Arthur Ngiraklsong. He was, like Nakamura, dressed in a black suit and was seated at the back of the Palau dignitary section, reflecting his desire to be as far from the center as possible. In the aggressive, passionate world of Palau, fortune had found two soft-spoken, unassuming Palauans and elevated them to the bench. Judges Loren Sutton and Frederick O'Brien, the two white judges resident in Palau, less deferential to Palauan tradition, had taken off their jackets in the sweltering second-floor chamber and sat together in the center section, somewhat prominently, in short-sleeved, white shirts and ties.

Salii's relative by marriage, Alan Seid, conducted the program and occasionally translated the Palauan speeches and prayers. He announced the foreign dignitaries who had come to Palau for the funeral and read some of the condolences from Pacific Island governments. President and Mrs. Reagan and Secretary of State George Shultz sent messages of condolence that were well phrased. I detected Jim Berg's skilled hand. The Ibedul, one of Palau's traditional leaders, wore dark glasses which, together with his business suit, gave him an odd, hoodlumlike air. He seemed unsure how to handle the suicide death of his political opponent. When called upon to speak, he offered a long, rambling prayer in Palauan which, in stilted translation, appeared to say little about Salii.

President Remengesau's speech was the best, and it was very good indeed. He did not have a reputation as a good speaker, in either Palauan or English, but he delivered a well-phrased address in English, linking Salii to Remeliik as presidents who had given their lives for their country and who sought an agreement, the Compact, with the United States that had been fought over and negotiated for twenty years. It was the first and only time in all the speeches that any specific achievement of Salii was noted and the only time the Compact, which was the centerpiece of Salii's political career, was mentioned. Alonz, representing the OEK, read the legislature's memorial resolution. It sounded cold. He held out the paper to Mrs. Salii; she didn't reach for it. It fell to the floor. The bitterness between the OEK and the Salii family was well known.

Then a Palauan clan chief spoke. He recounted a story—I remembered it as a fable from Aesop—of an old man who brought his sons together and asked them each to break a stick. They did this easily. He then tied the sticks together and asked them to break the bundle, but they could not. Nothing more. No moral. No stated link to the present situation. But the Palauans understood. In the coming election, Palauans should rally around the Ta Belau's candidate for president of Palau, Ngiratkel Etpison, governor of a small state in the north, and a somewhat surprising choice, since he did not know English.

The moral of the story would go unheeded. Two men, Moses Uludong and Remengesau, had already declared their candidacies. Roman Tmetuchl, a perpetual presidential contender and longtime political opponent of Salii, had also declared. Ngiraked confided to me that soon he would announce his candidacy as well, and there were rumors that the Ibedul and Santos

Olikong, Speaker of the House, a strong opponent of the Compact, might also run. Salii's death had created a vacuum, and Palauan politics abhorred a vacuum.

At the end of the ceremony, which lasted about two hours, came the benediction. In tearful Palauan—it was not translated—Pastor Mokokiil Solomon spoke to the assemblage. His voice broke continually. At last, someone was expressing the emotion of the occasion. After the benediction, all present were given flowers. The casket was opened; and, as his or her name was called, each person stepped forward, paid last respects to Salii, laid a flower on the coffin, offered sympathy to the family, and exited the hall.

All those who had come, both inside and outside the hall, were asked to go to Salii's home for lunch. Embarrassingly, few people went. Almost all of the large quantity of food, enough to feed hundreds, remained covered and untouched. Close friends of Salii told me that the dignitaries had to catch planes or felt that this part of the observance was optional and a bit intrusive. Palauans would come later that evening and, according to Palauan custom, would chant and dance to distract the family and support them. But that night, again, few came. There was no dancing and almost no chanting. That the people of Palau would distance themselves from Salii in death was shocking, especially when compared to the mourning after Remeliik's death. Then, the government workers—who, in order to obtain a pay raise, had firebombed Remeliik's office and burned it to the ground—had camped out at his home, passionately singing and dancing, refusing to allow the funeral ceremonies to end. Where were these government workers—Salii's supporters—now?

Salii's burial on Sunday on his home island of Angaur was also sparsely attended. Attendance by outsiders was discouraged by the family. Only three patrol boats—fast but small—were officially available for mourners. At Remeliik's burial in Peleliu, a fleet of small boats had motored back and forth carrying hundreds of mourners.

Why had so many stayed away? Perhaps Salii's supporters saw his suicide as a betrayal. They had trusted him to persevere. They had fought with him against the U.S. Congress, against the local judiciary, and against the media who had mocked them and scorned their efforts. Now he had abandoned them. To Palauans, courage and style are important; they take great pride in both. Suicide by their leader brought shame not only on Salii, but on themselves. Perhaps it was more than that. Talk of corruption in his administration, of a possible indictment or even the arrest of Salii himself, had been bruited about.

The tension in Palau had grown as Salii pressed harder and harder to ratify the Compact. Each vote on the Compact—there had been three in the last year alone—heightened bitterness and the frustration of the people. Four court cases had been filed in the last twelve months; each judicial complaint, response, argument and decision further strained and wearied the general populace. The ties of family, clan, and village that bound the island had shattered; peace and tranquility gave way to violence and death. That the vast majority of the people wanted the Compact, as well as the political stability, the U.S. funding, and the Japanese tourism and investment that would come once the relationship with the United States was settled could not be denied. But not at the cost of peace. Had Salii gone too far? Had his opponents?

The people of Palau were somber, apprehensive, and uncertain. They were also exhausted; their energies totally spent in the attempt to build a new democratic nation in a society without a tradition of nationhood or democracy and at the same time negotiate a Compact with a sophisticated superpower over strong opposition in the U.S. Congress. It had been too much. We had let them down, brought their leader to his death, one whom we had supported and who supported us. They had tried, had given all they had. They deserved better than to be where they were now.

Notes

1. Page 1. *Palau*. The choice of whether to spell the island "Palau" or "Belau" or whether "Peleliu" should be "Beleliu" was once hotly debated. Island nationalists favored the *B* for a while, but that direction seems to have reversed itself. I have used the letter *P*, following Palau constitutional spelling and that of the documents produced for the Independence Day celebrations.

2. Pages 2-3. The text simplifies in two respects:

   (a) The text uses the name "Subcommittee on Territories." Technically, the Subcommittee of the House Interior and Insular Affairs Committee with jurisdiction over the territories is called the Subcommittee on Insular and International Affairs. The text is more descriptive if not precise. For readers not familiar with the Washington bureaucracy, it seemed easier to utilize the nomenclature "Subcommittee on Territories" and thus avoid confusion with the name of the full committee.

   (b) The text states that Jim Berg, as head of the Office of Freely Associated State Affairs (OFASA), succeeded Ambassador Fred Zeder, head of the Office of Micronesian Status Negotiations (OMSN). OFASA did succeed the OMSN, although its operating responsibility was somewhat different. Further, Fred Zeder held the title of ambassador of OMSN. Berg never served at the ambassadorial level.

3. Page 2. *I doubted the Palauans*. My skepticism was misplaced. Ms. Frank Quimby advises me that the Palauans do, indeed, have such a saying.

4. Pages 2-6. The text discussion of the funeral is based primarily on my own observations at the time, supplemented by subsequent interviews with a number of Palauans, both friends and foes of Salii. Newspaper coverage of the funeral rites was extensive but proved less insightful. K. Ola, "Mourners Gather for Salii Funeral," *Pacific Daily News*. Aug. 25, 1988, p. 1; K. Ola, "Salii Funeral Today," *Pacific Daily*

News, Aug. 26, 1988, p. 1; K. Ola, "Palau Mourns Salii's Death," *Pacific Daily News*, Aug. 27, 1988, p. 3; K. Ola, "Palau Looking to Future," *Pacific Daily News*, Aug. 28, 1988, p. 3; H. Graves, "Reconciliation Urged as Salii Tribute," *Pacific Daily News*, Aug. 28, 1988, p. 3.

5. Page 5. *President and Mrs. Reagan*. "Reagans Hail Palau's Salii," *Honolulu Star Bulletin*, Aug. 26, 1988, p. A-9.

2

Palau's Universe; The West Intrudes

To outsiders, the island world of the Republic of Palau appears extremely small: a population of less than 16,000, two-thirds of whom are concentrated in the urban center of Koror State. The Palau Islands stretch for about a hundred miles in a line from Tobi, Angaur, and Peleliu in the Southwest to the small circular atoll formation of Kayangel in the Northeast. Between them lie the beautiful Rock Islands; the larger islands of Koror and Malakal, the latter with its unique Micronesian resource, a sheltered, deep water harbor; and Babeldaob, the second largest island in all of Micronesia.

Traditionally for Palauans, this island world was a universe that ended just beyond the long barrier reef that sheltered almost all of the Palau islands. This universe was divided into two side heavens, northeastern and southwestern, corresponding to the political confederations and alliances of the Palauan precontact world. Fairly late in Palauan history, perhaps slightly more than 200 years ago, Koror, headed by its chief, the Ibedul, gained a tentative dominance over the southwestern-side heaven. The northeastern-side heaven was organized with its capital at Melekeok under the leadership of its chief, the Reklai. The Palauans had well-developed craftsmen's skills as well. The Palauan *kaep* were said to be among the fastest-sailing canoes in all Micronesia, and the *bai*, the large elevated meeting houses, were built with floor planks fitted so closely that the first European visitors failed in their efforts to slip pins between them.

Their world, though small, was not an easy one to master. The hostility of the side heavens was real, reflective of centuries of competition. At the village level there were continuous, serious disputes and, at times, open warfare. Although the Europeans who actively ruled Palau from 1885 onward, suppressed armed combat, the imposed peace between the traditional leaders, especially the Ibedul and the Reklai, remained a fragile one. The intense rivalry between the Ibedul and the Reklai continues to this day.

In Palau, the clan and family connections established by birth did not alone determine one's status, as they did in some other parts of Micronesia and Polynesia. They could be overcome by an individual's own exceptional accomplishments—showing unusual courage or a special skill—and this was expected.   Acquisition of wealth was proof of these exceptional achievements.   From this individual striving and competition, Palauans gained great selfconfidence, regarding themselves as the natural leaders of the Micronesian world, a world they believed they could control.   They pointed to the fact that during the early trusteeship period—in the 1950s and 1960s—when the United States governed all of Micronesia from Saipan, Palauans dominated the government of the Trust Territory of the Pacific Islands, occupying at times three-fourths of the department directorates.

I remember, and other lawyers have told me similar stories, how difficult it was to get any information—oral or written—from Palauan officials, even if necessary to advocate their cause. They understood that their world was fragile and easily torn asunder. Confidences, once given, could be betrayed. Guests were treated honorably but kept at a distance. If Palau was their universe, their heaven, Palauans were ever required to protect it and shield it from intruders.   The Palau world was an intimate island world.   It belonged to Palauans and was not shared with outsiders.

Prior to European contact, Palauans fashioned an impressive material culture with great stone causeways, monoliths, and terraced hillsides. When the Europeans arrived in considerable numbers, however, internal Palauan strife and Western disease had weakened their civilization.   The long population decline from, perhaps, as many as 50,000 prior to Western contact to about 3,000 in 1900 had begun.

The first important contact between Palau and Europe occurred when the British East India Company ship, the *Antelope*, commanded by Captain Henry Wilson, ran aground near Koror.   By great fortune, one of the *Antelope* crew knew Malayan, as did one of the islanders, permitting a rich discussion during these first contacts.   Significantly, the shipwrecked outsiders were helpless and had no ulterior purpose.   For three months, in the fall of 1783, the *Antelope's* crew stayed in Palau building another ship. A personal trust developed between Captain Wilson and the Ibedul. Captain Wilson regarded the Ibedul as a king, similar to British royalty. The comparison was not exact, however, either in terms of his selection or his position in Palauan society.

Although lineage was a factor, the title of Ibedul was conferred, not inherited.   Formally, the Ibedul was selected by the ranking clan women from Koror.   Once selected, the Ibedul became the head of the highest clan and the most powerful village official.   He was responsible for the care of the people under his charge, distributing work and produce to the clan.   In addition, Palauan chiefs, particularly a paramount chief such as Ibedul, had a sacred character. In the past, only these chiefs and designated mediums could communicate directly with the Palauan gods. While most Palauans are Christian today, including Ibedul, few would wish to undermine the powers of the local gods. Animal totems, such as the frigate bird, manta ray, and the fresh-water eel, are still respected in many Palauan communities. The Ibedul title itself acquired a sacred aura and power derived from its continuous transfer from individual to individual. At death, the title had a physical manifestation, a palm leaf, which the senior clan female removed from the Ibedul's body prior to its internment.

Captain Wilson was right in one respect. Like the British monarch, the Ibedul, to some at least, symbolized Palau. A recent, insightful travel writer recalls:

> One time I gave Kochi the news, a little too abruptly, that Ibedul Ngoriakl had died. Kochi was visibly shaken. I was surprised, for Kochi had never been one of those in awe of Ibedul. Then Kochi explained how important high chief Ibedul was to the well-being of the Palauan people, whatever you thought of the man who held the title.

At the Ibedul's request, Wilson and the crew of the *Antelope* weighed in on Koror's side in a number of local village battles against Koror's traditional rivals from Melekeok and the Northeast Confederation headed by the Reklai. Wilson's guns easily tipped the balance, cementing the relationship with the Ibedul and beginning the Ibedul and Koror's dominance of Palau. Thus began as well the islanders' view that they could manipulate for their own benefit the technology (guns, iron, and money) and interests of outsiders who came to Palau. In the Compact dispute this vision proved to be an illusion, as outsiders pierced Palau's world at will and, ultimately, destroyed Palau's self-confidence.

When Wilson departed, the Ibedul sent Lee Boo, reputedly his second son, back with the British to England while Captain Wilson left a sailor behind in Palau. The "noble savage" was the rage in intellectual circles in England, and Lee Boo quickly became, as had Omai, his predecessor from Tahiti, the star of London's intelligentsia and social set. When Lee Boo died of smallpox at age twenty, after less than six months in England, he had become more than just a curiosity. His graciousness left a lasting impact. Lee Boo's story was incorporated in the texts for British grade school children. At Lee Boo's grave in St. Mary's church in London, reflecting the depth of feeling of those who knew him, Coleridge wept at his epitaph:

Stop, Reader, stop!——let Nature claim a Tear——
A Prince of Mine, Lee Boo, lies bury'd here.

In 1788, a few years after Lee Boo's death, George Keate, who never traveled to Palau, using Wilson's notes and journals, wrote his idealized version of the *Antelope* crew's adventures. The book, *An Account of the Pelew Islands...Composed From the Journals of Captain Henry Wilson...*, entranced England and, in translation, Europe as well. The Palauans were "benevolent children of nature," "the mildest and most benevolent specimens of unenlightened men." If, in the West, the story of the wreck of the *Antelope* and the tale of Lee Boo retains a fascinating charm, in Palau the story is remembered for its political impact. In Melekeok, the home of the Reklai on the island of Babeldaob, they remember it as the time when they lost status to the Southwest, to Koror and the Ibedul.

Horace Holden's memoirs, *Narrative of a Shipwreck*, written fifty years later, told of his terrible experience when he was inadvertently caught up in the Reklai-Ibedul rivalry. Holden's ship, the New Bedford whaler *Mentor*, was caught in a violent storm and carried onto the reef off Kayangel at the northern tip of Palau in Reklai country. Half of the crew was swept away to their deaths. The eleven survivors clung desperately to the deck of the badly listing ship. Exhausted and frantic, they watched hopefully as canoes came from Kayangel to meet them. But instead of providing aid, the Palauans stripped the men and the wreck of muskets and other valuables. Holden and his shipmates temporarily escaped by launching a small boat and rowing frantically away. Pursuing canoes overtook them and forced them ashore at a village in northern Babeldaob. There, with the help of a resident beachcomber, Charles Washington, they were saved by persuading their captors that they were Americans, not Englishmen, and therefore not responsible for the English support of Koror and the Ibedul. Nevertheless, it was not until six months later that eight of the unlucky eleven Americans (three Americans were left on Babeldaob as hostages) and three Palauans accompanying them were finally able to leave. Once again, a storm blew them off course, their boat coming to rest on the very small island of Tobi in southwest Palau. There they were treated as prisoners and, effectively, as slaves. They were forced to submit to painful tattooing over their chests and arms and then distributed to different high-ranking men who dragged them as prizes from house to house, showing them off to their neighbors. In November 1834, two years after their ordeal in the Palau Islands began, Holden and his companions saved themselves again by seizing native canoes and paddling to the British ship *Britannia* when it appeared offshore. By then, of the original group on Tobi, three had died of starvation, another was clubbed to death after being caught stealing a coconut, and two had been pushed out to sea in canoes to perish.

The *Mentor* experience was an extreme, bizarre example of the Reklai-Ibedul rivalry. It has been rationalized in Palau and seen by some outside Palau in a racial, colonial context. The fate of the *Mentor* crew reflected the poverty of the islands as well. On the extremely small island of Tobi, semistarvation was the norm. Extreme poverty can change the soul of man.

The *Antelope* and *Mentor* experiences dramatized the continuing hostility between the northeastern half of Palau, the people of Babeldaob, and the southwestern side of Palau, the people of Koror. In the midst of this conflict, white men were valued for their weapons and manipulated for their support.

Walking around the Palau Islands, the casual visitor does not see this stormy past and the islands' domination by European powers, which lasted for slightly more than one hundred years. The early contacts were primarily commercial and primarily British. After the accidental contacts by Sir Francis Drake and the *Golden Hind* in 1579 in the course of his round-the-world voyage and Captain Wilson, the British came as entrepreneurs, generally trying to exploit the continuing strife among the various islands for their own commercial benefit. The British East India Company had a vague idea that Palau could act as a way station for expanding trade routes to China. The plan never materialized, so no continuing British governmental presence in Palau was necessary.

One of the most venturesome of the British soldiers of fortune was Andrew Cheyne, who tried to take advantage of the Reklai-Ibedul rivalry. Eventually, in 1866, the Ibedul had Cheyne killed for gun running to his enemies in Melekeok. The British government then sent a warship to Palau that summarily investigated the Cheyne killing and condemned the Ibedul. The Ibedul was shot and killed—Palau tradition holds that it was not the real Ibedul who was killed—and the British in 1883 forced the Ibedul and Reklai to sign a peace treaty, bringing to an end the warfare, if not the rivalry, between these chieftains and their allies.

Official Spanish rule and the beginning of a continuing European presence dates from 1885, when the Pope, arbitrating the conflicting claims of Germany and Spain, ruled in favor of the Spanish. A permanent Catholic presence was established in 1891 when the Ibedul gave two Capuchin priests an old *bai* for use as a permanent mission. A smattering of Spanish words and the continuation of the Catholic religion in Palau—today about one-third of the island is Catholic—is the legacy of formal Spanish rule.

Western imperialism began most forcefully in 1899, when Germany purchased Palau from Spain. German sovereignty was short, lasting only until the outbreak of World War I. German restructuring of copra production and phosphate exploitation had a strong impact on land tenure patterns. But physical remains of the German rule are few. Perhaps the greatest legacy of the German rule is the scholarship that resulted. Today—a hundred years and more after they wrote—the names of Johann Kubary, Karl Semper, and Augustin Kramer remain the great names in Palauan studies. There are a number of German words in the Palauan language, but other external vestiges of the German economic influence and direct cultural impact has disappeared.

After World War I, Japan received a League of Nations mandate over Palau and the rest of Micronesia. Japanese rule over Palau, lasting thirty years, would bring sharp change. Japan, with its population pressures, somewhat limited natural resources, and geographic proximity, viewed the islands as an extension of the Japanese homeland. It undertook a major program of economic development and acculturation of the islands based on Japanese migration. Within ten or fifteen years, Micronesians found themselves a small and unimportant minority, living by sufferance in the midst of a rapidly growing Japanese civilization. By 1940, 84,478 Japanese nationals were living in Micronesia. More than one-quarter of these (23,767) were in Palau. Koror, "Little Tokyo," became the headquarters from which the Japanese coordinated their rule over all of Micronesia. The Japanese had completed what Captain Henry Wilson had begun: Koror became the preeminent island in Palau and the Ibedul became the preeminent traditional chieftain. Until immediately before World War II, the Japanese permitted Western religious missionaries as part of their "civilizing" of Palau. The Church of the Sacred Heart, where Salii's funeral service was held, was built in 1935. At the time of its construction, it was the largest nongovernment cement building in Koror.

A nonviolent movement with religious overtones, Modekngei, emerged in Palau in 1914 directed toward a revitalization of Palauan culture and resistance to the adoption of the trappings of the Japanese civilization. Its founder, Temedad, a former policeman, and his successor, Ongesii, understood and expressed the frustration of the Palauans at the discrimination, the arrogance, and the methods that the Germans and the Japanese used to dominate Palau. Modekngei adherents continued the movement underground until the final days of World War II.

The Japanese era endured physically and psychologically. By the end of World War II, nothing remained except the concrete foundation and a few stone steps of the Japanese colonial headquarters building, which once had sweeping verandas and a graceful courtyard flanked by nipa palms, and the grand Shinto shrine, which opened in 1940 in a three-day ceremony that included an official representative of the emperor. But on Koror, one could still see a number of former Japanese colonial buildings, now used for different purposes. The impressive Palauan courthouse building served under the Japanese as a Palau government office, the OEK once housed the Japanese telecommunications building, and the Palau museum structure served formerly as a Japanese weather station. If you knew where to look and you removed the overgrowth, there were other Japanese markers, remnants of schools, shrines, and memorials.

Psychologically, the Japanese era lives on, and Palauans are conflicted about it. Many remember vividly the patronizing attitude of the Japanese. During Japanese rule, very few Palauans were permitted schooling beyond the three-year public schools. The noteworthy exception was the Carpentry

Apprentice Training School established in Koror in 1926, but even this prestigious educational institution was geared only to the manual arts. There were no middle schools, no colleges, no normal schools. Few Micronesians could enter the flourishing commercial fishing, cultured-pearl, or commercial agricultural industries. Even in the phosphate mines of Angaur, where laborers were forcibly recruited to work the open pits, a practice the Japanese had to defend year after year at the League of Nations, the wages were openly discriminatory. Japanese were paid the most, followed by Chinese, Korean, Okinawan, and, finally, the lowest paid of all, Micronesian workers. Public works were also frequently the product of forced labor.

Nevertheless, older Palauans, most of whom speak some Japanese, accord to the Japanese period a nostalgia that softens, even erases, the memory of the cultural slights and the forced labor. They remember the construction boom of the late thirties which transformed Koror into a bustling small town with many Japanese-owned, small shops. Under the Japanese, storyboard wood carving reemerged as a native Palauan craft. Traditionally, Palauans carved and painted their myths of creation, local history, and romantic tales on the *bai*, the Palauan meeting houses. But the skill died out. Only as a result of the initiative and concern of the Japanese artist and anthropologist Hijikata Hisakatsu did Palauans relearn what is today their major woodcraft. Palauans born after 1945 cannot accept the patronizing attitudes their fathers knew and accepted. The much younger Palauans, those under 35, are neutrals in this debate. They are drawn to Japan for financial and geographic reasons and find to their pleasant surprise that in Japan they are accorded a special affection.

Japanese attitudes toward the Mandate Period are also mixed. Older Japanese view the Palauans and the other Micronesians as old friends with a shared experience. Younger Japanese, on the other hand, are embarrassed about the Japanese colonial period and appear eager to make amends. The Tokyo government has begun a foreign aid program for Palau and the Japanese tourists are coming to Palau, albeit in modest numbers. Guam and the Marianas are undergoing an economic boom resulting from Japanese tourists. These islands are the closest tropical islands to Japan and, like Bermuda and the Bahamas to the eastern United States, they represent to the young Japanese uncrowded beaches that easily accessible and safe. Palauans know this economic boom could be theirs as well. The Japanese have been cautious, however. They wait for political stability in Palau and political acceptance by the United States. Then there would be time for the large hotel deals that the aggressive Palauans thrust upon them. Then Palau could expand its airport to permit jumbo jets from Japan to land. With the Compact, Palau would be very attractive to Japanese investment. Without the Compact, Japanese investors stayed away.

Notes

1. Page 9. *The Palau Islands stretch*. The text is not quite accurate. The hundred-mile distance refers to the main archipelago from Angaur, Peleliu, to Kayangel. Tobi is one of the very small outliers, 300 to 400 miles to the southwest. I mentioned it in the text because Tobi reappears subsequently in this chapter in a prominent way.

2. Page 9. *Babeldaob, the second largest island*. Guam is the largest.

3. Page 11. The title transfer at death is described in D. R. Smith, *Palauan Social Structure* (1983), p. 308.

4. Page 11. The quotation is from K. Brower, *A Song for Satawal* (1983).

5. Page 11. *Coleridge wept at his epitaph*. D. Peacock, *Lee Boo of Belau*, 1987, p. 2.

6. Page 12. *Eight of the unlucky eleven Americans and three Palauans*. Of the fourteen, as noted in the text, six were to die on Tobi (four Americans and two Palauans). Edward Barnard, captain of the *Mentor*, and Bartlett Rollins, a crewman, escaped from Tobi in February 1833. Horace Holden and Benjamin Nute, another crewman, escaped from Tobi in November 1834. Calvin Alden, one of the three Americans left as hostage on Babeldaob, escaped as well. In addition to the Holden memoirs, the text relies on Captain Barnard's narrative. K. Martin ed., *Naked and a Prisoner: Captain Edward C. Barnard's Narrative of Shipwreck in Palau, 1832-1833* (1980), p.38. The remaining two Americans on Babeldaob, and one Palauan on Tobi were rescued by the *Vincennes* in December 1835. For the final events of the *Mentor* story, see M. McCutcheon, "The Great Hostage Caper," *Washington Post*, Sept. 4, 1988, Outlook, p. 1 and Martin, ibid, Appendix A and Appendix B, pp. 43-44.

7. Page 12. *The Mentor experience*. As related in the text, this is considerably foreshortened from the Holden memoirs and Captain Barnard's narrative. For U.S. newspaper reports of the *Mentor* shipwreck and the encounter of its crew with Palau, see R. G. Ward, ed., *American Activities in the Central Pacific 1790-1870*, Vol. 5, passim (Gregg Press).

8. Page 13. *The contact by Sir Francis Drake*. The question of whether Drake encountered Palau is not without controversy. I am persuaded by W. A. Lessa, *Drake's Island of Thieves* (1975).

9. Page 13. *Palau tradition holds*. K. Nero, "Cross-Cultural Performances: A Palauan Hoax," 1 *ISLA* 37 (1992).

10. Page 13. *Official Spanish rule*. Mary McCutcheon has pointed out to me that actually Palau fell on the Portuguese side of the line created by the Treaty of Tordesillas, although it is very close and navigators were not very good at calculating longitudes in those days.

11. Page 14. I have classified Johann Kubary as a German because he wrote his books in German. By birth, he was a Pole. D. Ballendorf tells Kubary's depressing story—his suicide after the death of his son, destruction of his home, and inability to sustain a museum interest in his work in the Carolines—in D. Ballendorf, "The Obscure Johann Stanislaus Kubary and His Estimable Discourses on Palauan Money," 14 *J. of Pacific Society* 19 (1991). See also W. Price, *Japan's Islands of Mystery* (1944), p. 148.

12. Page 14. Semper came to Palau as a result of a shipwreck. He stayed in Palau from March 1862 to January 1863, writing an insightful, detailed account of

Palauan daily life and culture. K. Semper, *The Palau Islands in the Pacific Ocean* (1982).

13. Page 14. Views of the Modekngei religion's origins and beliefs vary. I have relied primarily on a somewhat sympathetic account in M. Aoyagi, "Gods of the Modekngei Religion in Belau," in Ushijima and Sudo, eds., *Cultural Uniformity and Diversity in Micronesia* (1987), and K. Brower, *With Their Islands Around Them* (1974), pp. 53-55. For a less sympathetic account, see E. J. Kahn, Jr., *A Reporter in Micronesia* (1966), pp. 174-76.

14. Page 15. The conclusions with respect to the Japanese and Palauan attitudes toward the Japanese colonial period and toward each other at present are based primarily on my own interviews both in Palau and Japan. I am indebted as well to my discussions with Professor Dirk Ballendorf, the first Peace Corps director in Palau and the author of a number of articles on Palau. W. Price, *America's Paradise Lost* (1966) also comments on this, throughout.

15. Page 15. D. Ramarui, *The Palauan Arts* (1980) and Palau Museum, *Bai* (1969) are very useful locally published and authored publications describing the modern storyboard. Hera Owen, in her catalog of the work of Charlie Gibbons, the Palauan primitivist painter, notes as well the Japanese and German painters that came to Palau during the earlier colonial periods. H. W. Owen, ed., *Charlie Gibbons; Retrospective Exhibition Catalog* (1980), pp. 1-2.

3

The United States Invades Palau; The Brutal Battle for Peleliu

The United States invaded Peleliu and Angaur, two of the southern islands of the Palau Islands, in mid-September 1944: Peleliu on September 15, 1944; Angaur, two days later. Coincidentally, these were the home islands of the two men who were to become the first elected presidents of Palau: Remeliik from Peleliu and Salii from Angaur. The purpose of the invasion was to seize the small airfields on each island, thus protecting against flank air attacks on U.S. troops proceeding to free the Philippines. Optimistic estimates expected the fighting to be over in three or four days. That estimate may have been accurate six months earlier, when U.S. bombing had left the Palau Islands helpless, but by September the Japanese were well prepared.

The battle for Palau would be the most brutal battle of the Pacific War. The United States had waited too long to invade or, as it is now generally felt, should not have invaded at all. The combatants were as fine as the Pacific would ever see. Spearheading the amphibious landing was the First Marine Division, the Old Breed, officers and men who had fought together in the South Pacific for more than twenty-four months. At Guadalcanal, after bitter fighting, they had achieved the first Pacific victory by American ground forces in World War II and then moved on and captured Cape Gloucester on New Britain Island. Their regiments were headed by men such as Lewis "Chesty" Puller, the Marine Corps' most decorated officer, and Herman Hanneken, who already had earned a Congressional Medal of Honor. On Guadalcanal, Puller's regiment alone earned two Medals of Honor, five Navy Crosses, eleven Silver Stars, twenty Bronze Stars, and 364 Purple Hearts. These men were not just Marines and patriots, they were battle hardened, having proved to themselves and to the world they were men of extraordinary courage, dedication, and fighting skill. Backing up the

Old Breed was the Army's Eighty-first Infantry Division, the Wildcats, facing combat for the first time.

Opposed to them were 5,500 troops of the Japanese Fourteenth Infantry Division, the Sunlight Division, with battle honors stretching back to the Russo-Japanese War. The division had been reinforced in late April by Colonel Nakagawa Kunio and 6,500 troops of the elite Second Infantry Regiment. Nakagawa, in his early forties, had received nine medals for bravery and leadership and was recognized by his superiors as a brilliant tactician and combat commander. The Japanese had no illusion about the ultimate result. Tojo, Japan's Supreme Commander, made that clear in setting forth the Japanese objective to Major General Murai Kenijiro who, with Nakagawa, was in charge of defending Palau: "Your objective is to hold the island as long as possible to deny its use by the enemy to support their future plans, and kill as many Americans as you can before the last Japanese soldier dies at his post."

Murai and Nakagawa were on a suicide mission.

Terrain and time favored the defenders. By mid-September when the U.S. invasion fleets appeared, the Japanese had been preparing their defenses for six months. The U.S. troop landings were preceded by a thunderous naval and aerial bombardment that smashed all buildings and facilities above ground and blasted away some of the jungle cover on both islands. Angaur, ten miles south of Peleliu, approximately two miles long and one mile wide at its widest point, generally was flat, but its northwest corner held an area of rugged terrain, the Ramuldo. Ramuldo's landscape, a series of wooded coral ridges one to two hundred feet in height, was honeycombed with caves. Major Goto Ushio, commander of the island's garrison, had available to him only 1,400 troops and no heavy artillery, resources barely sufficient to defend just one possible landing area. Preinvasion intelligence photographs made the difference, as the U.S. invasion forces avoided the heavily fortified Green Beach.

Establishing a beachhead at Angaur was relatively easy, but destroying the enemy was difficult. Fighting on Angaur lasted almost a month. Remnants of Goto's force were compressed into the caves in vine-covered ridges of the Ramuldo at the island's northwestern tip. From there, in slowly diminishing numbers, they resisted the attempts of the 81st Infantry Division to dislodge them. It was late October before the last of Goto's forces succumbed. Two days before the last underground strong point was blasted, Major Goto and his 130 remaining soldiers launched an abortive counterattack. All were killed.

Peleliu was to be far worse. Peleliu was nearly six miles long and two miles wide. The southwestern base of the island was fairly level, but the northern arm was serrated by a series of tortuous ridges, called, in Palauan, the Umurbrogol, a maze of peaks, cave-pocked cliffs, and rubble-strewn defiles. The Marines would christen the ridges Five Brothers, Five Sisters,

Walt Ridge, Death Valley, and the two most famous: Bloody Nose Ridge and the Pocket, the site of the Peleliu Japanese command. The ridges and most of the island outside the airfield were thickly wooded. The scrub so completely masked the terrain that aerial photographs and preinvasion-day photos taken by U.S. submarines gave intelligence officers no hint of its ruggedness.

The beaches were mined with mine belts extending inland as much as 100 yards. Barbed wire and antitank ditches, backed up by well-camouflaged pillboxes and reinforced concrete blockhouses, barred the approaches. Nature provided the most formidable invasion obstacle; the coral reef of Peleliu extended over 600 yards. Because of the reef, troops and equipment making the assault had to be transported in slow amtracs. In the first ten minutes twenty-six had taken direct hits. In the next hour and a half, sixty were damaged or destroyed.

The Marines reached the shore exhausted, having taken a terrible battering. Late that afternoon, the Japanese counterattacked, led by thirteen light tanks. The Marine infantry line held and fired back with Sherman tanks, bazookas, antitank guns, and flamethrowers. Normally, casualties of 15 percent are considered more than enough to relieve a regiment. Puller's regiment suffered 33 percent in forty-eight hours. By the end of the third day, Puller's regiment alone had lost only six fewer men than the entire First Marine Division had lost at Guadalcanal.

By incredible determination and extraordinary courage the Old Breed established the beachhead. The fighting had just begun.

In earlier battles, the Japanese had based their defense on preventing the invaders from establishing a beachhead. On Peleliu, Nakagawa deployed only one-fourth of his men to repel the invasion and then let the Marines come to him. With dynamite and pickax, the Japanese had enlarged the hundreds of caves on Peleliu and blasted out new ones. The result was honeycombed caves with staggered levels, multiple passageways, and well-camouflaged and well-sited gun positions. Blast walls of reinforced concrete or oil drums filled with coral protected their small, well-concealed entrances. Most of the caves sloped steeply downward or had sharp turns just inside their mouths to protect against flamethrowers or tank attacks. Some caves were large enough to hold only one man. Others held hundreds. From mutually supportive positions, the Japanese covered nearly every yard of Peleliu from the beach inland to the center of Nakagawa's command post, deep beneath the coral rock in the center of the ridge system. In effect, the Japanese had constructed a defense-in-depth with the whole island as a front line.

The Japanese garrisons had laid in plentiful supplies of ammunition, food, and water, all stored in deep, subterranean caches. The defenders were ready for a long, drawn-out battle of attrition.

Paths that the Marine infantry had to use to scale the ridges were covered by positions sited to unleash a devastating crossfire. The Marines were permitted to scale the bluff, and then the Japanese would open fire with mortars, antitank guns, and machine guns, killing the Americans and throwing them down the gorges. Progress was painstakingly slow. The Americans sealed one cave with a TNT charge. The Japanese escaped to another through an unseen tunnel. If, finally, the cave's occupants were cornered, the Americans were subjected to a sudden suicide charge. The death throes were accompanied by grenades thrown at distances of less than three feet, bayonet attacks, and hand-to-hand fighting.

Finally, on September 30 the United States proclaimed the island "secured." The battle was to go on for almost two more months.

The island of Peleliu is solid coral. The Marines found it virtually impossible to dig through the coral. They had to lie on the surface with almost no cover and try to withstand the Japanese mortar and artillery fire. Each time a Marine hit the ground, the jagged coral cut his skin. Crawling along the ground painfully abraded a man's knees and chest. Because digging the usual toilet holes was impossible, excrement was everywhere, its stench blending with the noxious odors of uncovered corpses and discarded, rotting food, the whole hellish scene baking in the hot sun. Despite continuous spraying with DDT, flies and insects were everywhere on the battlefield spreading serious disease and irritating skin rashes. Water was strictly rationed. The U.S. ships, offshore, sent barrels of fresh water ashore. The barrels had been used to store diesel fuel. They were supposed to have been steam scoured, but under combat conditions, the barrels were not cleaned properly. The water seriously poisoned all who drank it.

In early October, for a few days winds cooled the air, but the relief was deceiving. The winds reached almost gale force, blowing clothes, weapons, excrement, food, and skeletal remains in a bizarre whirlwind. The storm passed. A few days later, the blazing heat returned. By the morning of November 25, seventy-two days after the invasion began, crushed by high explosives, cremated by flamethrowers, or entombed when their caves were sealed, the defenders occupied only one ridge. Nakagawa cabled the prearranged code words—Sakura, Sakura—that resistance was no longer possible. Having been refused permission by divisional headquarters to make a final annihilating charge, Nakagawa and Murai disemboweled themselves in their cave command post with ancient jeweled daggers in the traditional last rites of Japanese samurai warriors. Over 12,000 Japanese had died.

There were 6,336 First Marine Division casualties suffered on Peleliu: 1,252 killed, 5,274 wounded. Eight Marines won the congressional Medal of Honor, five posthumously. The Eighty-first Division suffered 2,433 casualties—542 killed and 2,736 wounded—in its first bitter exposure to battle.

There are monuments on Peleliu to the valor and sacrifice of these fighting men. At the base of Bloody Nose Ridge, the Japanese government has constructed a Peace Park of bleached cement surrounded by a grove of trees. Within the park stands a small Shinto shrine with an inscription in Japanese and English: "To all countries' unknown soldiers." The American Eighty-first Infantry Division is remembered by a granite column; some of the letters from its white limestone inscription faded now: "Lest we forget those who died here." Close by, on the southern end of Bloody Nose Ridge, stands a four-by three-foot red granite monument, dedicated in 1984 on the fortieth anniversary of the battle. Below the globe and anchor, the Marine Corps emblem, is a simple epitaph: "In memory of the Marines who gave their lives in the seizure of Peleliu."

Notes

1. Page 19. I want to thank Benis Frank of the Marine Historical Center in Washington, D.C., who reviewed the chapter as a former combatant and knowledgeable archivist. He was kind enough to discuss with me many of the details of the battle in addition to guiding me to important archival material.

2. Page 19. *Palau would be the most brutal battle.* Comparisons like this could be regarded as inappropriate. The verdict is not mine but that of a number of military historians. G. Garland and T. Strobridge, *Western Pacific Operations* (1971), pp. 284-286.

3. Page 22. *Nakagawa cabled the prearranged code.* The prearranged code signal is the interpretation of H. Gailey, *Peleliu 1944* (1983), p. 181. The Marine Corps official monograph of the battle interprets the final words solely as an indication of an inability to make contact and the word *Sakura* as the name of a city in Japan. F. Hough, *The Assault of Peleliu* (1950), App. F, p. 201.

4. Page 22. *Over 12,000 Japanese had died.* The number of Japanese killed is in dispute, at least from American sources. The U.S. Marine Corps official history cites 10,900 killed, while the army estimates 13,600. The precise American casualty totals are also still being changed. G. Garland and T. Strobridge, *Western Pacific Operations* (1971); Vol. 4 of U.S. Marine Corps, *History of the U.S. Marine Corps Operations in World War II*, p. 285, n. 81 and n. 82.

5. Page 22. *Eight Marines won.* The eight congressional Medal of Honor winners were Corporal Lewis K. Bausell, Private First Class Arthur J. Jackson, Private First Class Richard C. Kraus, Private First Class John D. New, Private First Class Wesley Phelps, Captain Everett C. Pope, Private First Class Charles R. Roan, and First Lieutenant Carlton R. Rouh. Corporal Bausell and Privates First Class Kraus, New, Phelps, and Roan died in the actions for which their medals were presented.

4

The "Nuclear-Free" Constitution; The Compact Fails

When World War II ended, the United States gained control of the 2,000 small islands of Micronesia, spanning an ocean area the size of the continental United States. In World War II, Micronesia as a whole, and Palau in particular, played crucial logistical roles. From Palau the Japanese attacked the Philippines and Indonesia; from the Marianas they launched the invasion of Guam; and from Truk, strikes on the Solomons and New Guinea. Subsequently, the Japanese used the Micronesian islands as a great defensive barrier to the liberation of the Philippines, Wake Island, and Guam.

To American planners and to the American public, Micronesia and Palau also were valued in relation to the pain of their conquest. The wounds in these battles were not yet healed. Loved ones still mourned their dead in personal terms. The U.S. ambassador at that time, Warren Austin, told the newly formed United Nations: "Tens of thousands of American lives, vast expenditure and years of bitter fighting were needed to drive the Japanese aggressors from these islands, which constitute an integrated strategic physical complex vital to the security of the United States."

The United States invented and gained U.N. approval for a new status to govern Micronesia: a strategic trust territory. As trustee of the strategic trust territory, the United States could fortify the islands to meet its military needs and report to the Security Council, where it had a veto. (Other trustee nations, governing ordinary trust territories, could not engage in military activities and reported to the General Assembly, not the Security Council.) In short, the United States could do pretty much as it pleased.

From the outset, some U.S. military men doubted Micronesia's military importance. In their opinion, the acquisition was justified solely on the grounds that it would prevent other nations from using the islands as a base of operations, the strategy of denial. General Dwight Eisenhower, testifying before the Senate Foreign Relations Committee, explained:

> We have here islands that in many instances are nothing but sandspits. They are of very little economic value. . . . But they are the spots on that great ocean surface that to-day provide a capacity and an ability for a nation that would seek to conduct aggressive operations across that ocean. They would have to use them. So long as we have them, they can't use them, and that means to me, even in their negative denial to someone else, a tremendous step forward in the security of this country.

Military goals and prospects drove Micronesia policy. The United States built a major missile tracking base at Kwajalein in the Marshalls and developed a variety of smaller training and surveillance bases elsewhere in Micronesia. In Palau, the military presence remained distant and abstract. No bases were built; only contingency plans formulated. U.S. ships and submarines—some nuclear, some not—moved swiftly through Palauan waters on the way to the Indian Ocean or returning to the States.

Little thought was given to the people of the islands. Social services were held to a minimum. During the fighting on Peleliu and Angaur, for example, the Palauans fled or were evacuated to the north to Babeldaob, the largest Palauan island. Now, the fighting over, they remained unnoticed. Their numbers were so small. Micronesia's population in all of its 100 inhabited islands then totalled less than 100,000 people; in Palau, slightly more than 5,000.

Although noncombatants, the Palauans had suffered greatly during World War II. Koror, the capital of the Japanese Pacific empire, was bombed to rubble. The islands of Peleliu and Angaur were denuded of vegetation. All Palauans on Peleliu were evacuated to Babeldaob, and the Angaurese, except for a few, were also sent to Babeldaob. On Babeldaob, the 5,000 Palauans retreated into the jungle, where they took shelter from the daily U.S. bombing of the 37,000 Japanese troops and military fortification. When it was safe, they could come forth and hunt for food. Endless famine was their collective memory. Palauans were reduced to living in the woods and scavenging for food while their islands were destroyed. The pain of the Palau population was constant. On the ground, the Japanese seized their farms and ordered them about with little concern for their welfare, while from the air, the United States continued their unrelenting fire. The pain of the Palau people, the experience of the horrors of advanced technological warfare, would have its consequence for the United States, but for the moment, it was ignored.

In the early sixties, the U.N. Visiting Mission to Micronesia sharply criticized the American administration, noting the inadequate economic development, poor educational programs, and lack of health care, the latter dramatically illustrated by the outbreak of polio in the Marshalls in 1962 at a time when antipolio vaccine was widely available in the United States. The next year a U.S. survey mission recommended accelerated development of

Micronesia as a prelude to permanent association between Micronesia and the United States. The United States increased funding for education, strengthened the schools with a large Peace Corps presence, established stateside standards for health, initiated the Micronesia Development Fund, and opened the islands to investors. For the first time, American citizens and flag vessels could enter Micronesia. Federal appropriations sharply increased from the $5-$6 million range of 1955-62 to $17-$36 million during 1963-69, $54-$81 million during 1970-75, and, finally, to $132 million a year before the trusteeship terminated in 1986.

While the United States was acting to preserve the status quo in the 1960s, the Micronesians had other ideas. They took the United Nations' concepts of "sovereignty" and "self-determination" seriously and began to act on them. In 1967, the Congress of Micronesia created the Joint Committee on Future Status and selected as its chairman Senator Lazarus Salii from Palau, a brilliant, young, political science graduate from the University of Hawaii, thirty years old. The Joint Committee's charge was to examine alternative status possibilities to end the strategic trusteeship.

The Joint Committee had to negotiate on two fronts at once: with the United States and, within Micronesia, among its own members. With the United States, the Joint Committee sought to create a new status in American law, that of a Freely Associated State (FAS), granting to the United States only those powers specifically enumerated in the Compact, the proposed agreement between the parties.

The Compact's basic structure was simple. The United States would receive the right to establish military bases, transship nuclear materials, and prevent foreign powers from engaging in any military activity. In exchange, the FAS would receive large amounts of money, the right of its people to enter the United States and work, and military protection.

The Compact, as the Micronesians envisioned it, granted the FAS the option to leave the union should the United States violate the agreement or, indeed, for any reason at all. The right to "opt out" proved to be a stumbling block. The Micronesians insisted on the right to opt out. To them it was the essential ingredient of the FAS status, permitting the islands' politicians freedom of action in the future and a feeling of dignity and self-worth. But opting out ran counter to American tradition, indeed to U.S. constitutional jurisprudence. Litigation after the Civil War decided the union was indivisible. The Johnson and Nixon administrations rejected the opting out provision. While these negotiations with the United States were going on, within Micronesia the Joint Committee struggled to hold the different island groups together while their geographical distance, their separate languages, and their economic disparities drove them apart. The Palauans, the Marshallese, the Northern Marianans, and the peoples of the island groups in the Federated States of Micronesia spoke totally different languages. Moreover, the smaller island chains—most notably, the

Marianas—were financially the strongest and fearful that the more populous and poorest would vote to tax them disproportionately.

After fourteen years, the Joint Committee's negotiation with the United States was successful. The Compact with the United States would accord to each FAS the right to "opt out," the right to leave the union. But the Joint Committee's negotiations among its own members failed. Micronesia split into four parts: the Northern Mariana Islands, the Republic of the Marshall Islands, the Federated States of Micronesia, and the Republic of Palau. In Palau, Salii and his followers supported continued Palauan federation with the other island areas of Micronesia. Roman Tmetuchl and his faction urged Palau to follow the example of the Northern Marianas and separate from the rest of Micronesia. The vote on this issue was to be the first in a number of votes over the next decade pitting Salii and Tmetuchl against each other.

Salii's entire career rested on the United States. He had been granted a scholarship to attend the University of Hawaii, and there was selected one of the University's outstanding students. He went on to obtain various jobs at the U.S. Trust Territory Government headquarters in Saipan. He spoke English fluently, most unusual in Palau. This was a tribute to his talent and his industry, since he first heard English at nine years of age when American soldiers captured Angaur in 1944.

Tmetuchl, the governor of Airai State, was an extremely wealthy, cultured man who, about fifteen years older than Salii, was the senior politician of Palau. His English was hesitant but his Japanese was fluent, reflective of his early schooling. He was a strong patron of the arts who promoted classical music concerts on the island. I remember a lunch he hosted at a restaurant for his local chiefs to meet President Tosiwo Nakayama of the Federated States of Micronesia and me. He had invited his local chiefs, most of whom spoke only Palauan and were quite non-Western in style and interests. At the end of the lunch, suddenly and astonishingly, a flutist was called in to play a few classical pieces accompanied by Tmetuchl's daughter. Many Palauans feared Tmetuchl's wealth and his reputation for strong arm tactics in his pursuit of power. He was said to have close ties with powerful interests in Japan. It was difficult to know if these tales were true. Palauans like to dramatize their politics for foreigners.

In the 1978 referendum on the Micronesian Federation Constitution, Tmetuchl led the separatists to victory, defeating the proposed constitution 55 percent to 45 percent. The Palauan decision to leave the Micronesian federation added to Tmetuchl's stature as a bold, assertive leader. His supporters controlled the OEK and appointed him chairman of the Palau Status Commission to complete negotiations of what now had to be a separate Compact between Palau and the United States. Palau then proceeded to draft its own Constitution to establish the Republic of Palau. Once the Constitution was ratified and elections were held, Tmetuchl, clearly the dominant force in Palauan politics, would be Palau's first president. So it appeared to all. It was not to be. The Palau Constitutional Convention met from January 28, 1979, to April 2, 1979. It destroyed Tmetuchl's power.

When the Palau Constitutional Convention convened, the local struggle for power was hidden beneath the euphoria of regaining power after 100 years of colonial rule. Villages vied for the right to bring food to the thirty-eight delegates, who found themselves draped in flower leis for the first few weeks. Traditional dances and chanting entertained the delegates, and hundreds of people from around the islands came to camp on the legislature's lawn, to observe the historic event and testify at the hearings. From the opening moment when the delegates jockeyed to elect a president of the convention, Tmetuchl was in trouble. In a major surprise, the disparate forces united around a single candidate, Haruo Remeliik, and elected him president of the Constitutional Convention.

Remeliik's rise to prominence was largely the result of the support of the Modekngei religious movement. Catholic missionary work in Palau began in earnest in 1891 with the support of the Spanish royalty and, subsequently, with the aid of the German rulers. To replace the native Palauan religion with Christianity as rapidly as possible, the houses of the Palauan gods in every village were destroyed and sorcery and divination were banned. By the time the Japanese Navy occupied the islands in 1914, very few diviners or shamans were left. Modekngei (Let Us Go Forward Together), an indigenous religious movement, with nationalist overtones that developed after World War I, filled the void. "Palau for Palauans" was their slogan. Modekngei preached the self-sufficiency of Palau's natural environment and the worship of gods from the traditional pantheon. Forced to operate covertly, Modekngei swept Palau nevertheless, one-third to one-half of the total populace becoming its adherents.

Remeliik differed from both Salii and Tmetuchl. He was less driven than they, less sophisticated, and less academic as well. He enjoyed the side of Palau that the people of Palau enjoyed. He liked to fish, to pigeon hunt, to return to Peleliu, his home island, drink *sakao*, and swap tales. He spoke English and Japanese but neither perfectly. However, of the three candidates, he was, perhaps, the one who moved most comfortably in all three environments: Japanese, American, and Palauan.

Although the legislation calling the Constitutional Convention required the delegates to draft a Constitution consistent with the Compact, convention politics propelled the delegates in a different direction. The convention delegates challenged the Compact being negotiated with the United States partly for ideological reasons but also as a way to weaken and embarrass Tmetuchl. They manipulated the convention so that eventually Tmetuchl would be forced to defend the United States and the Compact in the face of a Palauan nationalist movement that was just gaining strength.

As drafted by the convention, the Constitution contradicted the Compact in three ways. The first was an elementary, yet a surprisingly controversial, point. What were the boundaries of the new Republic of Palau? The draft Constitution defined Palau to include the territorial sea and the archipelagic sea. The Constitution extended the territorial sea out 200 miles, following Third World concepts later to be incorporated in the Law of the Sea Treaty. The United States limited the territorial sea to twelve miles. Moreover, the Palauan delegates argued that all the islands of Palau should be connected by an imaginary dotted line and all waters within that line should be Palau's alone, an archipelagic sea. The 200-mile limit would extend from that imaginary line. That argument, if accepted for all of Micronesia, meant cutting off over three million square miles of ocean and declaring it the property of the island governments. The United States rejected both the archipelagic sea theory and the expanded definition of the territorial sea. The Compact, following the U.S. approach, defined Palau's territory more narrowly, using neither either the archipelagic sea theory nor the 200-mile extension.

Under the Compact, the Government of Palau had agreed to transfer land if needed by the United States for military purposes. However, the Constitution barred the Palau government from expropriating private land for use by a foreign power. A second potential conflict!

Finally, the critical constitutional provisions, the ones which were to plague Palau and the United States for more than a decade more: the antinuclear clauses. These prohibited the Palau government from entering into an agreement to permit the United States to use, store, test, or dispose of nuclear weaponry or nuclear waste in Palau without the approval of three-fourths of the Palauan voters. In addition, nuclear-powered ships could not travel through Palauan waters without approval by three-fourths of the Palauan voters. The Compact, of course, envisioned unrestricted U.S. defense activity. The Compact provisions were no problem if the compact could be ratified by a 75 percent affirmative vote.

The author of the nuclear substance provisions, Tosiwo Nakamura, saw them as an antimilitaristic statement designed to avoid bringing the horrors of war to Palau. His view, simply stated, was that if the Japanese had not been in Palau in World War II, there would have been no attack by the Americans, and if there were no Americans today, there would be no attack by the Soviet Union. Nakamura took credit, as chairman of the Constitutional Subcommittee, for lobbying the provision out of his committee and bringing it to the convention floor. On the floor, the antinuclear clauses gained support because of external forces and local political pressures.

The external forces arose from the global fight over nuclear weaponry. From 1946 to 1958, the United States had experimented with its nuclear weapons, setting loose major nuclear explosions in the atmosphere in the Marshall Islands that impacted terribly on the lives of the people of Bikini, Eniwetok, Rongelap, and Utirik.

On January 26, 1946, the United States selected Bikini Atoll in the Marshall Islands as a nuclear test site. Bikini had been selected because (1) the atoll, one of the northernmost atolls in the Marshalls, was isolated; (2) the prevailing winds would carry any fallout to the north, further away from populated islands; (3) there was a protected deep-water harbor within the atoll to accommodate the naval fleet of Operation Crossroads; (4) it was within the 1,000-mile range of the B-29 bomber that would be flown from Kwajalein; and (5) Bikini had a minuscule population of 166 people. Commodore Benjamin Wyatt, U.S.N., Deputy Military Governor of the Marshalls, persuaded the Bikinians to leave their islands with a double-edged appeal based on the universal principles of peace and self-sacrifice: "For the good of mankind and to end all wars." Persuaded, or intimidated, or deceived—there is still much dispute about this—Juda, the high chief, agreed for himself and the other 165 inhabitants of the twenty-six islets of Bikini lagoon to relocate. First, they went to Rongerik Atoll, an uninhabited, smaller atoll to the east, and when that proved unsuitable, they went to Kili, a single island with no lagoon in the southern Marshalls. Meanwhile, the United States worked to clean up Bikini. By 1969 the Bikinians, anxious to return, were permitted to go home to their atoll. But the persistence of the radiation proved greater than expected and, ten years later, the Bikinians were forced to evacuate once more. Some Bikinians moved to Ejit, a tiny island near Majuro, some moved to Majuro, and the majority retreated to Kili.

In 1947 the military expanded its nuclear testing program to Eniwetok and relocated 142 people from Eniwetok Atoll to Ujelang Atoll. On the whole, that move went well. Yet a third population was affected by the U.S. nuclear test program when, in 1954, a thermonuclear explosion on Bikini caused considerable injury. The winds caused the fallout to engulf Rongelap, Utirik, and Ailinginae, injuring 249 Marshallese and leading in a few cases to thyroid cancer and leukemia. There have been charges that the military knew of the likely shift in wind direction and were using the Marshallese as guinea pigs, further embittering the atmosphere.

Between 1946 and 1958, the United States conducted sixty-six nuclear tests at Bikini and Eniwetok atolls as well as two upper-atmosphere tests at Johnston Island. The U.S. introduction of nuclear testing in the Pacific did not go unmatched. All of the original five nuclear powers used the Pacific as their test site. Three—the United States, the USSR, and China—launched missiles into the Pacific for test purposes, and Britain also exploded nuclear bombs there. France was the most active and persistent. France conducted forty-one atmospheric nuclear tests in French Polynesia between 1966 and 1975, and, from 1975 to 1992, after it ceased atmospheric testing, more than twenty underground nuclear tests there.

The Pacific nuclear tests provoked a tremendous outcry. Political opposition in the United States, Australia, New Zealand, and Japan pressed for a nuclear-free Pacific. The movement for a nuclear-free Pacific began in Fiji in 1970 with the formation of the ATOM committee (Against Tests on Moruroa) to protest French testing. Backed by the Pacific Conference of Churches, ATOM organized the first conference for a nuclear free Pacific in Fiji in 1975, and an important follow-up conference on the Micronesian island of Pohnpei in 1978, one that was very influential in Palau. The antinuclear activists embraced a broad, anticolonialist agenda, but in the nuclear area they challenged the utility of the tests themselves and the command facilities on the rim of the Pacific, and they pointed to the proved dangers of nuclear contamination.

Front and center in all of these arguments was the Marshallese experience. But there was the rub. However worthy the cause, and however passionate and concerned its partisans were, that intensity of antimilitary and environmental concern was not shared by the Micronesians, not even by the Marshallese. For example, in the Marshalls, Amata Kabua, the president of the Marshall Islands, later offered the use of his islands as a storage ground for Japanese and U.S. nuclear waste. It was a straight economic deal, as far as Kabua concerned. U.S. antinuclear activists were outraged.

A different environmental issue arose in the mid-1970s when Palau leadership flirted with the idea of a superport off Babeldaob designed to permit tankers from Iran delivering oil to Japan to dock, drop their cargo and return to Iran very rapidly. The original formulation envisioned pumping the oil directly into the substratum of land beneath the ocean. Under this plan, Palau would have required a vast network of storage tanks for petroleum. Environmentalists outside Palau protested against the introduction of oil facilities into unblemished tropical waters.

At the 1977 hearings on the superport plan before the Senate Energy and Natural Resources Committee, various environmental groups took the lead in opposing the superport, arguing for delay, for more information. In the words of David Roe of the Environmental Defense Fund, the dangers to "the beauty and scientific value of these islands and the way of life" had to be explained prior to a determination by the Palauans themselves. If the Palauans knew more, surely they would not sacrifice their environment.

The Ibedul also testified against the proposal "because of the adverse effects on our land, water." The Ibedul had another, nonenvironmental concern: the transfer of power over land from the traditional chiefs to the elected representatives.

The common ground between the Ibedul and environmental groups was their fear of development. Beyond that, their interests diverged. The environmentalists sought to keep Palau beautiful, to enshrine their vision of paradise; the Ibedul wanted to maintain the traditional land-use system and Koror's preeminent position in Palau, which would be threatened by a port complex on Babeldaob. Opposed to both the Ibedul and the environmentalists were Salii and Tmetuchl, who were seeking the economic viability of the islands above all. Congressman Philip Burton, the key voice in Congress on the territories, peremptorily announced he would never permit the superport and ended the debate.

If most Palauans—indeed most Micronesians—did not see environmental pollution and nuclear contamination as a high priority when weighed against the economic needs of their islands, there was one populace in Palau and Micronesia that did: the white judges. These judges almost uniformly shared the values and concerns of the antinuclear activists in the United States and abroad. These different views would have important political consequences.

In Palau, support for the antinuclear provisions in the Palau Constitution also was based on internal Palauan politics: it was hoped that they would prevent the first president of Palau—presumed to be Tmetuchl—from presiding over ratification of the Compact and obtaining the consequent funding and patronage that would go with this function. Tmetuchl realized what was at issue. He was fighting for the presidency of Palau. And he was losing.

On March 15, 1979, Tmetuchl, as chairman of the Palau Status Negotiations Committee, wrote to U.S. Ambassador Peter Rosenblatt, head of the Office of Micronesian Status Negotiations, inviting comments on the Palau Constitutional Convention's draft, including the proposed prohibition against nuclear substances. U.S. officials understood immediately the impact of the antinuclear clauses and were alarmed. At the Interagency Committee, the agencies took opposing views. Defense took a hard line: veto the Constitution. The United States had an overriding defense obligation not only to Palau but to the world. Free association was all well and good, but not if it meant weakening our security. The Interior Department argued that local self-government meant Palau would do at times what the United States didn't want it to do. The State Department came up with a middle course, one easier said than done: get the Palauans themselves to change the Constitution. In a cable, Ambassador Rosenblatt warned: "As drafted, proposal 91 might effectively prevent U.S. warships and aircraft from transiting Palau either in time of peace or war. We urge that this proposal be dropped. . . . Unless deleted or amended, the proposed language would create problems of the utmost gravity for the U.S."

To emphasize the depth of America's concern, Rosenblatt flew to Palau and personally addressed the legislature and the Constitutional Convention in a joint session on April 30, 1979. His message was tough and unyielding, his style ambassadorial and imperious. The Constitution as drafted was incompatible with the Compact of Free Association. "The provisions on territorial waters, eminent domain, and nuclear substances are unacceptable to the U.S. . . . We've come to the point of choice," the Ambassador said. "You can have an agreement of free association along the lines we have negotiated with your Political Status Commission or you can have the

Constitution in its present form."

Furious at the U.S. tone and its explicit threat, Remeliik and a number of delegates walked out in the middle of Rosenblatt's address. The Palauan delegates recalled the Federated States of Micronesia Constitution and its glorious preamble:

Micronesia began in the days when man explored seas in rafts and canoes. The Micronesian nation is born in an age when men voyage among stars: our world itself is an island. We extend to all nations what we seek from each: peace, friendship, cooperation, and love in our common humanity. With this Constitution we, who have been the wards of other nations, become the proud guardian of our own islands, now and forever.

Palau's preamble was not as grand or as eloquent, but it expressed what the people of Palau cared about: their selfconfidence, their desire for sovereignty, and their national pride: "In exercising our inherent sovereignty, We, the people of Palau, proclaim and reaffirm our immemorial right to be supreme in these islands of Palau, our homeland."

When the convention reconvened, the delegates refused any change in the nuclear ban. The voter approval requirement remained essentially the same: "three-fourths (3/4) of all votes cast." Forced to choose between the Compact and the Constitution, the Palauan delegates chose their Constitution. It was an easy choice. Bonifacio Basilius, Chairman of the Civil Liberties Committee to the Constitutional Convention, reflected on the nuclear ban in the Constitution:

When we talked about the nuclear ban, in all honesty we did not intend a "nuclear free" Constitution. We wanted a strong power to negotiate with the U.S. At that time we did not think that 75% was an obstacle. It was our intention to put a strong case in the hands of our negotiators for the best deal from the U.S. . . .

Then, the U.S. Ambassador heard about the clause and U.S. negotiators came here and tried to pressure us to take the clause out, which had the opposite effect.

The United States missed the importance to the Palauans, indeed to all Micronesians, of their Constitutional Convention. The Constitutional delegates were nationalists, building a nation, a very small nation to be sure, but they were intense, proud nationalists nevertheless. They had been able to create their island nation by holding firm and overcoming the sixteen-year resistance of the United States to the concept of free association. Facing down the United States had become a welcome rite of passage for the delegates.

The United States would never be able to rectify totally Rosenblatt's initial misstep. Tmetuchl and the United States tried. The popular vote on the Constitution was scheduled for July 9, 1979. The OEK, controlled by Tmetuchl and under pressure from the United States, repealed the

Constitutional Convention's enabling legislation, intending, as a consequence, to void the Constitution and, thus prevent the ratification vote.

Five hundred angry Palauans, joined by 200 older women of the leading clans, protested the repeal outside the OEK. The protest was unusual and the presence of the women stranger still. The protest had an effect. The Constitution was put to a vote despite the OEK action. The issue was simply framed in the popular mind: the United States (the Compact) v. Palau (the Constitution). The Constitution was overwhelmingly approved by 92 percent of the voters. Palau and the Constitution had won, at least temporarily.

The Constitution's supporters filed a lawsuit to void the OEK legislation. Two weeks later, the Trust Territory High Court, comprised of United States-appointed judges, upheld the OEK action and voided the popular vote approving the Constitution. The constitutional drafting process had to begin anew.

The OEK then created the Palau Constitutional Drafting Commission to "eliminate any inconsistencies" between the invalidated Constitution and the Compact. The United States got what it wanted in the new draft Constitution. The Drafting Commission proposed changing the three-fourths requirement to a majority of the votes cast so it would be easier to approve the Compact.

The people of Palau voted on the Drafting Commission's version of the Constitution in a second plebiscite held on October 23, 1979. The United States lost again. The new Constitution obtained only 31 percent of the vote. After the people of Palau rejected the Drafting Commission's version of the Constitution, the Constitutional Drafting Commission reinstated the three-fourths requirement that was in the first draft Constitution. The third draft of the Constitution, virtually identical to the first, was approved by 78 percent of the Palau voters on July 9, 1980.

With the language of the Palau Constitution finally settled, United States and Palauan officials met to reconcile the Constitution's provisions with the Compact. Two of the problems were eliminated by changing the Compact. Palau agreed that its boundaries would be consistent with international law. Since Palau's archipelagic views and 200-mile law, that issue evaporated. To limit the danger of the military land acquisition problem, the United States agreed to list in the Compact the specific pieces of land that might be subject to military use. There was still a possibility that the United States would seek additional land, but it seemed remote.

With respect to the nuclear ban, the United States was stuck. The United States would not change the national security provisions of the Compact. The Palauan and U.S. negotiators had to hope to get a 75 percent approval vote. Palau appeared to be relatively unanimous in favor of the Compact. Tmetuchl and his supporters were strongly in favor, as was the coalition of former Constitutional Convention delegates headed by Remeliik, Salii, and

Alfonso Oiterong. Although these latter were anti-Tmetuchl, they were pro-Compact. Further, since the Palau Constitution had been approved by 92 percent and 78 percent, a 75 percent vote did not seem overwhelmingly difficult. But the numbers were deceiving. The high percentages in the previous votes reflected a very low turnout. When the opposition was organized and got out their vote, these percentages would no longer be obtainable.

The first Palau presidential election was held the next year. The leading candidates were Tmetuchl, Salii, and Remeliik, dubbed the Japanese candidate, the American candidate, and the Palauan candidate. Although personal ambition was to keep Salii and Tmetuchl at odds, their visions of Palau were very similar. They both saw foreign investment as critical to Palau's growth. Tmetuchl's contacts and cultural sophistication and Salii's intellectual brilliance made them both confident of obtaining and managing large foreign investment. Both viewed the Compact as essential to provide the political stability that would induce the necessary foreign—primarily Japanese—investment. Remeliik was less closely associated with the Compact. As president of the Palau Constitutional Convention, he was associated with the Palau Constitution and Palauan nationalism. Environmental and antinuclear opponents of the Compact later spoke of him as being one of them, but that was not true. With his more local outlook, he simply viewed the Compact as being less important in the Palau scheme of things.

More than nationalism and ideology were involved in this election, however. The character of the two men, Tmetuchl and Remeliik, could not have been more different. Tmetuchl was assertive where Remeliik was consensual; Tmetuchl inclined toward secrecy, whereas Remeliik was more open and participatory. Tmetuchl's sophistication contrasted with the populist unpretentiousness of Remeliik. Salii, like Tmetuchl, was strong, but more open in style and personality. Remeliik and Tmetuchl had lived all their lives in Palau. Salii had studied and worked outside of Palau much of his adult life.

Tmetuchl had a status somewhat higher than either Remeliik or Salii. Tmetuchl was the Governor of Airai State near Koror city, an important place in the Palau landscape. Remeliik was from Peleliu, a small island somewhat distant from the main island of Koror. The word Peleliu is a contemptuous term, meaning "under house," reflective of the low status the island holds in Palauan eyes. Salii was from Angaur, even more remote from the center of power. Angaur, known as "the Village of the Dead," has always had an unhappy reputation among the Micronesians. Its rather unearthly-looking guano waste was thought to be the promenade of ghosts, a purgatory where the dead came to be tested before those who qualify were taken to heaven. A few spirits, caught in the uncertainty of whether heaven or hell was to be their final destination, remained in Angaur in terrible agony.

Palauans, natural and compulsive political analysts, on hindsight argued that leaders from the small out-of-the-way places, like Peleliu or Angaur, were more likely to think of Palau as a whole than to be driven by their single home constituency. But there might be a simpler explanation for the rise to power of politicians from those areas. Peleliu and Angaur, the first two islands in Palau captured by the Americans, by 1946, in an astonishing reversal of fortune resulting from the American influence, had the highest standard of living in Palau. For example, they were the first islands to have twenty-four hours of electricity and twenty-four hours of running water.

Perhaps critical to the election was the Modekngei religion. Freed from governmental persecution by the end of World War II, Modekngei spread rapidly throughout Palau. The religious tensions between followers of Modekngei and the larger Christian groups (Catholic and Seventh Day Adventist) paralleled Palau's politics. Modekngei followers generally favored the original draft constitution and opposed those leaders like Tmetuchl (an active Seventh Day Adventist) and Salii (a Catholic) who argued for the United States-supported draft Constitution. Modekngei threw its weight behind Remeliik, president of the Palau Constitutional Convention.

Remeliik and Alfonso Oiterong emerged from the five-man presidential and vice presidential fields as winners in the 1980 election, with marginal pluralities; 31 percent and 32 percent, respectively, of the total votes cast.

Tmetuchl's loss embittered him. He withdrew his support for the Compact, arguing the need for additional benefits for Palau, and turned on Remeliik, carrying the election struggle into Remeliik's administration. The Senate, controlled by Tmetuchl, paralyzed Remeliik's government for six months by holding up confirmation of all cabinet appointments. There were strikes by government workers in 1981 and 1982 against the Remeliik administration. During the first strike, a mob of government workers firebombed Remeliik's office, angry because of Remeliik's refusal to negotiate a salary increase. With the first constitutional government about to collapse and his office in a shambles, Remeliik surrendered. He agreed to a three-point program: a $50 biweekly increase in wages, additional salary adjustments in future, and no sanctions against the strikers.

But Remeliik had no money to fund his promised wage increases. He had to renege on the deal. The government workers struck twice more, each strike more unruly than the last. During the third strike, one worker was shot and killed and three other workers were wounded by the police. President Remeliik declared a ten-day state of emergency and ordered the workers back to their jobs. He asked the Ibedul to help restore order. The Ibedul responded by deputizing his men's clubs. For the moment there was an uneasy peace.

Finally, the United States came to Remeliik's rescue, voting a special appropriation to pay the increased wages.

Remeliik came to realize he needed the Compact. The Compact satisfied Palau's nationalism and also its financial needs. Neither Remeliik nor Oiterong had the technical expertise to deal with the complexities of the Compact and its many subsidiary agreements. Therefore, they appointed Salii, Micronesia's chief political status negotiator from 1969 to 1975, as Palau's Ambassador for Status Negotiations and Trade Relations, to negotiate the final details of Palau's Compact with the United States.

Salii successfully concluded the negotiations in a year. On August 26, 1982, the United States and Palau signed the Compact of Free Association.

Under the Compact with Palau, the United States was granted the right to use four defense sites: the middle third of Babeldaob Island, Airai Airfield, Malakal Harbor, and Angaur Airfield. The United States announced it had no plans to use these military bases and viewed them as a contingency only to provide logistical support for possible military action in South Asia. Many questioned the U.S. need for these sites, even on a contingency basis. Even now, after the loss of the Philippine bases, the United States has no concrete plans for military bases in Palau. These military base rights were combined with military transit rights through Palauan waters, permitting ships and submarines to cruise from the northern Pacific to the Indian Ocean, and the right of strategic denial, the right to bar rival countries from using Palau for military purposes.

The ratification vote in Palau was scheduled for February 10, 1983. In Palau, the opposition was comprised not only of local people but also—quite different from the case elsewhere in Micronesia—off-island groups from Japan, Australia, England, and the States. The local opposition, in general, was better educated and wealthier than the average Palauan. Its members could afford to cast aside the right to immigrate to the United States and to defer or forego the riches seen under the Compact. Some remembered what happened in World War II as well: the destruction of Peleliu and Angaur and the bombing of Koror. They saw the Compact as repeating history. Once more they would be attacked because a great power had military bases in their islands.

The off-island groups—some church groups, some antinuclear organizations, and some leftists generally opposed to the United States—were hardly unified. But the antinuclear groups had as their goal elimination of the military base and transit rights under the Compact since, they reasoned, these were of questionable value anyway. Barring the military use of Palau to others—strategic denial—alone might satisfy the United States, they thought, if ratification of the Compact as negotiated proved too difficult.

The opposition first sought delay, arguing for a fuller local education program than the three months allowed. The challenge failed. The American Enterprise Institute, which sent impartial observers to the election, felt the education campaign was fair. A U.N. Trusteeship Council team

resigned to the fact that Palau's failure to obtain a 75 percent vote of approval on the entire Compact meant that the Compact of Free Association with the United States had failed due to lack of ratification.

Notes

1. Page 26. *Although non-combatants, the Palauans*. K. Nero, "Time of Famine, Time of Transformation: Hell in the Pacific, Palau," in G. White & L. Lindstrom (eds), *The Pacific Theatre: Island Representation of World War II* (1989).

2. Page 27. *Federal appropriations sharply*. Hezel, "A Brief Economic History of Micronesia" in *Past Achievements and Future Possibilities* (Pohnpei, Federated States of Micronesia: The Micronesia Seminar, 1984), p. 36.

3. Page 32. *The Pacific nuclear tests*. For details of the Nuclear Free Pacific movement, see S. Firth, Nuclear Playground (1987), Chapter 12.

4. Page 32. *The antinuclear activists*. The 1978 conference drafted a document which, with minor revision, remains the popular charter for the movement: "Peoples Treaty for a Nuclear-Free Pacific." Its preamble states in part:

The western imperialistic and colonial powers invaded our defenseless region, they took our land and subjugated our people to their whims. We note in particular the racist roots of the world's nuclear powers and we call for an immediate end to the oppression, exploitation and subordination of the indigenous people of the Pacific.

Quoted in B. Aldridge and C. Myers, *Resisting the Serpent* (1990), pp. 12-13.

5. Page 32. The testimony commented upon in the text is found in U.S. Senate, *Palau Deep Water Port, Hearings before the Committee on Energy and Natural Resources*, 95th Cong., 1st sess., March 24, 1977, p. 29.

6. Page 32. Some of the drama of the Palau Constitutional Convention is conveyed in F. Quimby, "The Yin and Yang of Belau," in R. Crocombe & L. Mason (eds.), *Micronesian Politics* (Institute of Pacific Studies, University of the South Pacific, 1988).

7. Page 34. *Remeliik and a number of delegates*. Professor Shuster believes only Remeliik walked out. Rosenblatt, Quimby, and Tmetuchl confirm the text.

8. Page 34. The preamble to the FSM Constitution was apparently written by Fred Kluge. F. Kluge, *The Edge of Paradise* (1990), p. 43.

9. Page. 36. *Peleliu is a contemptuous term*. Two readers of the text in manuscript have pointed out that the translation is technically incorrect. I have relied, both for the translation and the accompanying stories, on W. Price, *Japan's Islands of Mystery* (1944), pp. 147, 158-59.

10. Page 37. *Remeliik and Alfonso Oiterong emerged*. D. Shuster, "Elections in the Republic of Palau," 35 *Political Science* 117 (1983).

11. Page 37. The Tmetuchl actions and the Remeliik administration are discussed in D. Shuster, "The Politics of Free Association and the Politics of Violence." (Paper presented at the Pacific Islands Political Studies Association Conference, May 23-25, 1988).

12. Page 38. *They appointed Salii*. B. Elbelau, "Ambassador Nominee Calls for Unity," *Pacific Daily News*, April 27, 1982, p. 4.

13. Page 38. For a review of the Palau ratification process, see A. Ranney and H. Penniman, *Democracy in the Islands: The Micronesian Plebiscites of 1983* (1985), pp. 25-50.

14. Page 38. *But the antinuclear groups had.* H. M. Schwallenberg's "After Palau's Plebiscite What Comes Next?" sets forth the military compromise discussed in the text (Micronesian Seminar, 1983).

15. Page 39. *A U. N. Trusteeship Council team.* J. Simpson, "U.N. Team: Palau Vote Held Fairly," *Pacific Daily News*, Feb. 14, 1983, p. 3.

16. Page 39. *Despite the organized.* F. Quimby, "Deja Vu: Outsiders Not New to Palau's Political Tempests," *Pacific Daily News*, February 13, 1983, p. 16; L. Caldecott, "Between the Crocodiles." *New Statesman*, Feb. 25, 1983, reports on Roman Bedor's campaign in London for a nuclear-free Pacific.

17. Page 39. *Any hope for 75 percent.* J. Simpson, "Ibedul Urges Compact Rejection," *Pacific Daily News*, Feb. 9, 1983, p. 3; "Pact Draws More Fire from Chiefs," *Pacific Daily News*, Feb. 10, 1983, p. 1.

18. Page 40. *William Butler.* For details of the 1983 U.N. debate, see R. Clark and S. Roff, "Micronesia: The Problems of Palau." (Report of the Minority Rights Group of the International League for Human Rights, New York, 1984); "Speakers Criticize Conduct of Palau Plebiscite," *Pacific Daily News*, May 27, 1983) p. 4.

19. Page 41. *Valid act of self-determination.* Quoted in M. Mechem, "United States Argues Palau Compact Valid." *Pacific Daily News*, Aug. 20, 1983, p. 1. Christopher, *Ibid*, p. CRS-17.2.

5

Remeliik's Reelection Campaign; The Role of the Compact

Salii managed Remeliik's 1984 presidential campaign. His strategy was to polarize the Palau electorate into vigorously competing pro-Compact (pro-Remeliik) and anti-Compact factions. Key to the success of this approach was the plan to call a second plebiscite to ratify the Compact on September 4, 1984, just three months before the election in late November.

During August 1984, Remeliik's task force, promoting the Compact, visited all the Babeldaob rural villages. The Task Force brought in Ambassador Zeder, the head of the Micronesian Office in the State Department, to answer villagers' questions; thereby using his considerable stature as President Reagan's personal representative to support the Compact ratification effort and, indirectly, President Remeliik.

The Compact opposition continued to be active as well, focusing not only on the plebescite in Palau but also on public opinion in the States. The Public Broadcasting System aired *Strategic Trust: Making of Nuclear Free Palau*, a film utilizing old footage showing World War II tanks invading a beach, a nuclear mushroom cloud arising from Bikini and graphic pictures of burns and birth defects caused by radiation as a result of the U.S. nuclear bombing of Hiroshima.

In the second plebiscite, the Compact received 66 percent, not sufficient for ratification, but more than sufficient for the election of Remeliik to a second term in the upcoming presidential election. Remeliik campaigned for reelection not only as pro-Compact but also as the people's candidate, a common man with no high title or great wealth who had successfully weathered the turmoil and turbulence of the workers' strikes. Tmetuchl and the Ibedul, Remeliik's opponents, argued that they supported the principle of free association with the United States, but not the Compact in its present form. Greater Palau control over land, increased funds in exchange for the

U.S. military use, and the continuation of United States-sponsored student scholarships and federal programs were the major areas where the Compact, in their view, needed improvement. The Remeliik campaign portrayed Tmetuchl as a fiercely competitive opponent whose power, if he won the presidency, could endanger Palauan freedom. Tmetuchl's supporters depicted Remeliik as weak, a man unable to manage the affairs of the state.

The Ibedul's decision to run for the presidency was somewhat unusual, since the traditional leadership had generally avoided campaigning for elective office. He had been successful in several Koror state elections in the seventies but was inexperienced on the national scene. In his campaign, the Ibedul was projected as a unifier, a bridge between tradition and modernity, a peacemaker who brought the strikers and President Remeliik together during Palau's civil unrest of 1981 and 1982.

Remeliik and Oiterong won surprisingly easily. Remeliik, who received 50 percent of the vote to 31 percent for Tmetuchl and 18 percent for the Ibedul, attributed his success to his pro-Compact position and his door-to-door, personal approach. Oiterong took 53 percent of the vote.

After his election, Remeliik took up the old U.S. position and argued that the 66 percent vote of approval in the September 1984 plebiscite was sufficient for Palau to ratify the compact. The OEK House rapidly voted to approve the Compact. The Senate stalled.

Salii had won a Senate seat in the November election with the stated desire of softening the opposition of the OEK Senate to the Compact. Under pressure from Remeliik and Salii, the Senate finally went along with the Remeliik plan and approved the Compact.

However, Zeder, head of the U. S. office negotiating the Compacts, would not accept the procedure. He had been burned once. Not again. The United States insisted Palau needed a 75 percent vote of approval unless it changed its Constitution.

Notes

1. Page 43. For the discussion of the Remeliik reelection campaign in this chapter, I am indebted to D. Shuster, "The Politics of Free Association and the Politics of Violence: An Essay on Recent Palauan Political History," (Paper delivered at the Pacific Islands Political Studies Association Conference, May 23-35, 1988).

2. Page 43. *Salii managed Remeliik's.* D. Shuster, "Election, Compact and Assassination in the Republic of Palau," 12 *Pacific Studies* 23 (Nov. 1988).

3. Page 43. *The Public Broadcasting System aired.* "Antinuclear Film Clouds the Issue," *Washington Times*, August 24, 1984, p. 2B; Unger, "A Provocative Look at a Tiny Republic's Nuclear Defence Controversy," *Christian Science Monitor*, May 22, 1985, p. 24.

4. Page 44. *The Remeliik campaign portrayed.* D. Shuster, "Palau's Elections:

Image Figures High in Presidential Race." *Pacific Daily News*, Nov. 29, 1984, p. 3.

5. Page 44. *Remeliik and Oiterong won.* D. Shuster, "Remeliik Wins Palau's Election," *Pacific Daily News*, Dec. 13, 1984, p. 3; "Remeliik President, Election Certified," *Pacific Daily News*, Dec. 18, 1984, p. 5.

6. Page 44. *After his election, Remeliik.* "Remeliik: Compact Resolved, No Need for Ambassador," *Pacific Daily News*, Feb. 6, 1985, p. 3.

7. Page 44. *Salii had won a Senate seat.* F. Quimby, "Palau Ambassador Seeking Senate Seat," *Pacific Daily News*, Nov. 5, 1984, p. 3.

8. Page 44. *The Senate finally went along.* "Palau Senate O.K.s Compact," *Pacific Daily News*, Feb. 23, 1985, p. 3; Editorial, "Clear Issue Remains on Palauan Question," *Pacific Daily News*, Feb. 25, 1985, p. 18.

6

The Power Plant Purchase; Great Britain Seeks a U.S. Guarantee

The IPSECO scandal, which was to engulf Salii, began innocently enough. From the onset of the trusteeship in 1946, Palau had suffered from a severe shortage of electrical power. Blackouts were frequent and power hours necessary. The absence of power paralyzed all efforts to develop economically. Power was essential politically for Remeliik as well. The Ibedul and Tmetuchl had acquired small generators for their followers. The homes of their supporters shone while much of the rest of Palau sat in darkness.

The OEK passed a resolution in 1979 protesting the limited supply of electric power in Palau during the thirty years of U.S. trusteeship. On May 16, 1979, the Interior Department responded. The Army Corps of Engineers loaned Palau for one year a power plant (three generators with 0.5 megawatt capacity each).

In 1981, Remeliik, just having been elected president, appointed a Task Force headed by Vice President Oiterong to solve Palau's power problem. The International Power Systems Company, Ltd. of London (IPSECO) sold high-quality, very high priced, electrical generating plants. Trying to sell the Rolls Royce of power plants to the Third World, it lost out to Westinghouse and General Electric. IPSECO turned to Palau. The need was great; competition small. The one hitch: Palau didn't have money to pay for the power. That problem came second; first, they had to make the deal.

Surprisingly, that didn't turn out to be too difficult. IPSECO had sold an electrical power plant to the Marshall Islands only a few years before. In August 1981, two members of the Palauan task force visited the Marshall Islands and saw the facility then being built. The Marshallese recommended IPSECO, influenced by the fact that IPSECO would arrange very favorable terms for financing: no down payment. Remeliik contacted Gordon Mochrie, president of IPSECO. Two of the Palau task force members then visited him in Hawaii and solicited a proposal.

In September 1981, Mochrie proposed the construction of a 16 megawatt diesel power plant and a six million gallon fuel-storage facility on Koror. He went further. He would immediately provide, at no charge, a mobile generator twice the size of the one loaned Palau by the Corps of Engineers. Mochrie was a tall, well-dressed, sandy-haired man who spoke very slowly with a heavy British accent. In Palau, where everyone wears an open shirt and no jacket, he stood out in his hand-tailored silk suit and tie. He looked like he had answered central casting's call for a British officer. The Palauans were impressed. The Palau Task Force quickly responded to Mochrie. In less than three months, on December 15, 1981, Palau and IPSECO signed an agreement to enter into good faith negotiations. Mochrie invited the Palauans to London at IPSECO's expense.

After President Remeliik told High Commissioner Janet McCoy of the Palau delegation's forthcoming London visit, the United States government realized the importance of what was happening. The State Department cable of January 28, 1982, sent by its status liaison officer in Micronesia, agreed that the United States had not addressed Palau's need for power but argued that Palau would be unable to pay for the IPSECO generators. "The time is approaching when USG must decide whether we will seriously object to this deal, or let events take their course."

The U.S. government concluded that Palau needed power but IPSECO's plant simply cost too much. The U.S. estimate was that Palau needed 5.2 megawatts of power. A 1.5 megawatt plant for $500,000 rather than a 16 megawatt plant for $27.5 million was what was in order. The U.S. solution: sell the Palauans the plant the Army Corps had loaned them. To the Palauans it seemed like more of the same: too little and too late. Just when Palau could go first class and satisfy its power needs forever, the United States, to save money as it had done for thirty years, was going to sell them a generator that was too small.

The Senate Energy Committee staff visited Palau in late 1981 and pressed for that more modest approach. They assured the Palauans that money for the purchase would be in the next appropriations bill. The final meeting was an accidental, but dramatic, one. At the Koror airport, the Senate staff, on the way back to Washington, met the Palau delegation on its way to London. To the Senate staff, the sight of the Palau delegation, some holding overcoats in the tropical heat, reinforced the fantastic aspects of the IPSECO negotiations. To the Palauans, the Senate staff consternation proved at last, for one important moment, that they had broken loose from U.S. tutelage and were going first class as a result. The Palau delegation were the first official emissaries to London since Lee Boo more than two centuries before. Unfortunately, their host was not as caring as Captain Wilson or George Keate. Mochrie turned London into a sybaritic bacchanal with opportunities, for the unsated few, to go on to Paris.

On February 2, 1982, Palau and IPSECO signed a contract for the construction of a $27.5 million, 16 megawatt, diesel power plant and a six million gallon fuel-storage facility. The fuel-storage facility consisted of eight 750,000-gallon tanks. Two tanks were to supply oil to the power plant and six tanks were intended to store oil to be sold to fishing fleets and other customers. The contract was contingent on obtaining financing. Financing was no small matter. Palau was bankrupt and the United States was unwilling to help. Mochrie, with a salesman's confidence, stated that the project would be self-financing, primarily from the sales of fuel to the Japanese fishing fleet. U.S. officials knew Mochrie had argued in this same fashion to justify the Marshall Islands project. They doubted Mochrie then. Were there enough Japanese fishing vessels needing to refuel in Micronesia to pay off *two* IPSECO power plants?

Mochrie continued to try to arrange financing for Palau, finally approaching Stephen Syrett of Morgan, Grenfell Co. Syrett also believed IPSECO's revenue projections were wildly optimistic. His financing package looked to Compact funds as the solution. Syrett did not comment on the IPSECO projections but emphasized that if the project revenues were not sufficient, the banks would look to the Palau general treasury, and, since those cupboards might well be bare, to Compact funds as well. To ensure that the banks got paid, the Compact funds had to be deposited directly into a special escrow account. The Palauans protested. Compact funds, they thought, could not be deposited directly into a special escrow account. The Compact funds first had to be given to the government of Palau. Morgan, Grenfell held firm, the Compact fund payment had to be made directly to the banks. The Palauans eventually conceded.

Based on the Syrett financing structure, Morgan, Grenfell put together a syndicate to insure against the failure of Palau to repay the loan. The insurance structure of the deal was two-tiered: the British government guaranteed repayment of the IPSECO plant loan by Palau, and the five major banks, headed by Morgan, Grenfell, guaranteed the British government.

In November 1982, another Palau delegation headed by Haruo Willter, Palau's minister of finance, and Patrick Smith (stateside counsel to the Ibedul) traveled to London to meet with IPSECO and Morgan, Grenfell. The parties replayed the earlier record. Again, Mochrie stated that project revenues would be sufficient to repay the loans. Again, Syrett avoided the issue. Morgan, Grenfell was not looking just to project revenues but in the last analysis expected the government of Palau to repay the loans possibly with Compact funds.

On Palau, not only was the suggestion of mortgaging Compact funds financially bad business, it was politically very dangerous. At Palau's initiative, the word "Compact" was eliminated from the loan documents so that it would appear that Compact funds were not to be encumbered. The deal would appear as Mochrie painted it: it would cost Palau nothing. On the other hand, the Palauans were not told the actual cost of the proposed two-tiered insurance, only that it would be part of the package. The interest rate on the loan was 11.25 percent, considerably higher than that in Mochrie's initial presentation. The interest charge, insurance, and reinsurance costs meant a total Palauan debt obligation for the IPSECO plant of $47 million to be paid over nine years.

The Palau delegation prepared a trip report stating that they successfully resisted efforts to make the project other than self-financing. Smith, the Ibedul's counsel, protested: that's not what the agreement actually provided. The agreement actually envisioned the use of Compact funds to repay the banks. Smith tried to call Syrett. Willter, alarmed, conferred with Victor Uherbelau, the acting attorney general; and, shortly thereafter, Smith was cut out of the deal. In January 1983, Morgan, Grenfell sent revised drafts of the loan agreements to Oiterong, who distributed them to the OEK. In an unusual move, the Palau task force called in six Palau attorneys to examine the loan agreements. The next month, Remeliik signed them and Uherbelau issued his legal opinion confirming the validity of the agreement and pledging Palau's full faith and credit.

Almost immediately, the Ibedul sued to prevent the deal, arguing that the loan had to be authorized by the OEK. Further, Palauan competitive bidding requirements had not been followed. The lawsuit frightened the banks. They demanded that Palau enact new legislation specifically authorizing the loans. At this point, unless Palau passed the legislation the banks demanded and the Ibedul's litigation were defeated, the IPSECO project would unravel. On April 12, 1983, the Ibedul suddenly, almost mysteriously, withdrew his lawsuit.

On April 21 the OEK began its legislative hearings. Mochrie appeared at the hearings, asserting that the project would be self-financing and basically would not cost Palau anything. The OEK then passed legislation authorizing the president to waive Palau's competitive bidding requirements and award the contract directly to IPSECO. Both houses of the OEK in their reports on the new law emphasized that the IPSECO project would be self-financing. Nevertheless, the new law waived Palau's sovereign immunity so that if the project revenues were not sufficient, the Palau government itself could be sued and would pay. There was considerable political doublethink going on. Many of the key players in Palau's executive and legislative branches saw through Mochrie and had grave doubts about his projections. After all, the OEK legislation had as its express purpose allowing the banks to sue Palau if the project were *not* self-financing.

Thus, at the April 21 OEK hearings, Senator Nakamura commented, "You say the project will not involve appropriations from national government, but when you look at the bill it authorizes appropriations. So when I look at this report, it conflicts with the bill itself."

If fuel sales were the basis of Mochrie's self-financing projections for the IPSECO project, Alan Seid's testimony at the OEK hearings destroyed that prospect:

Mr. Seid. . . . I would like to cite certain examples which are reflected in those projections. In year one of the initial sale of fuel, IPSECO claims that it will sell 7 million gallons of fuel to Van Camp. Van Camp will buy 7 million. Our research indicates that Van Camp bought a million gallons on the average in the last four or five years at the most. It is rather inconceivable how Van Camp would be able to buy 7 million gallons of fuel which would provide for funding—for income to the project—when in fact you gentlemen know that Van Camp is closed today.

If Palau knew this, why didn't Palau look elsewhere?

In fact, Seid and Smith, representing the Ibedul and the State of Koror, recommended a careful study of alternatives. But the process of investigating alternatives would be very lengthy and very costly.

Sen. Rechucher. . . . [W]hat I am asking is that, how long will it take if we are going to negotiate for another power plant? If you know from your own observation and study?

Mr. Seid: Okay. We don't know at this time how long will it take.

Sen. Tarkong. My last question is addressed to the Vice President and Minister of Administration. If this deal with IPSECO does not go through . . . how long will it take for the Administration to replace this transmission need? This is my last question.

Vice President Oiterong. . . . [Y]ou can calculate the time element involved if we were to renegotiate, taking into consideration the past two-year negotiation time, a new deal—it will be a long time.

Koror's opposition had its own political hooker. Whatever the merits of the Ibedul's opposition to IPSECO, working out an alternative with him would not be easy. The Ibedul had made that clear when he wrote to the OEK demanding 40 percent Koror ownership of the power plant plus half of the utility fees if it were located in Koror. What about changes in the IPSECO deal as already negotiated? Koror and the Ibedul would not agree to that.

In short, the OEK was stuck. Take IPSECO, warts and all, or go back to politics as usual and an absence of electric power in Palau for years to come. The OEK reported out the legislation with only two dissenting votes. The OEK House and Senate reports emphasized the project was self-financing. The reports would protect the legislators against local criticism if the Palau government had to use its own funds to repay the IPSECO loan.

The high commissioner of the trust territory may veto any Palau legislation within twenty days of its passage. Uherbelau traveled to Saipan, hand carrying the new OEK legislation to the high commissioner of the trust territory—Ms. McCoy—to gain her prompt approval and to answer any questions she had concerning the OEK law and the project. As it happened, she had quite a few. What if additional funds beyond the project revenues were needed to repay the banks? Would Palau use Department of Interior's funds intended for Palau's general government operations? Uherbelau responded that Palau would use local revenues only.

The high commissioner remained skeptical. On May 5, 1983, Ms. McCoy vetoed that part of the law permitting Palau to be sued if the project were not self-financing. Although she could have vetoed the waiver of the competitive bidding and award of the power plant contract to IPSECO, thus voiding the IPSECO deal altogether, she let that part of the law stand. The United States seemed to care only about potential U.S. liability.

At the OEK hearings, Mochrie had said that the "international banks and the British Government have examined all of IPSECO's projections in detail and have assured the Presidential Task Force on Palau Power that the project is in fact self-financing." After the OEK hearing, the Ibedul, on the advice of Smith, sent a letter to each of the banks asking for their written confirmation of Mochrie's representations. The Ibedul's letter included a critical analysis of IPSECO's revenue projections.

The banks met. Should they answer the Ibedul's letter? They agreed they should contact President Remeliik, pointing out that the banks had not examined IPSECO's revenue projections. But they did nothing. The Ibedul's letter remained unanswered. A week later the banks learned of McCoy's veto of the OEK law. "What did it mean?" Syrett asked Oiterong. "What was the U.S. position? Could the banks be paid out of Compact funds or not?" The project was near collapse.

Oiterong, accompanied by Lazarus Salii, joined Mochrie in Washington, D.C. There they met with Assistant Secretary of Interior Pedro Sanjuan and Ambassador Fred Zeder, head of the Office of Micronesian Status Negotiations, in the State Department. It was the project's last gasp.

The views of Zeder and Sanjuan were well known. Zeder saw the islands, potentially, as "real centers of commerce." Power was essential. In pressing for IPSECO, Zeder emphasized his own business experience.

Sanjuan had testified the year before against the IPSECO project. It was too big and too costly; eventually the United States would be stuck with the bill. Moreover, the Marshall Islands' project was already in trouble. Both Zeder and Sanjuan were right. The Palau Islands could be "centers of commerce," and the United States would have to pay for power.

Mochrie was the lead spokesman at the meeting. He emphasized that "Her Majesty's government" was behind the project and he, personally, was looking forward to a long-term, continuing partnership with the United States. That was, indeed, the point. Mochrie had much at stake here. He hoped to put IPSECO plants in all of Micronesia and American Samoa. The one in the Marshalls was up and running; Palau was next, then American Samoa and the Marianas. If the United States blocked the Palau project, his entire plan for the future of IPSECO vanished.

Mochrie's opening speech reaffirmed all of the Interior Department's fears. The Marshalls and Palau IPSECO plants were bad enough, but Mochrie was going to push the United States into a host of these overpriced projects for which the United States would eventually pay.

Mochrie continued to speak with anger and bewilderment. What did McCoy's veto mean? The Palau OEK had passed the legislation. Didn't that bind the United States?

Interior replied with a basic question: Where did the deal stand? Had Palau signed an agreement with IPSECO? The Palauans gave an ambiguous reply. Interior would not let the matter go. Was the deal consummated?

Finally, the Palauans replied. Yes, they had agreed to it; the agreements were signed. It was easier to lie and get on to other matters. The Palauans emphasized their need. Power was essential, and now they were going to get it. The United States should support them.

Mochrie and the Palauans asked the United States to reverse the high commissioner's veto so that the banks, if the project turned out not to be self-financing, could sue Palau. The United States refused. The United States knew that any lawsuit against Palau eventually would have to be paid by the United States. Mochrie and the Palauans came at the issue another way. Would the U.S. government itself assist the project? Perhaps the United States could guarantee the repayment? Once again the United States turned the Palauans down. As a matter of policy, the U.S. would not guarantee credit or underwrite default for the island governments during the trusteeship.

Finally, Palau fell back to its last hope: the Compact. Could Palau use its Compact funds to finance IPSECO? On this issue, as Palau knew, Sanjuan and Zeder took opposing positions. In response to the question, Sanjuan resisted any U.S. commitment. Zeder's view was that Palau should be treated as an independent country making its own decisions. If Palau wanted to pledge its own Compact funds, that was Palau's business. As long as U.S. funds were not involved, the United States should not intervene. Zeder's view prevailed. The State Department sent a note to the British government stating that Compact funds could be used.

That did not settle the matter. What Compact funds could be used by Palau to stand behind the IPSECO deal? This was not a trivial question. Interior was cynical about the Compact. It felt that in twelve to fifteen years, when the funds were about to run out, the islands would be asking for additional U.S. funds. For this reason, the Compact was fairly specific, setting forth separate accounts for special purposes. Interior had insisted that Compact funds should be spent as mandated in the Compact agreements to ensure that the Micronesian governments would not overrun their budgets

Under the Compact, Palau would receive $28 million for energy. Alone, these funds were not sufficient to fund the IPSECO project. Could other Compact funds be used for IPSECO? The Compact granted Palau $36 million for capital needs during the first year of the Compact, and until the Compact was approved, Palau received additional U.S. funds annually for power. Zeder, in the State Department telegram, stated that these funds all could also be used to service the IPSECO project. From a financial point of view, this was sufficient; but, just in case, the U.S. note ended with a vigorous endorsement of the project.

Please be assured that the Office for Micronesian Status Negotiations and the Office of the Assistant Secretary of the Interior for Territorial and International Affairs fully support the efforts of the Government of Palau to improve its present power-generating capability.
Ambassador Zeder sends.

To this day, Interior Department officials say that this last paragraph and the possibility of using Compact funds other than the amount explicitly set aside for energy were inserted by Zeder at the last moment and not cleared with them. Cleared or not, it was the go-ahead the banks wanted. The Zeder telegram saved the IPSECO project.

On June 6, 1983, by telegram the Department of the Interior (DOI) inspector general advised Remeliik *not* to sign the loan agreements because a DOI review of revenue projections showed that Palau could not service the debt. The inspector general repeated this advice the next month in a draft report analyzing the electrical power plant and fuel storage facility.

On September 2, President Remeliik belatedly acknowledged receipt of the inspector general's telegram and report. Remeliik's response was, at best, not forthcoming. For the first time, he disclosed to the Department of the Interior that it was not until "June 8, 1983, [that] Vice President Oiterong executed the loan agreements and other related documents on behalf of the Republic of Palau."

If, as Remeliik admitted, the Department of the Interior telegram was received two days *before* Palau executed the loan agreement, why had Palau gone forward? Remeliik had not even notified Oiterong in London of the inspector general's letter. Why not?

Remeliik responded that he did not see any other way for Palau to get power.

During this period, Palau had repeatedly requested for sufficient funds to upgrade, improve or otherwise ensure reliable source of electric power to serve our people not only for the present power requirements but for the future as well. Both the . . . OEK . . . and my Administration determined that to borrow money on Palau's public credit to finance this vital developmental project was the only avenue open to us.

Subsequently, Compact critics questioned U.S. actions. They argued the

United States refused to intervene in order to create an economic dependency that would require Palau to ratify the Compact in order to finance the IPSECO project. This assumes that the Palauans were passive, not really comprehending what was happening. In my view, the Palauans were as aware as any of the players involved in the IPSECO machinations. They had thought out the IPSECO deal rather carefully and arrived at the conclusion that from a Palauan perspective, the deal was not a bad one at all. The Palauans knew their need for power and they knew as well the U.S. failure for more than thirty years to meet that need. Pledging their future resources was a gamble. If the Compact were ratified, there would be enough funds. If the Compact was not ratified, the United States could be looked to for additional funds. Either way, Palau would finally have power in place and the United States would be addressing the question of how to finance Palau's power needs. A key OEK Senator in 1983 put it well: "If we default, the plant cannot be repossessed, and the United States will pay. It is debatable whether the United States would, indeed, pay; but, in light of the need for reliable electric power to develop Palau, the risk may be one worth taking."

In sum, Palau was acting reasonably, even shrewdly, to meet its priority need. Some, in the United States at least, and perhaps a few in Palau, knew how important it was for a Palau-elected government to produce visible benefits for the people if democracy on the island was to survive. The Remeliik government had very few chances to deliver any benefits. IPSECO, high cost or not, provided such an opportunity. Nevertheless, IPSECO was not certain if Palau politicians would view the IPSECO project as within their self-interest.

Between July 1983 and November 1984, IPSECO paid five Palauan officials a total of $775,000: Carlos Salii, then Speaker of Palau's House of Delegates, received $250,000; Lazarus Salii, Carlos's brother and then Ambassador for Trade Relations and Status Negotiations, was paid $200,000; the Ibedul, $100,000; Hokkens Baules, a private businessman, $121,000; and, finally, $175,000 was given to Polycarp Basilius, the president of the Palau Economic Development Bank. These payments have been used by critics to cast doubt on the value of the IPSECO deal to Palau, suggesting that the bribe turned the Palauans around on IPSECO. One fact stands out: except for the Ibedul (whose primary political concern was the ownership of the land on which the IPSECO project was to be built) no one in a position of power in Palau viewed the IPSECO deal as a bad one either before or after the IPSECO payment.

Lazarus Salii received two payments from Mochrie: $100,000 on July 19 and $100,000 on September 20, 1983. Salii explained the two payments subsequently in December 1987 in testimony before the House Foreign Affairs Subcommittee:

In 1983, I was interested in the establishment of an airline in Palau on a private venture basis. At that time I was owner of BELTA Travel Agency and proposed with Gordon Mochrie (the IPSECO project manager) that we joint venture this airline. Mochrie agreed. . . .

This was purely a business venture, not in any way connected to the IPSECO Power Plant. The money advanced was for the services of the BELTA Travel Service Company which was a privately owned and licensed Palauan company.

After the failure of the Compact in the first referendum held that year and the political uncertainties for Palau that ensued as well as the various difficulties that Mochrie began to encounter, the project [the Belta Travel Agency] was not aggressively pursued. The project has been dormant since then.

The Salii testimony appears incredible. There was no evidence that Mochrie ever spoke about a travel agency, and there was no contract to suggest Mochrie contemplated any such investment.

Assuming Salii was being paid to assist in the IPSECO project, what did IPSECO get, or hope to get, in exchange? At the least, support in Babeldaob for the plant. With Koror doubtful because of the Ibedul's opposition, Polycarp Basilius and Lazarus Salii were politically strong enough to permit IPSECO to locate the project on Babeldaob. (In fact, the IPSECO plant was eventually located on Babeldaob, permitting the Ibedul, who had been paid as well, to discreetly withdraw his opposition to the project.) Lazarus Salii first appears in connection with the IPSECO project in the winter of 1983 when he flew with the Palau delegation to London. Later that year, in May 1983, he returned to London and Washington for meetings with Sanjuan and Zeder. Mochrie and IPSECO may have been hoping that Salii's prestige with the United States was such that he could get the high commissioner to reverse her veto of the OEK legislation. If so, Mochrie was disappointed. Others believe that Zeder's support for the project was not certain and Salii's prestige helped bring him along. This seems unlikely. Zeder had always supported the IPSECO power contracts, both in the Marshalls and in Palau. Moreover, the meeting went as expected: Interior (Sanjuan) against; State (Zeder) in favor. By all accounts, Salii was not an active participant. If Salii's presence had any impact at all, it was a marginal one.

Nevertheless, IPSECO may have envisioned at least this marginal role for Salii as the quid pro quo for the payment. If so, was that improper? Here Salii's technical defense comes in. Salii's governmental position, Ambassador on Status Negotiations, provided that he serve without pay; it was obviously expected that he would continue to work in the private sector. Although virtually every member of the OEK does business with the Republic of Palau, Palau does not have a conflict of interest law. In sum, Salii violated no Palau conflict of interest law. Nor did Salii ever act contrary to the government of Palau's desires in the IPSECO matter; nor, for that matter, did Salii ever change his own views on the project. All this may be true.

But insofar as the IPSECO payment bought Salii's assistance in negotiating the project, duties he was to discharge for the government of Palau without payment, the receipt of the payments was clearly improper. He was, as the GAO report later suggested, using his public office for private gain.

Even if this were the case, why should Salii's receipt of the IPSECO payments affect Compact ratification by the United States? Congressman Stephen Solarz asked that very question in 1987 to Santos Olikong, the Speaker of the OEK House of Representatives and a strong opponent of the Compact:

Mr. Olikong. If it is held up, we would remain under the United States Congress. And in that way, we might be able to send the FBI to Palau and other investigative officials to investigate the whole thing from one to ten and then 100. If Palau becomes an independent government, no one in Palau can hope for things to be as in the past. We need the United States to help us investigate all of these allegations.

Olikong's response was in part candid and in part disingenuous. Some Compact opponents thought that the IPSECO payment to Salii was the tip of the iceberg. They believed there were other payments on other projects and perhaps other undisclosed legal violations. To that degree, Olikong's response was candid.

But of course all of the political figures were engaged in electioneering. Compact ratification was projected as Salii's strong card for November 1988. Blocking the Compact might deny Salii reelection. To the extent that Olikong was counting on the congressional Compact debate to damage Salii's reelection prospects, Olikong was misleading the U.S. Congress.

The IPSECO power project initially encompassed a power-generating station with five generators. After the relocation of the IPSECO plant from Koror to Babeldoab, Palau elected to cancel one of the five generators and to utilize those funds to construct transmission lines to carry the power from the plant site to Koror.

The IPSECO plant was built and began operations but revenues fell far short of the amounts required to repay the bank loans. Compact funds were needed. But the Palau Compact failed ratification in 1983 and 1984 when it could not get a 75 percent favorable vote. In 1985, when the first payment became due, Palau defaulted. Shortly thereafter, on December 17, 1985, the banks sued the government of Palau in the New York State Supreme Court. The banks had the contractual obligations in hand, and Palau had signed them. What was there to litigate? It was going to be an easy victory. Surprisingly, Palau mounted a strong defense: fraud. Palau said it relied on Mochrie's projections that the IPSECO project would be self-financing. Palau had even asked the banks whether the project was self-financing. The banks had said nothing. Their failure to tell Palau was an omission of a material fact: fraud. It was a matter of who said what to whom and when. It would be a long, drawn-out case.

With the case still being sorted out with preliminary motions, Congress weighed in. Congress's concern was the status of Palau's finances. As Congress saw it, Palau had been taken advantage of by (1) an English con man who sold Palau an overpriced power plant, and (2) unscrupulous bankers who watched greedily as Palau fell into Mochrie's trap. Compact money should not be wasted repaying these schemers. Senator McClure, the ranking Republican on the Energy Committee, in a speech on the Senate floor accused "Her Majesty's Government" of "sending out privateers to seek American assets with letters marque." Congress amended the law approving the Palau Compact so that effectively Compact funds could not be used to pay the IPSECO debt.

If Congress had for the moment saved Palau from the banks it had not saved Salii from IPSECO. Solarz might carefully separate IPSECO payments from Compact approval, but the Compact opponents would not. Salii was a knight errant warring for the Compact. After the IPSECO disclosures, his armor was tarnished.

Notes

1. Page 47. *In August 1981 two members*. Regarding the Marshall Islands IPSECO plant, see G. Johnson, "Marshalls Suing IPSECO to Recover Missing Funds," *Pacific Daily News*, July 9, 1986, p. 4.; Inspector General, *Ability of the Republic of the Marshall Islands to Repay Outstanding Loans* (Washington, D.C.: Dept. of the Interior, 1983).

2. Page 49. *On February 2, 1982*. For the basic chronology, I have relied on Judge Sweet's opinion finding the facts, *Morgan Guaranty Trust Company of N.Y. v. Republic of Palau*, 693 F. Supp. 1479 (S.D. NY, 1988), supplemented by Appendices I and II of GAO, *U.S. Trust Territory: Issues Associated with Palau's Transition to Self-Government* (1989). A useful Palauan perspective is found in the long letter from Senator Itelbong Lui to Congressman Morris Udall (March 16, 1988), in the author's possession.

3. Page 50. *Thus, at the April 21 OEK hearings*. All excerpts from the April 21 hearings are from the full transcript of these hearings which are available in English from the Olbiil Era Kelulau (OEK), Koror, Palau.

4. Page 51. *The reports would protect*. The House OEK report stated: "The most attractive feature of this proposal is that it is *self-financing*. . . . IPSECO claims and the Task Force has repeatedly maintained that the project will be able to generate enough revenues from the sale of fuel oil to pay off the loans to the bankers *without* any appropriations by the National Government" (emphasis in original). The Senate OEK report reiterated: "This project is intended to pay for itself through utility rates and the sale of fuel from the fuel storage facility. It should not require any appropriations from the national government."

5. Page 52. *The high commissioner.* The text uses the word veto because the reader is more likely to be familiar with that concept. Technically, the high commissioner can only "suspend" legislation, the theory being that when the trusteeship ends, the legislation would then come into force.

6. Page 52. Assistant Secretary Sanjuan's testimony is found in *Hearings and Markup before the Subcommittees on Human Rights and International Organizations, and on Asian and Pacific Affairs, Developments Regarding the Compact of Free Association Between the United States and Palau*, 98th Cong., 2nd Sess., 1984.

7. Page 54. The inspector general report in final form is found in Office of Inspector General, *Republic of Palau's Efforts to Obtain an Electrical Power Plant and a Fuel Storage Facility*, (Washington, DC: Department of the Interior, 1983). For a subsequent analysis, see: Office of Inspector General, *Power Plant and Fuel Storage Facility, Republic of Palau* (Washington, DC: Department of the Interior, 1989).

8. Page 54. *On September 2, President Remeliik.* Letter from Pres. Remeliik to Inspector General Richard Mulberry, Sept. 2, 1983, in Office of Inspector General, *Audit Report: Palau's Efforts to Obtain an Electrical Power Plant and a Fuel Storage Facility* (Washington, DC: Department of the Interior, Nov. 1983, Attachment 1.

9. Page 55. *Subsequently, Compact critics.* Transcript of ABC News, "20/20," July 2, 1987:

Tom Jarrel: . . . [B]ut the plant soon became the focus of controversy and the suspicion that the whole expensive project was conceived for one purpose—to force Palau into such a desperate financial situation that its only hope for economic survival was to rescind the nuclear-free constitution and get the money offered by the Compact of Free Association.

10. Page 55. The OEK Senate quote is found in the GAO report.

11. Page 55. *Some in the United States.* I am indebted to Ernest Downes of the Department of Defense for first making this point to me.

12. Pages 55-56. Salii, in his testimony before the Solarz committee, only admitted to $100,000, which was all that the newspaper article in the *San Jose Mercury News* had charged.

13. Page. 56. *Salii's governmental position.* The GAO in its report points out that the Palau executive order established the position without pay. GAO, *U.S. Trust Territory: Issues Associated with Palau's Transition to Self-Government* (1989). The OEK transcript of the hearings suggested a limitation of $25,000.

14. Pages 57-58. The joint resolution restricting the banks in seeking to force Palau to repay its IPSECO loans is found in P.L. 99-658, Sec. 104(e), 48 U.S.C.A. 1681.

7

The Assassination of Palau's First President; The Controversial Acquittal

In the early morning hours of June 30, 1985, assassins crouched in the bushes outside Remeliik's home. When the president drove home, the killers intended to surprise him, shoot him, and flee.

Remeliik's young grandson was fretful, finding it difficult to sleep. His mother, Remeliik's daughter, Patricia, walked with him outside. There she sat with him, talking to him quietly. Diagonally across the street, she noticed a burgundy pickup truck. A man sat inside smoking a cigarette. She could not quite make out who it was. The boy was ready for bed now. She went back into the house with him and put him to sleep.

A few minutes later, Remeliik drove up. The killer was ready. As the president opened the door, the killer raised the carbine and fired. The gun jammed. The killer had to reload. Remeliik had been warned. He cried out and ran in front of the car to enter the house. The killer jumped over the car and knocked him down. They scuffled. The president lost his footing. Another shot. This time it struck Remeliik in the thigh and knocked him down the hill. Three bullets to the neck and head, and the first elected president of Palau was dead.

A whole, misfired .30-caliber round was found about a foot from the top of the hill together with white and blue fibers on a coconut tree which came from the white tee-shirt and blue shorts Remeliik was wearing that night. Remeliik's pen, cigarettes, lighter, and car keys were scattered on the hill where they fell from his pocket as his body rolled down the incline. The murder weapon was never found.

The Palau people were stunned. This killing, the first murder of a Pacific Island head of state, frightened and angered them. The vast outpouring of affection at his funeral, the chanting and dancing through the night, were sincere. The people liked Remeliik, and in death they showed their deep affection for him.

Assassination theories abounded. *Newsweek* alluded to Remeliik's reputation as a "high-living womanizer" and surmised that the gunmen were hired by a husband or close relative of one of Remeliik's mistresses. It suggested as well "a more personal vendetta." In Palau, suspicion rested initially on Masanori Sugiyama, who had brutally murdered two men in Guam, torturing and suffocating one of them and stabbing and burning the other. He and an accomplice had been convicted and were sentenced to long terms in the Guam prison. Roman Tmetuchl, governor of Airai State, at the request of the Sugiyama family, had written the attorney general of Guam, Richard Opper, to ask that Masanori be transferred to Airai State prison to serve his prison term there. All costs of the transfer and imprisonment would be borne by the state of Airai. If Guam wanted him back, the attorney general had only to ask and Tmetuchl would return him. Opper had agreed to the transfer in the spring of 1985.

Three months later, in June 1985, the *Pacific Daily News* broke the news that there was no prison in Airai State. Masanori was in fact fishing, drinking, and pursuing his usual occupation: terrorizing the locals. Attorney General Opper was considerably embarrassed. He wrote to Tmetuchl and demanded Masanori's return to Guam. Opper noted in his letter that President Remeliik, on behalf of the national government of Palau, had supported his request. Then, together with two associates, the Guam attorney general went to Palau on Thursday, June 27, to bring Masanori back on the Monday morning flight. Tmetuchl suddenly had to leave the island. Negotiations proceeded with Tmetuchl's lawyer, Johnson Toribiong, and the Airai Council of Chiefs.

Opper tried to strengthen his bargaining position. He offered to credit the convict for time served if Masanori returned voluntarily; if not, Opper would obtain a writ of extradition and Masanori would have to serve his sentence from the beginning. Negotiations proceeded slowly. Opper had long, inconclusive meetings with Toribiong and various Palauan officials on Friday and Saturday. On Sunday morning, just before a scheduled breakfast meeting with Toribiong, federal officials called Opper and told him Remeliik had been shot. Palauans said that Saturday night Masanori had boasted he would kill the president. Based on these reports, the first thought of federal officials and, indeed, of the Palauan officials, was that Masanori murdered Remeliik.

The breakfast meeting with Toribiong was tense; introductory pleasantries very brief. Opper put the question: "Is Masanori going to be at the airport tomorrow morning?"

Toribiong avoided it. "Masanori has had some discussions with the council of Airai but there are no final decisions yet. Senator Sugiyama would like to speak with you." Senator John Sugiyama was Masanori's uncle. The family link was important. Family relationships—immediate family and extended family—were the ties that bound. In Palau, as in other Pacific

Islands, far from support communities and subject to typhoons that could devastate their world, the one rock on which to rely, the unbreakable tie, was family. Sugiyama was fulfilling a role demanded by tradition and by culture. He took on the task willingly; the passion of his plea was real.

Remeliik had supported extradition. The political picture had changed as a result of Remeliik's death. Perhaps there was an opening. Senator Sugiyama noted the changed circumstances caused by Remeliik's death. "When we first met in your office, Mr. Opper, you told me that it mattered not to you whether Masanori stayed in Palau. You told me that if our national government was not requesting his return to Guam, you would be just as happy to leave him with us under house arrest. Now, I believe that there is a possibility that the former hard position taken by President Remeliik, which I did not understand, may alter." Opper rejected this. It was too late now and too much had happened to allow Masanori to stay under "house arrest" in Palau. The meeting broke up. On Sunday night Toribiong told Opper that Masanori had fled. Toribiong did not think Masanori would join Opper at the airport the following morning.

Despite Masanori's boasts and unsavory reputation, and whatever the initial suspicions, the case against him as the murderer of Remeliik did not develop. Ironically, his actions were to be used against other suspects. Six months later, two relatives of Governor Tmetuchl were arrested and charged with first degree murder and a conspiracy to kill President Remeliik. They were Melwert Tmetuchl, his son; Leslie Tewid, his nephew; and Anghenio Sabino, a friend who worked for Melwert Tmetuchl. Francisco Gibbons was said to have actually fired the deadly shots. With their arrest, the murder became charged with local Palauan politics.

There are no jury trials in Palau. In late February and early March 1986, in accordance with Palau procedure, three judges heard the evidence against Tmetuchl's relatives. Two were specially appointed by the chief judge: Leonardo Ruluked, the principal of Palau High School, and Yoich Kohama, a Palau court clerk. The third judge was a statesider, a superior court judge from the Northern Mariana Islands, Robert Hefner.

The case lasted for 6 1/2 days. Close to seventy witnesses testified. Critical to the prosecution was a series of conversations overheard by two women friends of the accused. The women received drugs from the accused. One of them, Mistycal Maidesil, had first denied any knowledge of the killing, but now she said she was present when the accused plotted to kill Remeliik.

Q. Specifically what was said by whom with reference to the President?

A. That discussion, Meliong and Leslie were there during which Melwert said, "He is a bad President. We should find someone to replace him. He is a bad President; we should find someone to lead Palau. . . ."

Q. About how often, if more than once, did similar discussions take place where anyone made any comments about the President?...

A. I heard this about 15 to 20 times.

Q. When they occurred . . . who said what to whom?

A. Nothing much was said . . . except only that Melwert stated that, "He is a bad President. We should replace him with someone who can lead Palau." . . . Further, he stated, "For example. Let's take Masanori. He is supposed to be imprisoned or jailed here in Palau, but because the President refused to sign his documents, he was transferred over to Guam."

Q. Did those present react or respond in any way to that remark?

A. No. They only agreed.

In addition, the convicted murderer, Masanori Sugiyama, turned state witness. Masanori testified that several weeks before the assassination, he had sold to defendant Melwert Tmetuchl a .30-caliber carbine and ammunition for it. Maidesil described a similar weapon she had seen in the possession of Melwert several weeks before the murder.

The second woman, Namiko Ngiraikelau, testified that on her way home, about five to ten minutes after Remeliik was shot, she passed by a burgundy-colored, four-by-four pickup truck with tinted windows owned by Melwert's brother, Mlib. She saw two men walking and recognized one as Melwert and the other as Sabino. The two got into Mlib's burgundy truck, made a U-turn and drove away.

The dark red pickup truck was seen by others that night. Patricia Remeliik, the president's daughter, who was standing outside her home, and Isaac Bai, while driving on the main road on his way home, saw the truck with its lights off on a crossroad near the main road.

The defendants claimed they were elsewhere at the time of the crime. Melwert denied ever having any agreements with Sabino or Tewid to kill Remeliik. Melwert Tmetuchl testified that he was at home at the time of the shooting, although no witness saw him at home after about 11:45 p.m. that night. Sabino, similarly, testified that he never heard anybody say anything about killing or harming the president and denied being in the town that night. The three judges convicted all of the defendants of first degree murder and conspiracy and imposed lengthy prison sentences. Hefner said he discounted Maidesil's testimony, relying on the testimony of Ngiraikelau and the physical evidence.

The defendants appealed. To manage the appeal, the accused retained Stuart Beck, Governor Tmetuchl's attorney in Palau in the seventies. Beck brought in David Richenthal, who had ties to the American Civil Liberties Union (ACLU) which packaged the Beck/Richenthal appellate brief as an ACLU special report. With that ACLU report, Beck and Richenthal pressed their case before the *New York Times*.

On November 27, 1986, while the appeal was pending, the *New York Times* ran a front-page story headed "Doubts Cling to Pacific Assassination Verdict." The story, which tracked the ACLU report closely, quoted Richenthal: "The evidence in the case was so inconsistent and suspect that it would not have survived scrutiny by a grand jury in any American jurisdiction."

The *Times* story highlighted the weaknesses in the prosecutor's case—the limited physical evidence and the fact that no weapon was found—as well as noting the alibis of the defendants. The *Times* story focused on the two women, particularly Maidesil, the only witness to offer a motive for the murder, and she was described as a heroin user who failed three polygraph tests.

Richenthal mobilized congressional pressure as well. Congressman Don Edwards (D-CA), chairman of the Subcommittee on Civil and Constitutional Rights, wrote a series of letters between June and October of 1986 to the FBI protesting the lack of a jury trial, the use of the federal witness protection program for Maidesil, and the use of the FBI to assist the prosecution.

The ACLU report linked the Remeliik assassination to the Compact dispute, suggesting that the pro-Compact right wing, perhaps acting in concert with U.S. intelligence forces, was responsible. This theory, elaborated on by antinuclear activists and by a few Palau legislators, attributed to Remeliik strong antinuclear convictions. Remeliik had been president of the Constitutional Convention in the late seventies and he had helped to sponsor the Constitution's antinuclear clauses. Thus, they reasoned, Remeliik's killing was part of a cleverly engineered CIA coup carefully designed to oust a moderate leadership and replace it with a Palau executive more supportive of the Compact, one closely tied to the Pentagon and the IPSECO project.

This convoluted CIA theory was given credibility by "20/20," the nationally televised ABC news program, which, in an irresponsible display, argued CIA involvement with respect to both the power project and the presidential assassination, as part of a U.S. military plan to make Palau totally and helplessly dependent on the United States and the funds of the Compact. The "20/20" program staff reasoned as follows: Any sane populace was against assassination, against overspending, and against nuclear waste and nuclear war. Why would anyone in Palau want them? The answer: Palau was being snookered by the forces of evil: U.S. militarism. The program repeated the argument that Remeliik had planned to expose the machinations behind the power plant loan but was assassinated the evening before he was to go on local television. Although a planned television address was mentioned in the ACLU report and repeated as an article of faith by many anti-Compact advocates, no proof has ever surfaced that such an address in fact was planned. Those in the government at the time deny it. Further, Remeliik had initiated and strongly promoted the IPSECO project. Since his accession to the presidency, he had strongly supported the Compact as well. The conspiracy theory made no sense at all.

What permitted the CIA hypothesis to pass the "laugh test" was the fact that in 1975-76 the CIA, in an incredible act of stupidity, wiretapped the rooms of the Micronesians negotiating the Compact with the United States, presumably to try to manipulate Micronesian politics to their advantage. Since that time, almost all unusual events in Micronesia, especially in Palau, have been attributed to CIA intervention.

The appellate court was composed of three white judges, two of whom were not resident on Palau: Edward King, the Chief Judge of the Supreme Court of the Federated States of Micronesia (FSM); Paul Abbate, Chief Judge of the Superior Court of Guam; and Frederick O'Brien of Palau. The judicial panel appeared balanced. King was young, aggressive, bright: a sixties liberal with a strong antigovernment bias. He came to Micronesia originally as head of the litigation office of the Micronesian Legal Services program. Abbate was much older, soon to retire at age seventy. He had come to Guam from the Bronx, New York City, about twenty-five years before. His was the last stateside judicial patronage appointment to Guam. Soon after he came to Guam, his teenage son was murdered. The killing affected him deeply, so that on criminal matters he was strongly progovernment. O'Brien's background as defense counsel in the judge advocate general's office in Hawaii made him less predictable.

The appellate court reviewed the record, reversed the trial court, and ordered that the three be acquitted. The decision found that the prosecution's case depended on the testimony of two women. The appellate court examined their testimony at length. It characterized Maidesil as a habitual drug abuser who had failed a lie detector test three times and had changed her story so frequently as to make her inherently incredible. Similarly, the other woman, Ngiraikelau, contradicted herself at various times to the point that the court found her testimony not "reasonable evidence."

Maidesil testified that during June 1985 she smoked marijuana three times a week and used heroin twice a week, the heroin provided to her by Tmetuchl and Tewid. The prosecution argued that this drug use was not evidence that at the time of trial, or at any other time, Maidesil was under the influence of any controlled substance. Initially, on June 30, 1985, the day after the night of the President's shooting, Maidesil told the investigating Palauan police officers that Masanori was the assassin, the motive being Remeliik's refusal to prevent his extradition to Guam. About five days later, Maidesil denied having any knowledge of the assassination.

At the trial, Maidesil testified about hearing the defendants and another unindicted conspirator—Francisco Gibbons—talk about killing the President. There were similar contradictions elsewhere in her testimony. Prior to the trial she said she knew nothing about any guns, but at the trial she testified about going on a picnic with Tmetuchl and Sabino in early June, when they had three guns with them, "a .410 . . . a .22," and another "long gun."

Kenneth Vardell of the FBI interviewed Ms. Maidesil in Honolulu and administered a lie detector test three different times. The first Vardell report, dated July 29, discredited Maidesil. It said that she: "Confessed that she had fabricated her entire account of having heard the four men discuss plans to shoot President Remeliik. She admitted that she had not seen the men with guns on June 28th, had not heard any assassination plan on that date, had not seen Tmetuchl throw any weapon in the lagoon."

After this report, the defendants, who had been first arrested and indicted in early July, were released, and the case against them was withdrawn by the Attorney General.

Subsequently, Maidesil recanted her recantation and Vardell administered a second lie detector test to her. The second Vardell report said she "admitted that she had again lied on almost all of her new statement."

Four months later, on November 12, 1985, Maidesil testified before a federal grand jury in Guam. There, she basically repeated her earlier story that she had heard the same four men plan to kill President Remeliik. Tewid had told her following the shooting that Cisco Gibbons, a friend of Melwert and Tewid, had shot Remeliik and that he, Tewid, had driven Gibbons to Remeliik's home. Maidesil admitted having lied about certain details previously, but now, she said, she was telling the truth. Vardell, however, concluded after a third lie detector test: "The recorded responses are indicative of deception to all relevant questions."

The appellate panel reviewed Ngiraikelau's testimony as well. Ngiraikelau twice told the police that she had seen only one man walk past her house that night and that she was unable to identify that person. But at the trial she said she had seen two men: Tmetuchl and one she later picked from a photo array as defendant Sabino. Ngiraikelau also testified that Melwert Tmetuchl's truck with its distinctive burgundy color was there only fifteen minutes or so after the assassination. The appellate court dismissed the importance of the truck. A burgundy pickup truck with tinted windows such as the one linked to the murder scene was a "common sight on the roads of Palau."

Post mortems came quickly. "In fact, just about every Palauan knows there was only one such vehicle here, and that it belonged to [Melwert] Tmetuchl," responded Phil Isaac, the Palau attorney general who tried the case and argued the appeal. Isaac said the judges picked apart each individual witness's testimony but overlooked "the totality of the evidence" against the accused assassins and the mutually supportive character of the testimony.

The reversal expanded the distance between the courts and the Palauan people as well as between the courts and the government, especially when the Remeliik assassination decision became linked to Compact ratification. Anti-Compact partisans in the States referred to the Remeliik assassination as an unsolved murder on the violent island of Palau. The statement enraged the Salii government. To the government, the Remeliik murder was solved. It was the courts that let them go: those courts filled with white, stateside appointees.

Did the government prove its case? This is hard to assess even after reading the 800-page transcript of the trial. The case does, indeed, hinge on the testimony of Maidesil and Ngiraikelau. Hefner said he discounted Maidesil's testimony altogether and still found the defendants guilty. But from the transcript alone, without relying on Maidesil's testimony, an appellate court could find the evidence too thin to sustain a conviction.

On the one hand, the appellate court could have accepted the Maidesil and Ngiraikelau testimony as being that of two women extremely close to the accused who came forward with great misgivings, seeking always to shield their lovers and friends. The backing and filling of the women, even their lying, reflected this ambivalence and the conflicting pressures upon them. Maidesil's brother was a policeman who pressed her to testify, while she herself testified to her desire to remain silent in order to help the defendants. Lie detector tests are concededly poor indicators of truth in the best of circumstances. The failed lie detector tests in this scenario reflect Maidesil's changing state of mind. The appellate court could have discounted their importance and deferred to the trial court in judging the honesty of the witness.

On the other hand, the appellate court could have read the transcript itself and seen two women on drugs, one of whom failed a lie detector test three times. The physical evidence, the car and the gun, were linked to the defendants only through Maidesil and Ngiraikelau, witnesses of doubtful credibility. Read this way, lack of sufficient evidence was not an unreasonable verdict.

Whether the government proved its case or not, a more difficult question remained. Who killed Remeliik? Did the government try the right people but simply not have the ability to gather sufficient evidence to make the case hold up? Or did the government arrest the wrong men? For the moment, the question was largely ignored, as Compact ratification increasingly held the attention of the Palau people. But it was to return. One's views of the Remeliik assassination continued as a key factor in Palau politics and as a weapon.

The appellate court opinion sharply criticized Attorney General Isaac for placing Maidesil on the stand, thereby vouching for her veracity and making it appear that her testimony was less contradictory than it was. It faulted him further for preventing Vardell of the FBI from testifying as a witness for the defense.

Isaac was incensed. From one perspective, the Remeliik assassination case may have been Isaac's finest hour. Bucking enormous pressure, he had brought the case against relatives of the most powerful man in Palau. He saw the women not as vacillating drug addicts but as witnesses terrified at having to testify against powerfully connected defendants. The court was not only reversing a conviction but, in Isaac's view, unfairly tearing at his reputation.

In a petition for further review, Isaac characterized the opinion of the appellate panel as:

Discrediting the testimony of at least five prosecution witnesses, mischaracterizing their testimony, manufacturing facts not in evidence, and ignoring the totality of the evidence, selectively omitting much corroborative evidence and, finally . . . misapplying a U.S. case which discusses a "doctrine" of inherent incredibility . . . The end result is error causing substantial harm to the Republic for years to come.

Isaac went on radio and repeated his charges. Attacking the court publicly when the case was still to be finally decided went too far. The Supreme Court of Palau appointed a special prosecutor to look at Isaac's radio address. On the special prosecutor's recommendation, the Supreme Court filed a two-count criminal contempt charge against Isaac on the grounds that Isaac's comments obstructed justice by impugning the court in a pending matter. The government and the courts had not only lost faith in one other but were now openly at odds.

The Remeliik assassination decision was particularly painful to Salii. He understood that the release of the three suspects would be used by those hostile to the Compact to suggest Palau's incapacity to govern and to suggest as well a lawless society where wrongdoers were not brought to justice. A conviction would have given the national Palau government a certain stature, weakening the Palauan forces seeking disharmony. Instead, the acquittal continued Palau's terrible confrontational politics.

But the impact was greater than the Palau government understood. Stateside opponents of the Compact learned that major newspapers and television could rather easily be attracted to Palau and influenced to tell the story with the correct antigovernment spin. And it appeared to them that Palauan courts would respond to that media pressure. Thus, Sue Rabbitt Roff, one of the antinuclear advocates, in her 1991 book *Overreaching in Paradise*, referred to "considerable doubts summarized in the Defense Brief of the American Civil Liberties Union in the case and *reported in the* New York Times *in a major full-length article on November 27, 1986, which secured their acquittal* in July 1987" (Emphasis supplied). It was the beginning of the savaging of the Palau government in the press and in scholarly journals, as stateside advocates, savvy in public relations, went to work.

Notes

1. Page 61. *The Palau people were stunned.* D. Shuster, "Elections, Compact and Assassination in the Republic of Palau," 12 *Pacific Studies* 23, 36-39 (1988), describes the Remeliik funeral at some length.

2. Page 62. *Assassination theories abounded.* E. Rampell, "Assassination in

Palau," *Honolulu Magazine*, Aug. 1987, sets out these speculations in considerable detail.

3. Pages 62-63. For the details of the efforts to bring back Masanori Sugiyama, I am indebted to Richard Opper, the former Guam attorney general, who, at the time, wrote an extensive memorandum detailing the events and was kind enough to share it with me,

4. Pages 64-65. "Doubts Cling to Pacific Island Verdict," *New York Times*, Nov. 27, 1986, p. 1.

5.   Page 65.   American Civil Liberties Union (ACLU) Briefing Paper, "Assassination of President Remeliik of Palau, Subsequent Conviction of Three Defendants and Related Events" (New York: ACLU, Sept. 1, 1986).

6.   Page 65. *Remeliik had planned.* As far as I can discover, the idea of the Remeliik radio-television address exposing all surfaced first in the ACLU Briefing Paper, p. 10. It cited Martin Wolff, the Palau Senate counsel. The Department of the Interior, Office of Inspector General, attempted to interview Wolff on this point "but attempts to interview him have been unsuccessful." Memorandum from Asst. Inspector General for Investigations to File 5VI82, p. 11. (Made available to the author via a Freedom of Information Act request.) Wolff's subsequent memoranda treat the IPSECO project very favorably which tends to contradict the ACLU position. "The IPSECO project is not only a valuable asset to Palau, it is essential to the economic self-sufficiency of the future of Palau." Memorandum from Martin Wolff to Speaker Santos Olikong, Subject: IPSECO, Aug. 23, 1985. (Made available to the author by the Inspector General, Department of the Interior, after a Freedom of Information Act request.)

7.   Page 66. *The appellate court. Republic of Palau v. Melwert Tmetuchl, et al.*, Case No. 388-85, Palau Supreme Court, 1986.

8

An Unusual Legal Assignment; Greenpeace Enters the Fray

The special election to succeed Remeliik rapidly turned into a duel between Vice President Oiterong and Lazarus Salii. Roman Tmetuchl, depressed and tainted by the arrest of his son and nephew for the assassination of Remeliik, eschewed a run for the presidency. With Tmetuchl out of it, Oiterong seemed a shoo-in to succeed to the presidency as a result of his commanding win of the vice presidency in 1984. Oiterong obtained the support of both the Ibedul and Tmetuchl, Compact opponents. This support turned out to be a key tactical error, since it blurred his own position on the Compact and linked him even more closely to Tmetuchl.

Salii decided to run after gaining the support of Polycarp Basilius, perhaps the wealthiest man in Palau and a brother of the Reklai, the traditional leader of the northeastern portion of Palau. Thus, Salii complemented his strength in the Southwest, where his home island of Angaur was located and which was basically Ibedul country, with power in the Northeast, Reklai country.

Salii and his supporters vigorously endorsed the Compact. In this they outmaneuvered Oiterong, portraying him as slow and uncertain, an inadequate leader when placed against the bright and dynamic Salii.

Within the Palau Islands, the race was virtually even to the end. (Salii was to win by 100 votes.) Off-island, in the Palauan communities of Guam, Honolulu, Saipan, San Diego, Los Angeles, and Portland, which made up almost 20 percent of the entire vote and which tended to vote more on issues than on personality, Salii's proCompact stance was very appealing, leading to his significant victory. Salii beat Oiterong in the 1985 special presidential election, 4,077 votes to 3,484 votes, a margin of almost 600 votes. Salii was a wholehearted supporter of the United States. He was knowledgeable about the United States as a result of his work for the trust territory government, and enthusiastic about creating economic and political change in Micronesia and in Palau. From the time he was sent on a scholarship from Angaur to Xavier High School on Truk, he stood out as an unusual intellect. When the University of Hawaii in 1957 opened a special program for Micronesians, Salii was granted a scholarship by the U.S. authorities. He was the outstanding student in political science. He worked in the Palau district government and in the trust territory government in Saipan, where his work was highly praised by his superiors. "Brilliant" and "creative" were words commonly used to describe him. He combined this with a fluency in English and an aggressive "can-do" stance that endeared him to U.S. officials.

In the rest of Micronesia—in the Marianas, the Federated States of Micronesia and the Marshalls—there were no special nuclear substance bars in the Constitution and, therefore, their agreements with the United States had passed easily by majority votes of the populace. Embarrassingly, Palau remained still part of the U.S. trusteeship, the only Trusteeship remaining in the United Nations.

After Salii's accession to the Palau presidency in 1985, with his stated goal of completion of the ratification of the Compact, the United States did something quite remarkable: it agreed to change the Compact, including its key defense rights provisions.

The United States agreed to pay an additional $5 million a year for the first four years of the Compact to fund Palau's current operating account, increased the investment fund from $60 million to $70 million, and added $8.6 million for educational purposes. An additional $500,000 of the $2 million energy contribution was granted to those parts of Palau not served by the central power-generating facility, assuring energy funding for the outer islands. Road assistance was expanded from Babeldaob island to all of Palau.

These increased benefits and additional funds were combined with a new section committing the United States for the first time *not* to use, test, store, or dispose of nuclear, toxic chemical, gas, or biological weapons intended for use in warfare. This new language effected no substantive change from the previous Compact. But the new language had the advantage of paralleling the precise wording of the Palau Constitution.

This parallel was critical. The Palau Constitution required any agreement to "use, test, store, or dispose" of nuclear materials to be ratified by a three-quarters vote of the people of Palau. But—the U.S. government and the Palau government argued—the Compact with the United States was no longer such an agreement. As a result of the changes and the parallel language of the Compact, the United States had agreed it could not engage in any of the acts prohibited by the Palau Constitution. Therefore, only a majority vote was needed for ratification.

In February 1986, this new version of the Compact was submitted to the people of Palau for approval. In this third plebiscite, with the excitement of final ratification in the air, the Compact received 72 percent of the votes cast, more approval votes than ever before. This was still not 75 percent, but, of course, Palau argued that 75 percent was no longer required.

The Ibedul sued. In *Gibbons v. Salii*, the Ibedul challenged the vote approving the Compact, arguing that, *even as changed*, the Compact and the Palau Constitution were in conflict and, therefore, a 75 percent approval vote was still needed.

The Ibedul, strongly supported by Greenpeace, which provided outside counsel, pointed out that the United States was granted the right under the Compact to operate its aircraft and naval vessels within the jurisdiction of Palau without "confirming or denying the presence or absence of nuclear weapons within the jurisdiction of Palau." Was not transit of nuclear weapons "storage," which was prohibited by the Compact? For example, if a U.S. ship with nuclear weapons aboard docked in a Palauan port for several days, didn't that constitute storage? Salii, in his testimony in Washington, argued that permanent, in-ground storage of nuclear weapons was intended to be barred by the Palau Constitution, but temporary transit on ships or aircraft was not so barred.

The Ibedul and Compact opponents focused as well on the definition of nuclear power plants. Would not nuclear propulsion systems on U.S. ships be an unconstitutional "using" of nuclear power?

The outside forces allied against the Palau government were formidable, and they were fighting a fight Palau did not understand. Leading the fight was Greenpeace, the largest environmental organization in the world, with a membership of five million, offices in twenty-four countries, and revenues (in 1990) of around $157 million. It was an extremely powerful, determined opponent. One of its founders, Robert Hunter, said in a 1979 chronicle of Greenpeace, *Warriors of the Rainbow*, "It embodied at times a religious fervor, at other times a ruthlessness that bordered on savagery."

The Palau battle was one of a number of fights involving public relations and lobbying in which Greenpeace was now expert. The Greenpeace strategy was to simplify the analysis, embolden the contrasts. There were good guys and bad guys. The good guys, aligned with Greenpeace, were courageous saints; the bad guys, everyone else, were villains without any redeeming virtue.

The Palau government, the Palau institutions, and the Palau leaders—*all of them*—were painted as weak and corrupt. The Palauan people were depicted as unworthy, seeking money above all, even at the expense of family. Roff, writing in 1991, stated: "Palauans are not interested in kinship as such. Their primary concern is with wealth, and kinship for them is a vehicle for its manipulation. ... Even the murder of a close relative, in order to obtain his chiefly title and power, could be atoned for by paying the proper monetary fine." But the overarching villain was the United States.

Greenpeace depicted the fight as the big United States military machine against a few, helpless embattled stalwarts.

With Greenpeace as the Ibedul's champion, the Right Livelihood Foundation of Sweden awarded the Ibedul its peace award (touted as the equivalent of the Nobel Peace Prize) in recognition of his struggle on behalf of Palau to maintain the integrity of its nuclear-free Constitution. Greenpeace had found the Ibedul's weakness. He adored the spotlight. The receipt of the peace award in Stockholm, followed by side trips to Switzerland, Germany, and England, during which he was continually hailed as the indefatigable fighter for a nuclear-free Pacific, would have turned the head of a man considerably more cosmopolitan than the Ibedul. Given the Ibedul's limited background—except for a stint as an enlisted man in the U.S. Army, he had never left Palau—he was understandably thrilled by the international interest in his people's struggle and the adulation accorded him on this trip.

Having established the Ibedul in international circles as the spokesman for Palau, Greenpeace arranged for him to testify before the U.N.'s Trusteeship Council, where he was generally accorded the status of *the* high chief in Palau. (The Reklai, representing the northern confederation, was not mentioned. Moreover, the Reklai favored ratification of the Compact.)

My involvement with Palau and the Compact case began somewhat by chance. I happened to be in Guam in August 1986 counseling the Guam Commission on Self-Determination. Bob Rogers, executive director of the commission and a former teacher in Palau, told me that Isaac Soaladaob, Special Assistant to Palau's Minister of State and a former student of his, had called and asked me to come to Palau.

After a number of phone discussions with Soaladaob, I agreed to make the two-hour flight from Guam to Palau early Saturday morning, August 23, 1986. The Koror airport is very undistinguished. The terminal building has a few wooden benches to accommodate departing passengers, a tiny fast food outlet, and, beside the one gate, a small duty-free shop. The airport runway is still too small to take large jets, thus preventing large-scale Japanese tourism. Soaladaob, a warm, friendly young man, met me at the airport and took me to the Palau Pacific Resort, a first-class hotel in Koror.

The Palau Pacific Resort follows standard Pacific luxury hotel architecture: an expansive lobby, with an open vista from the entrance of the hotel to the pool, palm trees, beach, and the blue sea. From the lobby it looked like paradise. To the guests of the first-class hotel, Palau indeed was paradise: sea and sand, and good food flown in from Hawaii. But the view was misleading. To those who lived there, who had to earn a living there, Palau was not paradise. Rather, it was an extremely difficult place in which to live; the jobs were simply not there.

Soaladaob introduced me to his superior, John Ngiraked, the minister of state. In style, Ngiraked resembled the successful businessman. He wore a small goatee, unique in Palau. Ngiraked was one of the older, respected politicians in Micronesia. He, Tmetuchl, and Salii were the Palauan representatives to the first Congress of Micronesia in 1965. In fact, he had lost out as president of that Congress by a hair. He first had learned Japanese as the language of the governing power but now spoke a remarkably fluent and precise English. We ordered breakfast and Ngiraked explained where the case challenging the ratification of the Compact, *Gibbons v. Salii*, now stood. The government had lost in the trial court and had taken an appeal. My job, I surmised, would be to argue that appeal.

Ngiraked felt the only chance to win was to remove the Palau attorney general's office from the case. His own view was shared, he said, by the rest of the cabinet. President Salii, however, might not agree. Although he didn't mention it, Ngiraked and Salii were openly allies, but covertly political rivals. Ngiraked was extremely ambitious and widely regarded as opportunistic. The Ngiraked-Salii relationship was at best a marriage of political convenience. My coming to Palau at Ngiraked's request might not endear me to Salii.

Later that morning, Michael Mirando, Special Assistant to the President, talked to me as well. Mirando, a young statesider from Ohio, was a lawyer who was very close to the president. In the politically contentious world of Palau, he was probably the most controversial single individual. His motive for coming to Palau was clear and open: he wanted to make money. He looked forward to the approval of the Compact because of the Japanese foreign investment that would follow. Already he was the contact man in Salii's program of economic development for Palau involving the attraction of foreign investment. Palauans resented Mirando's open desire for wealth, questioned his integrity, and worried over his increasing power and influence with the president. They bitterly complained about him, privately among each other and to Salii directly. All to no avail. Salii's relationship with Mirando was extraordinarily close, some said like father and son. They vacationed together and frequently played high-stakes poker together. Their styles were similar: quick, bluff, and explosive, but Salii was less open, academically much stronger, and more thoughtful and more mature.

Mirando was less disparaging of the attorney general's office than Ngiraked but clearly favored my involvement in the litigation. Mirando brought me to President Salii's home. The president was outside seated on a trellis-covered, side patio in a beige safari suit: an epauletted short-sleeve shirt with matching Bermuda shorts and brown open-toed sandals. He was short and somewhat heavy. He wore his hair in a mild Afro, not that common in Palau, perhaps a tribute to both his stateside and his nationalistic ties.

I had met Salii some years before on Guam at a planning conference on the Pacific that I had arranged. He greeted me now with a warm smile. He said he remembered me and knew my work in Guam. President Salii was an extremely articulate, capable man. He was unpretentious, and thus access was easy. He understood the legal issues quickly, did not shy from complexity, and in reaching a decision, talked both personality and substance. He was quick to smile and quick to anger.

We discussed generally the politics of Micronesia and Washington, and then, in more detail, Mirando reviewed the substance of the Compact case. I said little. After a while, Salii said he wanted me to handle the case. But he was circumspect about the extent of my role and my relationship to the attorney general's office.

After the meeting with Salii, Mirando said we would meet at two o'clock that afternoon at the hotel with the attorney general and Phil Isaac, the assistant attorney general who was currently handling the Compact case. As scheduled, that afternoon I met Mirando who explained that the attorney general was out sailing and had pointedly not returned to meet with us. Isaac, too, did not come to the hotel to meet me. The idea of an outsider taking over any part of the case obviously was not going over very well with the attorney general's office.

I wasn't sure what could be done in light of their boycott, but, I said, if the files could be brought to me at the hotel that afternoon, I would look through them. My requirements for the files were very detailed and extensive. I didn't think I was going to get them. I also wanted the key to the judge's law library—the only law library on the island—so I could use it that night. By about 5:00 p.m., to my surprise, the files were at the hotel, with a key to the law library as well.

I thought there was an argument that could be made with respect to "ripeness," a procedural point that the case was not ready to be decided. There had been no intrusion by U.S. nuclear ships into Palau waters or land; nor was one threatened. Substantively, I could make no serious judgments from the briefs on other aspects of the case except that the Palau case was a strong one. One had to know a lot more about the Palau Constitution and the Compact than I to say more than that.

The next morning, I told Mirando I would be interested in involving myself in the case. We should ask for a thirty-day delay at a minimum to permit me to become familiar with the case. Mirando said he would talk to Salii about the request for a thirty-day delay. In response, Salii took a contradictory position. On the one hand, he said he very much desired my participation in the case. On the other hand, he was adamantly opposed to any delay.

What was the sense of having me participate if I couldn't prepare? Why would Salii want me to be involved under those conditions? Mirando was frank about the answer, and the answer was political. The government was going to lose, and it wanted to say it had lost with the best. That was somewhat flattering—just barely so—but without a delay I had doubts about the feasibility of my role. I told Mirando that I was not going to argue before the court unless I could make a contribution and conduct myself professionally. The way matters were shaping up, there was a real possibility of my looking foolish. The whole drama seemed to be the theater of the absurd.

I wanted to review the case one more time. That Sunday afternoon I visited the attorney general's office, which was on the second floor of the judicial building. The office was extremely limited in equipment. The Xerox machine worked one page at a time, without any automatic collator. Necessary law books were in the judge's law library. Computer research was not possible. Because of this, local government attorneys were always at a handicap when stateside attorneys were hired.

Isaac was waiting for me, or, more accurately, working on the case. He made no bones about the fact that he thought he didn't need any help, regardless of what anyone in Palau thought. For all I knew, he was right. Certainly, given the time constraints, whether he needed help or not, he wasn't going to get much from me. The meeting ended very unsatisfactorily. He didn't have the time or desire to give me any memoranda or materials. In any event, I couldn't argue Palau constitutional doctrine without careful preparation. I had to be in Manila the next day to sign a contract with the Asian Development Bank. While that would take no more than one day, it meant that preparation would have to be done on the plane and in Manila, without any discussion with anyone who knew anything about the case. My gut told me to stay away, but I was intrigued by the case and wanted to be involved.

I retreated to the ripeness doctrine, studying it with greater care. It was unlikely to win because this was such a heavily political case. The Palau Supreme Court was expected to decide it, not duck it on procedural grounds. But the ripeness argument was not trivial. I could make it. If that was what Mirando was willing to take, I could give him that.

Again I urged that a delay might make a big difference. Given the long delay that had already taken place in Palau's ratification of the Compact, thirty or sixty days more didn't appear significant. But Salii would not change his mind. He was too impatient to wait. There might have been internal Palauan politics at play here, but Salii's opposition to a delay also was consistent with his view that the courts were against him. Legal representation would make little difference. Ngiraked was very upset when I told him of Salii's decision. Ngiraked went to Salii's home to get Salii to agree to a lengthy continuance, which would have put me in total control of the case, but Salii refused. Ngiraked was still fighting to win the case; Salii had surrendered. Mirando then also went back to Salii to request a shorter, fifteen-day, postponement. Salii still said no.

I resigned myself to a very limited role in the case. I worked out a fee arrangement with Mirando, obtained copies of the cases and files I thought I needed, and the next morning flew to Manila. There was a plane back to

Palau on Wednesday morning that landed at 11:45 a.m. Oral argument was set for 2:00 p.m. If the airline schedule held, and it frequently did not, I would be back for the oral argument in two days, on Wednesday, August 27.

Since I was not a member of the Palau bar, I had to be admitted specially to argue the case. The request was delivered to Chief Justice Nakamura in his chambers. The chief justice was one of a number of Palauan families of Japanese ancestry. After the war, the United States had expelled all of the Japanese. Only a few, those with Palauan wives and children, were permitted to return on humanitarian grounds. These families rarely remained together. A Japanese man rarely could obtain work in Micronesia after the war, and Palauan women found life in Japan too difficult. Sometimes, a few children went with their father to Japan, but most stayed with their mothers in Palau. That had not been the case with the Nakamuras. Their father had found work in Palau and had returned to be with his family. All of these half-Japanese children married Palauans—Chief Judge Nakamura was married to Tmetuchl's daughter—and were regarded by the islanders as Palauan. Statesiders emphasized their Japanese character and gave it consequence, but generally Palauans did not.

I had met Chief Justice Nakamura before, although I did not know him well. In the past, in connection with some articles I had written, the chief justice and I had spoken more relaxedly about the role of the courts in Micronesia and the development of the Palau Supreme Court, and had even analyzed specific cases together. The motion to admit me was just a formality, but the chief justice was very gracious, stating how pleased the court was to have me argue before them. After a brief discussion of Micronesian legal developments, we went into the courtroom.

The courtroom in Palau is small. It consists of five or six rows of long wooden benches behind counsels' tables, the entire ensemble looking like a courthouse from American colonial days. The courtroom was full. Television producers from the United States and Australia were outside the courtroom, one asked to interview me after the oral argument. Adding to the tension were about twenty nuclear protesters from Nagasaki who rode around the island on large bicycles. Their presence made a huge impact on the small island.

The only native Palauan judge sitting on the case was Nakamura. The government's major concerns about the chief justice were that one of his brothers had introduced the nuclear substance ban and the other brother had designs on the presidency. But it was a tribute to him that no one could point to a specific instance or a decision—that he decided because of family ties or political bias. The other judges were white, stateside judges. Loren Sutton was a tall, easygoing American. He resided on Palau and had married a Palauan, a blind woman who sang in the local cabaret. Each night he went home and helped her prepare for her evening performance. The third judge was Edward King, the Chief Judge of the Federated States of

Micronesia, who had come to the islands as a neighborhood legal services attorney and been appointed to the FSM court. He was the youngest of the three judges and the most liberal of them. He liked the intellectual challenge of the law. On the bench he fidgeted about, constantly asking questions. I knew some of his opinions on the conflict between Micronesian custom and United States-imposed criminal law. They were carefully done, showing considerable scholarly effort. But the result was almost invariable: the overruling of Micronesian custom in favor of U.S. statutory laws. He was unlikely to defer to the Palauan majority vote. The U.S. and Palau government officials knew King's other opinions. In these he was a strong environmental advocate and very unsympathetic to the U.S. government and its activities in Micronesia.

The lawyers were overwhelmingly white as well. Outsiders provided counsel. The Center for Constitutional Rights, famous in the States for William Kunstler's criminal defense of left-wing politicians, contracted with Anne Simon to write the brief and then sent her to Palau to argue the case. She was an attractive woman, in her early thirties, I judged, and had written a number of articles on environmental law. She was absolutely humorless and made no effort to conceal her contempt for those who were arguing against her.

My own oral argument was relatively short. But I thought the judges considered it seriously. King asked me a couple of questions. But we had not been able to submit a brief on the subject, and the absence of written accompaniment to a technical procedural argument was fatal. Simon was not going to be snared by any procedural trap. She responded only briefly to my ripeness argument and then went on to the issues that were going to engage the court.

The oral argument was basically between Isaac and Simon, and it was a slaughter. I didn't know enough about the case to know whether she was really that good or the Palau case was really that bad. The judges were obviously sympathetic to Simon, and that helped considerably. King was an active questioner, and even Nakamura pitched in and challenged Isaac on occasion.

After the oral argument, Mirando and even Isaac congratulated me. They understood how little I knew and how little the time I had had to prepare. They thought I had done well. I was pleased that they thought so, but on the ultimate issue, judging by the court's questioning, Salii was right. The government of Palau would lose.

On September 17, 1986, the Court decided against us. The Palau Supreme Court reasoned that although the language was the same, the words used in the Palau Constitution were intended to be broader than the same words in the Compact. The Compact permitted transit of nuclear vessels through Palauan waters and envisioned that nuclear ships would be able to dock in Palau. Under the Palau Constitution, the United States could not "operate nuclear . . . vessels . . . within . . . Palau." In sum, the Palau Constitution barred certain nuclear activities that were permitted under the Compact. The Compact was still in conflict with the Palau Constitution. Since the Palau Compact had not received 75 percent of the vote, the Compact still had not been ratified.

Obtaining 75 percent of the vote was impossible. If the Salii government wanted to ratify the Compact, a different approach was necessary. The possibility of a constitutional amendment had been mentioned before in Palau, but the OEK would not agree to it. A constitutional amendment meant keeping intact the Compact—the U.S. instrument—while changing the Constitution, Palau's document. Perhaps, the OEK argued, the next plebiscite would obtain 75 percent in favor of the Compact. But it was clear to all—certainly to Salii—that obtaining 75 percent was hopeless. Nevertheless, Salii went through the motions to satisfy the OEK. Palau held another plebiscite on the Compact, its fourth, in early December 1986. This time the percentage voting yes decreased to 66 percent.

At about the same time, in December 1986, I travelled to Fiji to carry out work for the Asian Development Bank. Having had no contact with Palau since the court decision, I thought of stopping briefly in Koror on my way back. Therefore, prior to my departure from Washington in late November, I sent telegrams to Salii, Ngiraked, and Soaladaob, telling them I would be coming through Palau in December and hoped to see them. I received no response.

The work in Fiji took longer and was more exhausting than I had thought it would be. When it was completed, I was tired and more than ready to go home to Washington, D.C. If I returned via Palau, I would arrive in Koror on Christmas Day. Micronesia pretty well closes down during Christmas. It seemed unlikely that anybody I wanted to see would even be on the island, much less eager to meet with me at that time. Again, this time from Manila, I sent telegrams to Salii, Ngiraked, and Soaladaob saying I had to return home directly and apologizing for having caused them any inconvenience. It was an excess of courtesy. I was sure no one cared one way or the other.

Notes

1. Page 72. *It agreed to change the Compact.* Salii's first idea was once again to develop a treaty and thus bypass the legal controversy. After initialing a treaty, the United States and Salii chose the more direct approach in the text. "Salii Dispatches Delegation to D.C.," *Pacific Daily News*, Sept. 14, 1985, p. 3; "Treaty Could End Trust Territory," *Pacific Daily News*, Dec. 1, 1985, p. 3.

2. Page 73. *Leading the fight was Greenpeace.* L. Spencer, "The Not So Peaceful World of Greenpeace," *Forbes Magazine*, Nov. 11, 1991, p. 174.

3. Page 73. The Roff quotation is found in Sue Rabbitt Roff, *Overreaching in Paradise* (1991), p. 184.

4. Page 79. *But the result was almost invariable.* The decisions are analyzed in detail in B. Tamanaha, "A Proposal for the Development of a System of Indigenous Jurisprudence in the Federated States of Micronesia," 13 *Hastings International and Comparative Law Review* 71 (1989).

9

Two-Thirds of the Government is Furloughed; Palau Amends its Constitution; Salii Testifies Under Oath Before Congress

A few days after my return to Washington, Salii called me. To my surprise, he had been waiting to see me in Palau at Christmas. Salii wanted one question answered: Could Palau amend its Constitution *now* so that a majority vote would be sufficient to pass the Compact? Isaac, now Attorney General of Palau, had written an opinion that the Constitution could not be amended until the general election in November 1988. Isaac said that Article XIV of the Palau Constitution applied to *all* amendments and an Article XIV amendment could only be voted on at the general election for president. Salii wanted my views.

There was another section of the Constitution that allowed amendments but only in very limited circumstances. Article XV, entitled "Transition," contained only one section on amendments, and that section, Section 11, authorized an amendment to the Constitution to avoid an inconsistency with the Compact. Article XV said nothing about the time of the vote. Article XV's flexibility, I concluded, was purposeful; the flexibility on timing was necessary so that the Compact would go into effect at the earliest possible date. If the amendment had as its purpose removing a conflict or inconsistency between the Constitution and the Compact, as the proposed Salii amendment did, it was an Article XV amendment and could be voted upon at any time. I heard nothing more.

In April 1987, the House Territories Subcommittee congressmen, Chairman Ron de Lugo, Robert Lagomarsino (R-CA) and Ben Blaz (R-Guam), accompanied by Staff Director Jeff Farrow, made their first trip to Palau. The subcommittee presented a bipartisan, strong message to Palau: the Compact was fair and would not be renegotiated. De Lugo spoke to a joint session of the OEK: "We are not here . . . to negotiate changes in the Compact. It is our view that the Compact is generous already. . . .

[P]ressures . . . [d]elaying approval or changing tactics . . . regarding the Compact will not result in better financial arrangements."

De Lugo, as a territorial delegate from the Virgin Islands, had fought with the federal government and knew how difficult it was to win such battles. He also knew the difficulties of island politics. As a native Virgin Islander who traced his family's residence in the Virgin Islands back to the early nineteenth century, de Lugo understood island nationalism and the ambivalent attitudes toward race in all of the territories. After four terms as a delegate, de Lugo ran for the governorship of the Virgin Islands and lost. De Lugo was white. Race was a major reason for his defeat. After two years on the sidelines, he had run again for Congress and was overwhelmingly elected. He was forced back into the "white" world of the House of Representatives in Washington. Personally, he was more relaxed than during his earlier terms. Some years before, de Lugo's only son had been killed in an automobile accident. There had been a divorce. Since then, he had remarried happily. He had just been appointed subcommittee chairman, his first chairmanship role, and he was relishing the assignment. Although he upheld congressional committee prerogatives, he was, on the whole, a moderate and conciliatory force.

De Lugo and Farrow asked Salii what his political plans were? In light of the September 1986 Palau Supreme Court decision, how did Salii expect to ratify the Compact? Salii gave them my legal opinion. He planned on a constitutional amendment. Salii initially was delighted at the congressional mission, which he believed would give Palau the prominence the islands deserved. The subcommittee's message also pleased him. Many of his political opponents engaged in Palau doublespeak. They did not oppose the Compact in principle. It was just that this Compact, as negotiated so far, was not quite good enough. De Lugo's speech barred further negotiations.

There was also a disturbing aspect of the visit, from Salii's point of view. Salii and the counsel to the Office of Micronesian Status Negotiations of the Department of State, Howard Hills—who acted as advance man for the trip—wanted the visit to be seen as a congressional statement in favor of the Compact and ratification. Nothing more. De Lugo's speech to the OEK accomplished that. But de Lugo and Farrow viewed this as an orientation trip as well. They sought a broad exposure to Palau's politicians, including the Compact opposition, especially the Ibedul. The subcommittee made that clear at the outset. Somehow or other, it couldn't be arranged. Farrow asked again, Hills stalled, Farrow insisted.

Farrow was a longtime territories expert and the driving force on the subcommittee. His dominance over the Subcommittee and his obsessive secrecy were an embarrassment to de Lugo on occasion. But he was very intelligent and an extremely hard worker, and his knowledge of the issues made him a valuable staffer. Further, he was tenacious. In opposition on an issue, he was a powerful and unrelenting opponent. His politics were both strongly partisan and personal. In 1984 at the Democratic National Convention, Farrow served as Vice President Walter Mondale's floor whip for the territorial and overseas voter delegations, a position he also would hold for Michael Dukakis in the 1988 convention. He was ever on the alert to embarrass the Republicans. Stagnation in Palau would be such an embarrassment. If the Democrats won in 1988, his ambition was an open secret in Washington: to be appointed Assistant Secretary of the Office of Territorial and International Affairs.

The congressional visit was to end badly. Salii had arranged an elaborate dinner for the congressional delegation at the Palau Pacific Resort hotel to cap their visit. While Salii and a large number of invited guests waited, and watched, de Lugo and Farrow conversed with the Ibedul at the Palau Pacific Resort pool. De Lugo and Farrow had finally gotten their meeting.

Salii was furious. Such a visible conference with the leading opponent of the Compact sent a supportive signal to the opposition and undercut de Lugo's stated message. It confirmed Salii's suspicions of the subcommittee. De Lugo and Farrow, on the other hand, blamed Salii and Hills: Why hadn't they arranged a meeting earlier in a more discrete place as de Lugo and Farrow had asked? Why had Farrow been forced to squeeze the Ibedul into the schedule at the last minute?

In June 1987, the government of Palau made one last effort to ratify the Compact by a three-quarters vote. The vote was 67 percent in favor. Not enough. Hardly a surprise.

On July 1, 1987, immediately after the failure of the Compact referendum, Salii furloughed 900 employees of the national government of Palau, about two-thirds of the entire labor force of Palau. Salii made no bones about the reason for the furlough. If the Compact were approved, the financial constraints would be eliminated and the employees would get their jobs back right away in addition to back pay. Otherwise, the government did not have the money. No one would be rehired until the new fiscal year, October 1. He had warned of the firings back in January when he had asked the U.S. Department of the Interior for an additional $1.7 million. Interior refused.

The Compact's opponents, particularly the Ibedul and the OEK Speaker of the House, Santos Olikong, charged that the layoffs were unnecessary, reflecting governmental mismanagement and political manipulation rather than a real financial crisis. They waited for the inevitable reaction by the fired workers against the president.

Salii had met individually with each agency and each organization to explain the firings at great length; beginning these meetings in February and March. He explained that the government could not keep up the level of services without Compact funds. If blame were to be placed, he said, place it on the opponents of the Compact; on the OEK, particularly Olikong, and on the Ibedul. It was a daring move, and it worked. The government workers who were laid off did not blame Salii but rather placed the blame on the opponents of the Compact. Despite the weight of the Ibedul's title and personality, he was losing the political battle. His opposition to the Compact was costing him dearly. If he were seeking to be elected president of Palau in 1988—and most thought that was his goal—continued opposition to the Compact was no longer the way to get there.

The furloughed government workers started a vigil around the OEK urging action; namely, the passage of a constitutional amendment. A vigil in Palau is different from one in the United States. In the United States, there would be chants, signs, marching, and endless media coverage. In Palau, there were signs, it is true, but there was little marching and no chanting. Maybe it was simply too hot for that. To a passerby, if one could not make out the signs (and they were not easy to make out), the vigil looked like a Sunday picnic. Outside the OEK was a large tent with long benches underneath. There were no weapons—at least, I never saw any. Men in colored tee-shirts sat on the benches, talking very quietly and, once in a while, as the time passed, ate lunch or supper.

But their continued presence was significant and, as in the States, sent a message. The message to a Palauan might be quite different than it appeared to an American. Palau is neither a society of the written word nor an open one, and therefore to outsiders who didn't speak Palauan, interpreting the dynamics of the events, even at the time, was not easy. There was no media coverage to aid you. To reconstruct the situation months afterwards, which many have tried to do, you would be dependent on stories told by participants, probably biased, with their own political agendas and sometimes faulty memories to boot. The opposition argued that the furloughed workers intimidated the OEK and threatened the anti-Compact opposition. Their strongest case to that point was that of Belheim Sakuma, who charged that his house had been burned to the ground after he played a program on the radio explaining the right to oppose the Compact. But the government disputed Sakuma's charge.

I was called to Guam in mid-July. While there, I telephoned Salii to see if he wanted to see me. He asked me to come to Palau right away. The OEK was debating legislation proposing a constitutional amendment. The House had already passed it, but the legislation seemed stalled in the Senate. Salii asked me to go over to the Senate, talk to the senators, and see what I could do to ease passage of the amendment.

I met with almost all the senators in two day-long, continuous meetings in the Senate conference room on the ground floor of the OEK beneath the chamber. The deliberations progressed slowly. The Palauan senators wanted the Compact, but the crucial question was, Did they have to amend their Constitution to ratify it? Politically, the Palau Constitution was very popular. The protests outside were referred to frequently by various senators, never to suggest that the senators were afraid, but as evidence that they could not avoid a decision. The people wanted something done.

The amendment was not a surprise. Since early June, Salii and his supporters had discussed the amendment possibility, while opponents had devised ways to attack it. How was an amendment to be placed on the ballot to be voted on by the people? The OEK rules required a three-quarters vote by the OEK before any amendment could be passed by the OEK and placed on the ballot for a popular vote. If the three-quarters requirement applied to an Article XV amendment, as the proposed one was, it meant we had to get 12 out of 16 votes in the House and 11 out of 14 in the Senate. My legal opinion stated that the three-fourths vote was not necessary under Article XV, but obviously if we did get a three-quarters vote in the OEK, we were a lot safer.

In 1987 the OEK was divided on the Compact. The Senate had a pro-Compact majority, with eight of the fourteen members supporting implementation of the Compact. The House of Delegates had an antiCompact majority, with eleven of the sixteen members opposed to the Compact. Getting three-fourths vote of both houses in these political circumstances did not seem possible. Sure enough, in the Senate we got ten votes, one less than three-fourths. In the house, the constitutional amendment passed 9-2, with five delegates absent, far less than the 12 required if a three-quarters vote were necessary. The legislation envisioned two votes: one on August 4 to pass the constitutional amendment eliminating the three-fourths requirement and a second vote on August 21 passing the Compact by majority vote.

Commentators at the time, and later, stated that the OEK was intimidated by the furloughed workers. Legislators opposed to the Compact said they received threatening letters and telephone calls. Some of their cars and houses were damaged. One legislator alleged that the furloughed workers threatened him physically. On the other hand, the pro-Compact supporters in the Senate stated that legislators, although subjected to some pressure, were free to vote their conscience. Indeed, the OEK vote exactly reflected the popular vote on the Compact: somewhere between 62 percent and 72 percent.

Immediately after the law's passage, a case, *Merep v. Salii*, was again filed, this time to declare the constitutional amendment procedure invalid and prevent the vote on August 4. The opposition seemed to me less vigorous, almost as if it were going through the motions. The heavy mainland representation was not there: no stateside lawyers; no television cameras. Kaleb Udui, a longtime Palauan opponent of the Compact, was attorney for the opposition. He was a lawyer of great dignity and prestige, the first Micronesian from the trust territory to earn his law degree.

If Greenpeace was throwing in the sponge, the Territories Subcommittee was not. The subcommittee traditionally had advocated special financial benefits for the territories while opposing status change, which involved a transfer of power. Congressman Philip Burton had openly opposed all of the compacts—even those with the Federated States of Micronesia (FSM) and the Republic of the Marshall Islands. Burton had died in 1985 just at the moment when these compacts were presented to the U.S. Congress for ratification. Many felt that if he had lived, they would never have been approved.

Congressman John Seiberling (preceding de Lugo as chairman of the subcommittee) held stultifying hearings for 2 1/2 years to delay ratification of the compacts with the Marshalls and the FSM. (The hostility of the subcommittee was so strong that the heads of the two Micronesian governments refused to testify before it. Today, representatives of the FSM and the Marshallese governments still will not appear before the subcommittee.) The pattern of hostility to the compacts set by Burton and Seiberling continued in the case of the Palau Compact. The Subcommittee on Territories, under the leadership of de Lugo, had held up the ratification of the Compact with Palau in the last Congress despite administration pressure.

Suddenly, the Subcommittee on Territories called an oversight hearing for July 23, 1987. The timing would provide a forum for the opposition as well as make it difficult for Salii to campaign for the constitutional amendment.

The Territories Subcommittee hearing room is a small one: relatively narrow, with only six rows of seats for the public. Invariably, no matter what the topic, the room is full, with spectators standing around the press table on the one side or in front of the rear doors on the other. Usually, besides de Lugo, there are only one or two congressmen present. They stay for only a short time, to ask a question or two or make a statement, and leave.

This hearing was different. Right at the outset, nine congressmen were there, sitting in an elevated semicircle in front of the witness table. Something was up. Because of the publicity with respect to Palau and the Compact, the small hearing room was jammed. The rear doors could not be opened. In the last row sat Sebia Hawkins, the head of the Washington office for Greenpeace. Her actions during these hearings were always the same; she came very early and took a seat in the center of the last row, taking extensive notes. A tall, slim woman, she plaited her hair and the very long pigtail was a striking counterpoint to her otherwise unobtrusive presence. In the crowded chamber, with its large congressional presence, everyone waited expectantly for the dramatic confrontation between Salii and the Territories Subcommittee.

To find out what was going on in Palau was tough. The subcommittee, of course, could reach out and did reach out through their own channels. But there were few who were unbiased and even fewer who knew what, indeed, was going on. The congressional assessment of Salii and Santos Olikong, the sole witness for the opposition, might well be determinative. In addition to coping with problems of time and distance, the subcommittee was somewhat limited in another way: de Lugo was out of his element. He was a legislator and a conciliator, not an investigator. He was uncomfortable in such a combative role. Farrow was another matter. Farrow enjoyed the inquisitional role, ferreting out facts from hidden crevices. But Farrow could only prepare the questions. He could not ask them or follow up on them if the testimony led in unexpected paths.

De Lugo, in a long opening statement set out his view: Palau should exercise self-determination but the United States should meet its trusteeship responsibilities first.

> Our commitment to self-determination requires that Palauans make their own decisions. . . . [T]he [Palau] government now faces a tremendous budget shortfall in the remaining months of this fiscal year. . . . The situation raises the question of whether U.S. trusteeship responsibilities are being met. The United States must ensure that these responsibilities are lived up to.

Republican Congressman Ben Blaz of Guam set out the administration view. Let the government of Palau and the people of Palau handle their own affairs. "Four times the majority of the people have agreed, and we still have in my view a minority wanting to take control of the whole situation. And I hope that will be changed with this new action [the constitutional amendment] that the President is contemplating." De Lugo got to the purpose of the hearing. This was to be an investigation of the Salii administration. "In preparation for this hearing, the committee received all sorts of conflicting statements, and the committee received some very serious charges."

Then the bombshell: sworn testimony.

I had attended hearings of the Interior and Insular Affairs Committee since 1962. I had never seen or heard of the committee taking sworn testimony. To force Salii to testify under oath was a public relations coup for the opposition and terribly demeaning to Salii. It infuriated him. Some said the pain of this hearing never left him. Outwardly, at the time, he never blinked. Although the swearing-in process was sprung on him without warning and therefore surprised him—it stunned me—Salii took the oath and proceeded as if this were all commonplace. First, he noted, disarmingly, the unusual, large attendance of the committee. "In my many years of travel over here I have never appeared before a hearing where as many members as today are sitting in."

Salii addressed first the governmental layoffs, their necessity and the timing.

> A few weeks ago I was forced to lay off some 900 executive branch employees of the government. . . . Every year we have been pleading with the administration. . . to face the reality of the situation in Palau, and make available a meager $2 million to see us through to the end of the fiscal year.

During the oversight hearing which followed [the December 2, 1986 plebiscite] in

February [1987] . . . we advised the committee that we would need, instead of $10 million for 1988, $13 million.

The question might be properly asked if the situation as I have outlined it was true, why didn't Palau run into a crisis prior to today. And the answer simply put is this, that under the strength of the [C]ompact . . . approval, the government was able to obtain some credit . . . to make up for the shortfall in the budget available to the government.

Salii was basically right on the numbers. Despite the doubling of Palau government wages since 1984, funding from the Department of Interior had only increased from $8 million in 1981 to $10.8 million in 1987. Palau had increased its own taxes from $4.7 million in 1981 to $7 million in 1987, a 49 percent increase.

Salii went on to testify about the actions of the furloughed employees demonstrating before the OEK. He placed their role in a traditional U.S. setting: poor, jobless people petitioning their legislature for their rights.

The government employees . . . conducted themselves in a very orderly, in a very peaceful manner. . . . And their request is simple and clear, to those members of our [C]ongress who have been lying to the people about the [C]ompact, who have been claiming . . . that we can negotiate additional funding for the [C]ompact.

They are not violent people, they are people in hardship, they are people without jobs, without the means of income to support themselves and their families.

Then he discussed specific incidents reported in the *Pacific Daily News*, particularly the burning of the house of Belheim Sakuma. Salii regarded it as a publicity stunt; his anger was evident in his testimony.

There was one incident where a so-called house was burned down, the gentleman whose house that is, I am sure he is in the back of the room. And he has told the media that the pro-[C]ompact people burned that house.

Well, first of all that is no house, that was an eyesore shack that had absolutely no value. The night of the incident the police found his wife driving their car full of household things.

I take some time to point this out, because I am sure they will be making all kinds of claims and making all sorts of charges.

Belheim Sakuma did not testify in person, although he submitted a written statement, and the incident, widely reported in the press, seemed to fade away after Salii's testimony.

Next Salii addressed the passage of the constitutional amendment, the issue of intimidation, and his own role in Palau.

[I]t has been stated openly . . . that members of our Congress who voted for the . . . amendment of the constitution were intimidated to do so. And that, perhaps, the President of the government had something to do with that intimidation. . . .

I have been involved in the negotiations for the future of Palau for 18 years, and I haven't given up. . . . I haven't seen it necessary to resort to violence, and I don't think I will ever do that.

It was a very strong statement delivered in large measure extemporaneously. There were holes in it: a much milder depiction of the actions of the furloughed government employees than others might sketch, and no discussion of his own link, if any, to the furlough committee. But as usual, Salii's vigor was impressive, and the thoroughness of the discussion and his command of the material equally so. De Lugo seemed affected by it. His first comment changed the tone of the hearing completely: "I am sure that Mrs. de Lugo, who is sitting behind you, joins me and Mrs. Lagomarsino in returning best wishes to Mrs. Salii, your very charming and able wife. We enjoyed very much the hospitality while we were there, and I can tell you that we fell in love with—at least this member—fell in love with Palau."

Then de Lugo reverted to the questions prepared by Farrow for him in advance. They disclosed where Farrow, at least, was coming from. First de Lugo challenged Salii on the timing of the furloughs. If the Compact had been ratified in June, how would that have solved anything? Given the procedures for congressional approval and various supplementary agreements, no money would be available anyway for many months. How could Salii say Compact approval would save the day?

Salii's answer was to the point. The issue was bank credit: "In talking to those potential lenders, we were assured by them . . . once the Compact was approved by the voters, they would immediately make loans available to Palau. Every one of them made that commitment."

Olikong, the OEK Speaker, was the sole Palauan representing the opposition, and he blew it. If there was an intimidation argument to be made against Salii, Olikong was not the person to make it. His opening gambit made it clear to all that he placed Palauan politics first, issues of personal safety second. He took the position that he supported the Compact; he just wanted a few more changes. That position might play in Palau but in Washington the committee wouldn't let him get away with it.

Mr. Olikong. . . . Nobody in Palau is opposed to the Compact, sir. . . .

Mr. De Lugo. Mr. Speaker, you are saying that you . . . believe everyone you know in Palau, supports the [C]ompact?

Mr. Olikong. Yes, sir.

Mr. De Lugo. But there are certain problems that exist . . . for instance, scholarships for students. . . . And also, land compensation, that is a major concern.

Mr. Olikong. Especially for the chiefs, the traditional leaders, yes.

Mr. De Lugo. But these are issues that can be addressed outside of the [C]ompact. They can be addressed legislatively. . . .

Mr. Olikong. Yes, as long as they are addressed, and we really see that they will be accommodated, that will be fine with us.

Olikong's argument underscored, if it needed underscoring, how small a part antinuclear thinking and environmental concerns played among Compact opponents in Palau. Even de Lugo didn't mention it, speaking instead of student scholarships.

Olikong next argued that Palau could renegotiate the Compact, although de Lugo, Blaz, and others had gone to Palau three months before and said no additional negotiations were possible. Then the issue of intimidation was reached and, remarkably, Olikong lost the high ground. It seemed to the committee that he, rather than the government, was seeking a breakdown in law and order. Congressman Fofo Sunia of American Samoa articulated the congressional response to Olikong.

Mr. Sunia. You say that if that [renegotiation of the Compact] is not possible, it would mean the death of democracy in Palau and a severe strain, possibly to the breaking point in the friendship between our two countries.

Can you elaborate on that, what are you suggesting there?

Mr. Olikong. Well, if the crisis in Palau is not taken care of, anything can happen in Palau. . . . Maybe somebody gets killed, or other factions start fighting, which is something that we have been trying to keep from happening.

Mr. Sunia. Well, Mr. Speaker, sitting here and listening to you...this sort of statement, I think, runs very close to agitating the people to do what might not have been there or might not have been in their minds to do, when they hear elected officials make these kinds of statements.

You know, it is almost as if you were suggesting to them something that they hadn't thought of in the first place....

The arguments against Salii having evaporated, de Lugo retreated to pressing the administration on the financial issue, bringing up the fact that in 1984, in Remeliik's administration, Palau had been brought close to anarchy. De Lugo questioned Kittie Baier, the Department of the Interior's representative, on why the department would not increase Palau's funding. Baier replied that it was an overall budgetary squeeze; Palau didn't merit that high a priority. De Lugo didn't believe her reply. He was sure the administration was purposely squeezing Palau, forcing the people of Palau to ratify the Compact.

I was angry about the timing and style of the hearing, but the hearing was proper. The hearing might be embarrassing to Salii and helpful to his opponents, but the committee, whatever its biases, certainly had the obligation to explore charges of intimidation. But then Farrow overreached himself. Salii may have deflected his congressional critics in what was a tour de force performance, but he had not moved Farrow an inch. Immediately after the hearing, and only a week before the injunction hearing before the Palau Supreme Court, Farrow requested the Congressional Research Service to "rush" a legal opinion on whether the constitutional amendment was legal. With the case pending before the Palau Supreme Court, the Congressional Research Service (CRS) immediately responded to Farrow's request and issued a two-page legal opinion, almost without any legal reasoning at all, giving its views that Article XIV rather than Article XV applied. A constitutional amendment before November 1988 was not legal.

The CRS opinion was immediately leaked to the press. The *Pacific Daily News* prominently reported it. Hills, of the Department of State, responded, noting the selective and incomplete analysis of the CRS opinion. He then issued his own legal opinion, reaching a contrary conclusion: Article XV did apply, and the constitutional amendment was legal.

The subcommittee hearing, the CRS opinion, and the Hills opinion were part of a broader pattern. Both sides tried, unfortunately, to influence the Court by manipulating public opinion. The Palau government was somewhat limited. Its pressure was primarily from influences on the island: the furloughed workers, the unstated but clear evidence of the desire of the people of Palau in the previous votes favoring the Compact. The opposition pressure came from groups off the island: the House Subcommittee on Territories, advocacy organizations such as Greenpeace, various academics, and the public media.

The courts in Micronesia in general and in Palau in particular had taken on a very visible role. Palau was by far the most litigious of the Micronesian Freely Associated States. For example, there was far more litigation in Palau than in the FSM, although the FSM has five times the population and the people of key FSM islands—Yap, Truk, Kosrae, and Pohnpei—spoke different languages, had distinct histories, and had strong strains of individual island nationalism.

Palau's litigiousness reflected the competitiveness and aggressiveness of Palauan society. The courts and judges—almost all of whom were off-islanders and white—were very visible and more intrusive in Palau than elsewhere in Micronesia. The local courts saw themselves as bringing integrity to a world where there was excessive political influence and physical coercion. As a result, the courts were inclined to be very activist, to do away with normal procedural restraints, if necessary, in order to check governmental power.

On the whole, the courts were regarded by the community as fair, even though Palauans, in many cases, might not actually follow through on the money judgments of the court. Palauans might choose traditional exchanges of modest gifts even after the court had decided in favor of a very large fine. But the Compact litigation was special. Its significance and visibility in the States affected everyone in Palau. The reputation of the Palauan courts, like the reputation of the other Palauan governmental institutions, indeed, of the Palauan people themselves, was to turn on the handling of this case.

The chief justice was sensitive to the Court's role and did not wish such an intrusive role for the Palau Supreme Court as, perhaps, the stateside members of the Court did. But whatever his own desires for the Court, the spotlight once again was on the Palau Supreme Court and on him. Proponents of the Compact in Palau, within and outside the government, saw none of this struggle in Nakamura. They viewed him and the Supreme Court as simply a stumbling block, hostile to the Compact, and to the people of Palau. I thought Mirando and Ngiraked, who talked openly—and scornfully—of the court, misread the chief justice. They thought Nakamura was weak and that his retiring nature reflected lack of courage. I read him quite differently. Nakamura would carry out his role and that demanded, in his view, a distance and a diffidence. But he was strong. Political pressure would only be counterproductive and make the government's legal position more difficult.

Seeing Nakamura as it did, the government had tried to personalize the issue. Isaac and the Palau Senate in July 1986 had written Chief Justice Nakamura, asking him to remove himself from the earlier case, *Gibbons v. Salii*, in which I had played a marginal role, on the grounds that the chief justice's brother was an active opponent of the president. But he had refused. Then he had heard the case and ruled against the government.

Plaintiffs in *Merep v. Salii* asked the Court for an injunction to prevent a vote on the constitutional amendment on the grounds that it was illegal. To grant an injunction, the judge must feel you are going to be damaged by the delay and that when you come to trial you will probably win. How the Court ruled on the injunction motion would tell us a good deal about how Chief Justice Nakamura was leaning. The chief justice ruled for us. He denied the injunction. The constitutional amendment process would not be delayed. Very few spectators—Palauans or off-islanders—were present in the courtroom.

The constitutional amendment was placed before the voters and passed on August 4, with fourteen of the sixteen states of Palau ratifying. The two states failing to ratify had less than 100 votes each. There had to be another vote on the Compact itself, but now that the amendment had passed, only a majority vote would be required.

The opposition then filed a second injunction request, this time to delay the vote on the Compact. The second injunction had no legal basis at all. I had argued the first injunction motion, and after we won, I flew back to the States. I planned on returning to Palau for the final hearing three weeks later. I thought we would win the second injunction motion rather easily, although Isaac and Mirando—ever distrustful of the courts—were skeptical. I was right; Nakamura denied the second injunction as he did the first. The vote on the Compact itself would go forward as scheduled on August 21. However, the chief justice also decided that the ballots should not be counted until the case was finally decided. Mirando called me, very upset at Chief Justice Nakamura's order. I was surprised at the order. Either the anti-Compact forces were entitled to an injunction or they weren't. The chief justice had decided they weren't. That should have been sufficient.

Eric Basse from the Palau attorney general's office, who argued the second injunction, believed Nakamura was simply trying to be fair. I could see that if the ballots were counted and the Compact approved, there would be additional pressure on the Court to decide in our favor and the Chief Justice might not want to subject the court to that pressure. I agreed with Basse and remained unconcerned. My feeling about Nakamura's decision to permit the vote but not to count the ballots was, so what? All of this was intermediate jockeying of little consequence. The chief justice had denied both injunction motions. Those were his most critical rulings. We were still on track. The final decision would also be in our favor.

Mirando didn't see it that way. He interpreted Chief Justice Nakamura's ruling as meaning that once again the courts would rule against the government and prevent the Compact from going into effect. My respect for Nakamura was greater than that. I didn't think he was tipping his hand. My advice to Mirando was, "Let it be." I was still confident that we would win.

Against my advice, Mirando pressed Basse to file a motion requesting that the ballots be counted immediately after the election before the case was finally decided. Nakamura reversed himself. The ballots would be counted before the case was finally decided. We would know which way the people had voted before the judiciary finally ruled in the case. Basse had found a section of the Palau Code requiring ballots to be counted immediately after an election. The chief justice was playing it by the book. If that is what the statute said, that's what he would do. But the reversal was unfortunate. It convinced some in the furlough committee that the chief justice could be pressured.

The Compact was put to a vote on August 21—the sixth vote—and passed by its greatest margin yet, receiving slightly more than 73 percent aye votes. U.N. observers had been present to supervise the voting, as they had the five previous times Palau had voted on the Compact.

All that was left was one more argument on the summary judgment motions before Chief Justice Nakamura. We had won on the injunction motions. The government of Palau would win again. We were very close to the ratification of the Compact and the end of five years of litigation.

Notes

1. Page 83. The relevant language of Articles XIV and XV of the Palau Constitution is:

ARTICLE XIV. AMENDMENTS

Section 1. . . . (c) by resolution adopted by not less than three-fourths (3/4) of the members of each House of the Olbiil Era Kelulau.

Section 2. A proposed amendment to this Constitution shall become effective when approved in the next regular general election by a majority of the votes cast on that amendment and in not less than three-fourths (3/4) of the states.

ARTICLE XV. TRANSITION

Section 11. Any amendment to this Constitution *proposed for the purpose of avoiding inconsistency with the Compact of Free Association* shall require approval by a majority of the votes cast on that amendment and in not less than three-fourths (3/4) of the states. (Emphasis supplied)

2. Page 83. *Article XV's flexibility.* For the curious reader, let me elaborate a bit more on the reasoning of the legal opinion. Amendments under Article XV would obviously be few since Article XV, Section 11, could only be used to remove inconsistencies with the Compact. Article XIV amendments were likely to be many since the amendments could touch upon anything. Restricting the time when Article XIV amendments could be put to a vote would assure that the large number of proposed amendments would not involve excessive cost or be beyond the ability of the government to educate the voters. Thus, I reasoned, the two amendment provisions, Article XIV and Article XV, were independent of each other.

3. Page 87. *In 1987 the OEK was divided.* GAO, *U.S. Trust Territory: Issues Associated with Palau's Transition to Self-Government: Supplement to the Report to Congressional Requesters* (1989), p. 54.

4. Page 87. *In the House. Ibid*, p. 53.

5. Page 87. *Commentators at the time. Ibid*, pp. 55-57.

6. Page 89. *Salii addressed first.* The GAO said, "We found that Palau was experiencing a cash shortfall in 1987 and cost reductions were needed." GAO, *U.S. Trust Territory: Issues Associated with Palau's Transition to Self-Government, Supplement to the Report* (1989), p. 62. The GAO noted that Palau had been turned down in its efforts to obtain a bank loan by the Bank of Hawaii. It was not until September 8, 1987, that the Bank of Guam granted the Bank of Palau a line of credit. *Ibid*, p. 64.

7. Page 90. *The burning of the house.* Statement by Belheim Sakuma in House of Representatives, Subcommittee on Insular and International Affairs, *Palau Oversight Hearings*, 100th Cong., 1st sess., July 23, 1987.

8. Page 92. *Farrow requested the Congressional.* The "rush" characterization is that of the CRS. Legal Opinion, Zafran to Farrow, CRS, July 21, 1987.

9. Page 93. *Hills of the Department.* Letter, Hills (Dept. of State) to Salii, Aug. 13, 1987.

10

The Ibedul and Salii Settle the Compact Case; The Palau Women Refile the Lawsuit

There is only one plane to Palau on Saturday. It leaves Guam at 5:00 a.m., arriving on Koror at 7:00 a.m. I had first sent a fax to Salii and then, in order to be sure, since the Palau telephone system every once in a while goes on the blink, I telexed him to say I would be arriving early Saturday morning, August 29, 1987, bringing with me the briefs in the case of *Merep v. Salii* before my final oral argument on summary judgment.

The Minister of Natural Resources, Wilhelm Rengiil, a man of considerable dignity and insight and past president of the Micronesian Occupational College, met me at the airport. As his first name implied, he traced his ancestry back to the Germans who ruled Palau from 1885 to the outbreak of World War I. He was the product of Micronesia's first compulsory public education system, which was started by the Japanese shortly after they arrived in 1914. Although there had been schools under Spain and Germany, the schools were run by missionaries and attendance was not required. Because Rengiil was the top student in his class of twenty-five for three consecutive years, as a reward he was permitted to continue his studies for an additional two years. His daughter had just become the first female Palauan member of the bar and, upon joining the Palauan attorney general's office a few weeks before, became the first Palauan in that office.

Rengiil brought startling and wonderful news: the case had been settled the night before. The plaintiffs in the suit, together with the Ibedul, had proposed a settlement order on Friday afternoon to settle the case. The Ibedul was the most powerful Palauan opponent of the Compact. From the first, he had campaigned against its ratification. An accommodation with him was a major breakthrough.

The settlement order had been discussed at a Cabinet meeting Friday afternoon. The ministers wanted to be sure the settlement order was, indeed, final and would prevent any further legal challenge to the Compact. To be sure the matter was settled once and for all time, the president and the cabinet had decided to hold a breakfast meeting with me on Sunday to go over the order before Salii signed it. It was a wonderful result, a political compromise bringing about a victory without the bitterness and anger attendant upon a court decision. It was also a reflection of the traditional Palauan way of governance and decision making, one based on consensus and a complex series of checks and balances.

Rengiil and I went immediately to see President Salii. Rengiil told me not to let on that I knew about the settlement of the lawsuit, since the president would want to tell me himself.

Salii's office was in a cinder-block building, badly in need of a coat of paint, with a corroded tin roof. It was a disgrace and reflected the U.S. lack of concern, indeed scorn, for Palau and Palauan officialdom. That was the U.S. pattern. The graceful executive buildings in the other U.S. territories had been built by previous colonial governments for their governors. La Fortaleza in Puerto Rico, the elegant Spanish mansion overlooking the ocean, or Government House in the Virgin Islands, the Danish-built, charming white structure with its red-tiled roof, nestled in the hills of St. Thomas, showed the esteem these islands had in the eyes of their colonial rulers. In the Pacific, all of the United States-built buildings were run-down, reflecting not inadequate budgets, but inadequate concern. The United States hated its own imperial role and seemed to take out its anger by providing stingy budgets for the islands.

Inside, Palau's executive office building was equally shabby, with metal desks and chairs in some offices and old, badly worn wooden desks in others. Salii's office was separated from the others. Some dignity, even elegance, was lent to the room by the presence of a large imitation leather desk chair and a cloth desk covering.

As Rengiil had predicted, Salii immediately mentioned to me, with a broad smile, that the lawsuit had been settled; indeed, he had signed the order the night before. I thought I had misheard. I repeated, contrary to my instructions, what I had learned from Rengiil: an order had been presented, but we were going to discuss it on Sunday to be sure of its legal soundness before Salii signed it.

That was true, the president explained, as of Friday afternoon. After the cabinet meeting, there had been a subsequent meeting, when a new order was presented by the Ibedul and his supporters. Late Friday night, without further discussion with the cabinet, Salii had signed that later order and presented it to Chief Justice Nakamura. Nakamura had signed it last night as well.

We had forced a legal surrender, after having beaten back all earlier efforts to stop the August 4 and August 21 referenda. We knew that

Greenpeace had sent a legal adviser to assist the Ibedul. His advice was to settle; the Ibedul would lose. With the opposition begging us to settle the case—the Ibedul first approached Salii—the President hadn't been able to wait a day more to get the i's and t's dotted and crossed.

I blamed Mirando, the president's special assistant, who frequently acted as Salii's legal adviser, but when I looked into Mirando's office, his desk was clear. I was wrong; Mirando was not on the island. Mirando's wife was pregnant, in Ohio. He returned frequently, worrying especially because of a peculiar genetic blood defect that ran in their families and, if present in the newborn, resulted in death in early childhood. The president had acted alone.

I asked to see the order. Salii produced the document and anticipated my comment. He explained that the words "with prejudice," which were in the first proposed order, were not in this one. *Why not*? My unasked question hung in the air. If the words "with prejudice" were present, it indicated an intention that the lawsuit could not be brought again. Without the words, the settlement could simply mean the case was being withdrawn for the moment but could be started all over again at another time. The president was so fearful that the Compact agreement would get away that he weakened after the plaintiffs presented it to him again. He had bargained badly and avoided legal advice to boot.

The combination was certain to be disastrous. This was not the time for the president to be his own lawyer. A settlement of a lawsuit is a highly technical matter. The president understood the need to reach an agreement that would bar future lawsuits, but he had entered into an arcane world of legal formalism. Fine political analysis, strong intellect, and excellent intuition—the President's strengths—were not sufficient here.

Salii hated the legal aspects of the Compact dispute. The courts and lawyers had continually foiled him in his goal to get the Compact ratified. He completely distrusted the local judges. Salii saw the judges as foreign politicos in league with stateside opponents, fighting to retain power by preventing the local Palau government from gaining control. This was also the advice he was getting. His advisers were openly scornful of the judiciary. Isaac accused the courts of manipulating the evidence in the Remeliik decision to rule against Palau. Mirando frequently and publicly spoke of a constitutional amendment mandating that the judiciary, now appointed for life, be elected for limited terms as in the States. Ngiraked, the most sophisticated of those surrounding Salii, analyzed the courts in power terms: "The judges care only whether they get invited to the next international law society meeting." That invitation, Ngiraked understood, was dependent on "doing the liberal thing," keeping the Compact from being ratified by ruling against the people of Palau.

Salii was not a difficult man to read. His opponents knew his strengths and his weaknesses. The more he ignored the legal aspects of the Compact fight, the more they emphasized them. They were ever mindful of legal formalities. They had come to the negotiations with a skilled legal adviser. How like Salii to attempt to resolve the issue politically and totally discount the legal technicalities.

The principles behind settling a lawsuit are easy, their application is difficult. Did the parties intend to settle the case once and for all times? Did the parties decide all of the issues in dispute? And finally, were the parties the right people to settle the case in such a far-reaching way? Could they fairly be said to represent everyone? The answers were not easy. The absence in the order of those two words "with prejudice" was very damaging, but the words "with prejudice" were not the only ones that could indicate finality.

The Ibedul, the key opponent of the Compact, had agreed to the settlement in a lengthy memorandum signed by both the Ibedul and Salii. The agreement excused the Ibedul's sincere opposition to the Compact over many years. In short, Salii granted him political absolution. In addition, Salii gave the Ibedul power over what he really cared about: land. The president agreed that if land had to be taken by Palau and transferred to the United States under the Compact, then the Council of Chiefs, headed by the Ibedul, was to be in charge.

The Ibedul had tremendous status in Palau. He could be said to represent all of the opponents to the Compact. Did the parties intend a final settlement? Why enter into such an elaborate settlement agreement, which included the Ibedul, the highest traditional leader on the island, who was not a party to the lawsuit, unless the parties intended a final agreement? Yet nothing was said in the memorandum about the possibility of a future lawsuit that might be brought by others.

The memorandum made it clear that the parties were talking substance. But the order did not address the validity of the constitutional amendment process, the key issue in the lawsuit. All issues have to be settled. Was this one settled or not? At best, matters were unclear; at worst, Salii had bungled. If the settlement did not hold, he had lost a valuable opportunity to settle the Compact dispute forever.

I quickly wrote a couple of paragraphs and asked Salii whether he thought there was any possibility of amending the order to include them. The president exploded, reacting to my implied criticism in writing the paragraphs rather than to the value of the advice. His anger did not surprise me. Salii had a tremendous temper. One had to wait to see what Salii thought after he reflected a bit. I let the storm roll over. It usually passed as quickly as it had come.

"Arnold, there are not going to be any more lawsuits. There is nothing to worry about," he shouted.

"Mr. President," I answered, "it is a lawyer's job to think pathologically, to worry about what could go wrong. In all likelihood you're right and it doesn't make any difference. But it would be helpful, from a pathological point of view, just in case something does go wrong, if these paragraphs were included."

The president's temper covered a quick, analytical mind. Having gotten some of the anger and frustration out of his system, he reverted to his role as a problem solver, and he was quite good at that. He had the paragraphs typed up and went alone to meet with the parties. He returned in half an hour, unsuccessful. He suggested that I talk to Johnson Toribiong, a Palauan lawyer on the island and one of the best legal minds in Micronesia. He had acted as intermediary in the settlement of the case, a bit unfortunate since Toribiong himself and his key client were opponents of the Compact. For all I knew, Toribiong may have suggested striking the words "with prejudice" in the first place. (Subsequently, I learned that my suspicions were misplaced. Kaleb Udui, *Merep's* attorney, at the last minute insisted that the words "with prejudice" be stricken.)

Toribiong's major client, the uncle who raised him, was Roman Tmetuchl, the perennial runner-up for the presidency. Initially Tmetuchl was a proponent of the Compact, but after he lost the presidential election in 1981, he became a strong opponent. Switching about for political advantage was quite normal in Palau. All of the 1985 candidates, indeed, Remeliik himself, had been at various times both for and against the Compact. Only Salii had never wavered. On the Compact and relations with the United States, his position had remained firm. He was a strong supporter of both.

Toribiong grasped the significance of Salii's mistake immediately, but he felt the plaintiffs would not add to the order. I assumed that was the case. Obviously the plaintiffs had hurried to complete the settlement agreement before I arrived to avoid what I was trying to do now. Further, Toribiong doubted the chief justice would amend the order, even if the plaintiffs could be brought around. He suggested, however, that a different Compact case he had initiated, called *Inabo v. Republic of Palau*, be settled with these two paragraphs in the order signed by the judge. Toribiong's suggestion was creative; a good, albeit second best, solution. That Saturday afternoon Toribiong settled *Inabo*.

I summarized the legal situation for the president. Procedurally, we were better off than before. The *Merep* order, while not the best, might be regarded as a final settlement of all Compact litigation, and the *Inabo* case made that possibility even stronger. Perhaps we had muddied the situation sufficiently so that another lawsuit, if brought, would be won on procedural grounds. In any event, substantively we still had a very strong case.

The president was quickly bored with my legal analysis. Salii was confident that there wasn't going to be a lawsuit, so all of this sounded to him like the musings of a lawyer who was still thinking about legal contests and trials in Palau. Salii had already moved on to the next step. He was thinking of the actions required in Washington to get the Compact approved. He wanted to send a letter to Jim Berg at the State Department certifying that the Compact had been approved in Palau. This would get the final Compact approval process going in Washington. In Washington, the president of the United States had to refer the Compact to the Congress for approval.

Staff work in Palau was not easy. In all of Micronesia, both because of its small size and the general lack of fluency in written English, outsiders maintained undue control because of their linguistic skills. We were like the missionaries of old gaining control by means of our knowledge of the written word. Our presence was a constant reminder to Palauans of their inadequacy and the frustration of working with Washington and the States. That skepticism had been overcome in my case, I thought, as the president and a number of other Palauan officials had gone out of their way to indicate that they respected my work and my approach to Micronesia. For twenty-five years I had counseled territorial governments on status relations with the United States, always representing the territory, seeing the world from the small end of the telescope. I did not advise investors. Enough governments in the Pacific had seen me come and go to take my measure.

My role had shifted rapidly from a legal adviser to a guy who could write a letter, and the president wanted it written quickly. I drafted the letter that afternoon. It officially informed the president of the United States that Palau had ratified the Compact in accordance with its democratic processes.

The next day, Sunday morning, Salii talked to de Lugo. Word that the case was settled had reached de Lugo, and he telephoned his congratulations. Now that the battle appeared over, de Lugo and Salii pretended to be on good terms. At about the same time, Sunday morning, the Ibedul, in a radio address to his followers, explained that he had ended his long opposition to the Compact.

The president asked me when I would be leaving. He liked and respected me, but he understood it was cheaper to have me back in Washington than on Palau, especially if my sole function was to be a walking reminder of a faulty legal agreement. "Probably Tuesday or Wednesday. I have to work out my return airline reservations," I said. I was pleased that the case was settled, but frustrated that I had traveled twenty-seven hours (twenty hours in the air, with a change of planes in Hawaii and Guam) to get the news.

On Monday, I went over to see the Senate leaders. We had become friends as a result of our long discussions in late July when they had, with a great deal of reluctance, passed the law proposing a constitutional amendment. We had come out of these discussions with considerable respect for one another. Now I was there to say good-by and to get their reaction to the settlement. The president of the Senate, Joshua Koshiba, and one of the Senate leaders, John Sugiyama, were there. Senator Sugiyama said he heard the Compact opponents were going to file another lawsuit later that afternoon.

"I talked to the president just yesterday and he told me no lawsuit was going to be filed," I replied.

"Well, probably we're wrong," Senator Koshiba answered.

They were right and they knew it.

Late Monday afternoon, on August 31, 1987, twenty-nine Palauan women filed a new lawsuit copying word for word the complaint in *Merep*, the case that had just been settled. The women claimed that the August 4 referendum to amend Palau's constitution was illegal. Heading the list of plaintiffs was Gloria Gibbons Salii, the Bilung, the highest ranking woman in Palau. She was also the sister of the Ibedul and the wife of President Salii's younger brother, Carlos.

Interpretations of the complaint varied. Some felt it was a simple double cross. Most of the women were members of the Idid clan, the highest clan in Koror and the strongest supporters of the Ibedul. If anyone could be controlled by the Ibedul, it was these women. But others were not so sure. Compact politics were difficult to discern even in a small place like Palau. By now Palauans understood that this was no longer an internal fight against outsiders they controlled and could manipulate. These outsiders were highly motivated, well financed, and had the ability to come up with plaintiffs when they needed them. Some pro-Compact Palauans admitted that there were a few women who cared enough about the danger of nuclear contamination to continue to fight regardless of the Ibedul's position. Men might be unable to continue the case because of potential harm to their political advancement or because of possible retribution. For the women, there were no political jobs in the offing, and they were safe from retaliation.

Nevertheless, the new lawsuit was most un-Palauan. Women in Palau, as elsewhere in the Pacific, played subordinate roles. Traditionally in Palau, institutionalized concubinage was common. Arranged marriages were also commonplace; marriages with males from wealthier clans could determine a clan's status. Sexual servitude of that crude a character was no longer present, but the feminine dependency role that these practices represented died slowly.

Women did control the key, traditional leadership position in Palau; they selected the Ibedul. Some said their role was a formal one only, with men actually determining the selection behind the scenes. Perhaps so, but in the case of the present Ibedul, it was indeed the women who chose him, the younger, inexperienced man, over the older, more mature competitor, his uncle, a man who had considerable male support. Inheritance traditionally was matrilineal. The son of the sister of the Ibedul, not the son of the Ibedul himself, was the heir apparent to his title. In sum, leadership flowed through the loins of the women.

But once the women married and gave birth, once the selection of the Ibedul was made, political power, especially the visible exercise of political power, was a male prerogative. Only one woman had ever been elected to the OEK, and then only for a single term. Whatever a woman's influence might be behind the scenes, it was most un-Palauan for women to come forward and take a public, political initiative, especially in the face of statements to the contrary by the Ibedul and the president.

Un-Palauan or not, it had happened. The women had filed another lawsuit. We were starting over.

Notes

1. Page 97. *Wilhelm Rengiil.* A brief profile of Wilhelm Rengiil, emphasizing his academic gifts—he was one of the few Palauans permitted by the Japanese to study not only beyond three years of education but beyond five years of education—is found in W. Pesch, "Nan'yo," *Pacific Daily News, Islander Magazine*, Sept. 26, 1993, p. 8.

2. Page 101. In *Inabo v. Republic of Palau,* Johnson Toribiong had argued that the trusteeship agreement overruled the Palau Constitution, and therefore only a majority vote was required to approve the Compact.

3. Page 103. Regarding women in Palau: "That women in Palauan society hold a position subordinate to that of men seems to me to be a fact beyond question," writes H. G. Barnett in *Palauan Society* (1949), p. 167. More recently, D.R. Smith, *Palauan Social Structure* (1983), makes the same point: "Women's power is private; its locus is within the matrilineage where they are the sources of valuables, land, and children for this unit. In contrast, male power is public. Men are public spokesmen for their matrilinages, conveying decisions that have been made internally by male and female lineage members." (p.309). Regarding the role of women generally, see F. Hezel, "The Dilemmas of Development: The Effects of Modernization on Three Areas of Island Life," *Journal of the Pacific Society* (April 1987), p. 11.

11

The Case Proceeds to Judgment; Bedor Bins is Murdered

Whatever the politics of the situation, there was now a legal, tactical challenge: how to respond. There were two possibilities. First, we could go forward as if the settlement between Salii and the Ibedul in the *Merep* case had never occurred, answer the complaint, ask for summary judgment, and get on with it. This was Attorney General Isaac's preference, and, on hindsight, perhaps the correct course. It would have responded to the desire of the Congress and the people of Palau to resolve the constitutional question.

But from a political and legal point of view, at the time it didn't seem to be the correct approach. If we followed this course, it would pretty much admit that the president had been duped when he settled the *Merep* case, and I didn't think the president wanted that. Further, if we responded in that way, we would be making it easier for the women plaintiffs. Such an approach would permit the pattern of this case to develop like *Merep*, so that all the women had to do was copy the *Merep* documents.

We had the advantage of being lawyers. If we could propel the lawsuit into uncharted waters, the legal advantage to us would be greater. I favored, therefore, the alternative: to raise the procedural point. Then the women would not be able to bring the same lawsuit again. We would argue that the previous cases and the agreement between Salii and the Ibedul, had decided the issues and bound everybody.

I set forth the two choices to Salii: treat the women's lawsuit as a continuation of the *Merep* case and litigate the substance, or raise the procedural issue of his agreement with the Ibedul. I usually kept the president informed of what was happening. He liked that, I thought; it cemented our relationship and it also prevented others from getting in the way of what I was doing in court.

But I had never asked Salii to decide legal tactics. I made an exception here because it was his settlement we were discussing. There would be strong political ramifications in how we treated the women and their lawsuit. He liked my recommended approach, as I thought he would. We, therefore, filed a motion to dismiss on procedural grounds: the case had already been decided. (*Res judicata* is the Latin, legal term.)

We then met with Chief Justice Nakamura. He had a clear vision of what he wanted the Palau Court to be both as an institution and in its physical character. He sought a sense of dignity for the Court, like the sense of dignity in his own person. The law library was beginning to take shape, and he had arranged to publish the Palau cases in a regular loose-leaf reporter system similar to the publications of the courts in the States.

To accomplish his vision for the Court, he needed time, a respite from the limelight. He would build slowly, achieving respect from the people of Palau for its judiciary as an institution which decides fairly a series of cases that are unglamorous, but important to the everyday Palauan. The Compact case could not help him reach his goal. The Court was once again being placed in a highly visible role in Palau and being asked to overturn the popular will of the people.

As attorney for Palau, I now asked the chief justice to assign the case to a judge sitting in Palau, preferably himself, since he had handled the *Merep* injunction requests and, therefore, was familiar with the issues. The case could then be heard immediately, preferably the next day. But Nakamura refused to hear the case. He assigned the case to a judge from outside Palau. An off-island judge meant delay. That delay was to be catastrophic.

It was widely believed that Nakamura had been threatened. He had sent his wife and daughter to Guam. The GAO, in its later report, published in 1989, said of Nakamura, "He had experienced significant pressure but his action was motivated by a desire to maintain the court's integrity and *not by intimidation*. . . . He stated that although he received threats, he did not request police protection" (emphasis supplied).

The GAO investigators, whose opinion of Nakamura was very high, believed him. I have talked to the GAO investigators and others directly on the point, and I have no hard evidence on which to doubt their conclusion. Yet, unless he were threatened, or so angered that he felt he could not decide the case fairly, I can find no ready explanation for his refusing to sit on the case. If there were threats, and I believe on hindsight there were, he gave no indication of them.

Nakamura had assigned the case to Judge Robert Hefner, a white, stateside judge who normally held court in Saipan in the Northern Mariana Islands. The chief justice said he was going outside Palau in order to save the three other Palauan judges for the appeal. Hefner was a conservative Republican from California who had come to Micronesia from Los Angeles. He had been a judge in Palau from 1975 to 1979, so he knew Palau fairly well. The papers had to be forwarded to him, and then we had to wait until Hefner came to Palau. Travel time alone would take a couple of days. Hefner's appointment and the attendant delay angered many Palauans, who felt that once again it was an outsider, and, some thought, a biased one at that, who was going to decide their fate. The charge of bias was based on the fact that Judge Hefner had heard two prior cases in connection with the Palau litigation in 1983 and had ruled against the government each time. But these related to questions of ballot language and whether the nuclear sections could be separated from the other portions of the Compact.

The first case involved a crude effort by the United States to change the way the ballot was set out by the OEK so that the question was put in a way more favorable to Compact approval. Hefner found no power in the American or the Palau executive to change the OEK ballot language and, in addition, found that the rewritten language was intended to distort the question so as to mislead the Palauan voters. The decision was quite correct, I thought. Salii and Mirando were surprised when I said I would have ruled the same way.

The second case was a closer call. Palau had argued after 67 percent had approved the Compact in the first plebiscite that the vote approved the Compact. The nuclear provisions alone would remain unratified. The argument was a strong one. Hefner disagreed. He held that the OEK intended the question to be put to the people as a package in an all-or-nothing proposition. It would take 75 percent, not a simple majority, for any part of the Compact to take effect. I wasn't sure I would have ruled that way, but certainly it was a reasonable decision.

From these decisions, one could not charge bias by Judge Hefner or even an antigovernment attitude. But few in Palau read the decisions or knew the reasoning. It had come down to the bottom line. You were either for the Compact or against the Compact. Hefner had ruled against the Compact twice.

While waiting for Hefner, unbeknownst to me, efforts continued for a political settlement with the women. Gloria Salii, who was Lazarus Salii's sister-in-law and who held the female counterpart of the Ibedul title, the Bilung, was the most prominent name on the new complaint. Her status as a traditional leader required her to stand with the Ibedul and his settlement agreement. Only a day after the complaint was filed, she changed her position and withdrew her name from the complaint. Eight other women immediately followed her and withdrew their names as well.

On Wednesday, September 2, 1987, the women answered our motion in Palauan. They made two points: first, they were women and therefore not bound by the settlement agreements in *Merep* and *Inabo*; and second they wanted a delay to get an attorney since they were afraid at this point to go to the courthouse.

The answer was the first break in the dike. The first argument was absurd: women would be bound just as men were. With respect to the second argument, no judge could give a plaintiff a delay to some unspecified time in the future immediately after a lawsuit was begun. In effect, this would be granting the plaintiffs a permanent injunction without their asking for it. We pointed this out, arguing that at the very least the case should be dismissed, since the women didn't seem to want to prosecute it.

Whoever was advising the women saw the legal impossibility of their position. In their next filing, they narrowed their request, asking that the lawsuit be delayed for two weeks only, saying they had made contact with an attorney in the States who was helping them find a lawyer.

With the written legal interchange completed, we were advised that Judge Hefner would hear the case on Tuesday, September 8, at 2:30 p.m., flying in, apparently, on Monday night, the last day of the Labor Day weekend. The judicial system and Judge Hefner had moved expeditiously. Within a week of filing, the case would be argued. Nevertheless, the process was too slow. The people of Palau could not wait that long.

The women met regularly at Gabriela Ngirmang's house to discuss their lawsuit. The Ibedul continued to implore them to withdraw, bringing to bear his status, his commitment, and his opinion that the case had to be dropped or else there would be no peace in Palau. "How long could Palau engage in this internal warfare?" he asked. The Ibedul was not alone in pressing the women to change their minds. Government officials, furloughed workers, and neighbors all asked, pleaded, and angrily demanded that they withdraw. To no avail.

By now, the Furlough Committee was an organized force. It was structured as a legal entity, and had its own stationery. It could look back to the men's clubs of the Ibedul who, when government workers struck the Remeliik administration, acted in a semiofficial manner to keep order. The Furlough Committee saw itself by turns potentially as leading a revolutionary movement (Black September was one name it gave itself), a labor movement, or a political party. Palau was too small and undisciplined an island to contain a large group of angry people with political ambitions for very long. The Compact was now weighted with many goals, ambitions, and frustrations. The need to do something pressed on everyone. Around Salii were many who wanted the furloughed workers to be more active, not just to sit around. Many in the furlough workers' organization regarded violence as a legitimate tactic.

Normally, the weekend in Palau is filled with water. Fishing and boating are the standard pastimes, part of the local population's traditional experience. In Palau, like all of Micronesia, the water, like the land, is a world for men. Women rarely fish or boat. If they go along, they go as companions, not as active participants. This weekend was different. The water was forgotten. The people of Palau stayed home. The tension of the coming lawsuit dominated the thoughts and emotions of the furloughed workers. To many, the future was clear. They saw once again a foreign judiciary taking the Compact from them.

On Saturday night, September 5, four men in a red Mitsubishi Colt hatchback sedan drove to the home of Speaker Olikong, a leading opponent of the Compact, and fired at his house. Olikong was known to be off-island. The bullets struck harmlessly in the exterior walls of the house. Perhaps the men were only blowing off steam. Perhaps they were making a threat. The tension continued to build.

On Monday night, at 10:30 p.m., Koror suffered a sudden power outage. The red sedan, leased by the Furlough Committee, went forth once more. An explosive was thrown at the home of Ms. Ngirmang, the leading plaintiff for the women. It exploded on her front lawn: another threat, perhaps no more. Again, there was no damage. At about the same time, the Bai Ra Metal, an unoccupied building belonging to the state of Koror and formerly a night club under the Ibedul's management, was burned to the ground.

Later that night, the four men in the red car sped to the office of Roman Bedor, a Palauan legal adviser, a key opponent of the Compact, and co-counsel in the *Merep* case. His sister, Bernice Keldermans, was a leading plaintiff in the women's lawsuit. Two of the men, their faces masked, got out and banged on the office door. Roman Bedor's father, Bedor Bins, went to the door and opened it. A shot was fired. Bedor Bins was wounded seriously in the left side. He staggered toward his home. A second shot was fired. It hit him in the back, mortally wounding him. Bedor Bins was rushed to the Palau hospital, where he lay dying.

Salii heard of the shooting and drove to the hospital. He ran to Bedor Bins's room. Salii sat by his bed, took the older man's hand, and stroked it, saying over and over to him in Palauan: "It will be all right. It will be all right. It will be all right."

The next morning Bedor Bins was dead.

Notes

1. Page 106. *It was widely believed that Nakamura*. Professor Donald Shuster states that he talked to the chief justice at some length and was told there were threats. Letter from Professor Shuster to the author, Sept. 30, 1992.

2. Page 106. The quotation is from GAO, *U.S. Trust Territory: Issues Associated with Palau's Transition to Self-Government; Supplement to the Report* (July 1989), pp. 58-59.

3. Page 107. *The second case was a closer one*. Professor Roger Clark, an opponent of the Compact, concluded as well: "There are no obvious answers to these questions." R. Clark, "The Current State of the Trust Territory Negotiations: Who Has Tentatively Agreed to What?" (Working Paper Prepared for the Micronesia Support Committee, August 1981), p. 21. I am grateful to Professor Clark for making this paper available to me.

4. Page 109. The hospital scene between President Salii and Bedor Bins is based on conversations with Dr. Francesca Soaladaob, the attending physician at the hospital when Bedor Bins came to the hospital.

12

The Women Suddenly Withdraw; Judge Hefner Suggests Intimidation

Communication generally in Palau is informal. People learn of what is happening orally, usually at chance meetings, lunches, and social events. Some people have television, picking up sitcoms on the one available channel, but news is delayed. On occasion a special tape is played on the television, usually a political announcement or replays of hearings in the U.S. Congress. CNN had not yet come to Palau.

The *Pacific Daily News*, a Gannett newspaper published on Guam, is flown in daily and is the main source of outside news. Sometimes the paper doesn't make the plane and is received a day or two late. In any event, its Palau coverage is very limited, primarily covering those events in which statesiders would be likely to have an interest.

The local newspaper, an eight-to-sixteen page weekly put out by the Palau government's Public Information Office, focuses almost exclusively on activities of the Palau government, reporting them in as favorable a light as possible. At various times, more independent weekly or biweekly local newspapers—*Tia Belau*, *Palau Weekly*, *Rengel Belau* and *Palau Tribune*—have been started on Palau. All collapsed very quickly, partly due to the limited printing facilities and small size of the readership, partly due to the narrow political viewpoint of the newspaper, and partly due to local pressures, which frequently found muckraking reporting too upsetting.

The radio generally broadcasts music, but also airs special announcements and speeches by government officials. The telephone is still less than totally dependable. In sum, the news of local events gets out, but slowly and haphazardly.

Late Tuesday morning, on September 8, about 11:00 a.m., Isaac, the attorney general, told us of the Bedor Bins murder. He had learned of it from the police that morning.

Up to this point, the high road was ours. We represented the people. We were the good guys. The plaintiffs were a small minority, totally self-aggrandizing, seeking political advantage, uncompromising, and financed and supported from outside Palau by groups whose motives involved a series of movable left-wing targets. This might overstate matters, but not by that much, and such a portrayal could be argued persuasively to the judiciary. If we presented a reasonably good case on the merits, and we certainly could do that, I thought we would win. The killing of Bedor Bins changed that. It was not clear who was wearing the white hats now, but it certainly wasn't us.

The Palau courthouse structure, built by the Japanese, is a modest one of white cinder blocks, shaped in the form of a u. The open space in the center is used for parking and as a walkway from one side of the structure to the other. The rains, which had begun in August, had converted the ground in front of the courtyard into a series of small pools of water linked by stretches of mud. On one side are a courtroom, the Chief Justice's office, and the office of the clerk of the court; on the other side are additional courtrooms and judge's offices. Above, on the second floor, are the attorney general's offices.

Early that Tuesday afternoon, about an hour before the case was to be argued, John Tarkong, the head of the furloughed government workers who had kept a daily watch on the OEK to urge the passage of the constitutional amendment, came up and wanted to talk about the legal tactics of the case. It was not a friendly meeting. About fifty men and women had been driven to the courtyard in busses draped in black and gray crepe paper to resemble coffins. Most of the Palauans were wearing red headbands and lounging on benches along the side of the courtroom offices. What were they doing there? Who in his right mind believed, after the shooting and killing over the weekend, that a demonstration in front of the courthouse was in order? Tarkong answered that the furloughed employees were not responsible for the killing. But, I responded, the matter of who committed the murder was not going to be sorted out in the next hour and in the next hour a lot of people would blame the furloughed employees, especially since they had come to the courthouse wearing red headbands. What were the red headbands intended to signify, anyway? Couldn't they be removed? (In Fiji, under somewhat similar circumstances in 1977, the Nationalist party had put on red arm bands. There it had meant blood would flow. I thought something like that was probably the intended message here.)

Tarkong said he could not ask them to remove them. "This was their statement," he said.

When the case was called, at 2:30 p.m., the plaintiffs' table was empty. Judge Hefner asked that the case be called in Palauan and in English. He then stated that he did not know what to do, since none of the women had come to court. I suggested that the judge grant the government's motion to dismiss. Obviously, this would give us what we wanted, but it would not damage the plaintiffs significantly. If, indeed, as the women had said, they planned to obtain an attorney within the next two weeks, they would still have ample time to file an appeal, since appeals had to be filed within thirty days. They would file briefs 30 days after that. We would be in the appellate court, which is where the case would ultimately be decided anyway. The judge seemed intrigued and said, "It's a bit unusual, but I will hear you on the motion to dismiss."

I began my argument. The judge asked a number of questions about class action lawsuits and whether indeed the Ibedul-Salii agreement barred the new plaintiffs. Since I was unopposed, the questions were more in the nature of a quiz satisfying the judge's curiosity about me—in effect, testing the Washington attorney. At least, that was the way I took them. The spirit in which they were offered was friendly. Judge Hefner, it seemed to me, was stalling for time.

I was not more than ten minutes into the argument when Attorney General Isaac entered the courtroom and slipped me a note asking me to request a recess immediately. I was surprised and told the judge of the note. He turned to the attorney general, who rose and explained that the women plaintiffs were coming to the courthouse and were going to withdraw their lawsuit.

The judge granted a recess and left the courtroom. Isaac, Basse, the assistant attorney general, and I went upstairs to the attorney general's office to await the women. On hindsight, probably both the judge and I were at fault. We should have stayed where we were and held any discussion with the women in open court. This new settlement possibility had come up so suddenly, however, that no one was thinking perfectly clearly.

About ten minutes later Rafaela Sumang, accompanied by the Ibedul and an adviser to the Ibedul, and Salii joined us in the attorney general's office. Ms. Sumang said she wanted to withdraw the lawsuit to restore harmony once more in Palau. What was going on was not right. She hadn't intend to cause that kind of upset. I drafted an order that would have effectively settled the lawsuit. She asked whether the order was "with prejudice." I was not surprised at the question. Everyone in Palau was a Compact lawyer by now, and a pretty good one at that. I said that it was "with prejudice." The intent was to settle the lawsuit once and for all. There was some discussion by her in Palauan with the Ibedul and his adviser. Then she nodded. The order, with modest changes, was given to the Ibedul and his adviser to review and then to Ms. Sumang, and she agreed to it. Ms. Sumang understood perfectly what was happening. She was obviously tense, but she never mentioned that she was being threatened. I cannot speak to the dialogue between Ms. Sumang and the Ibedul. The Ibedul spoke only in Palauan and only to her. It appeared that he was reinforcing what I had said.

While the settlement agreement was being typed in final form, I went downstairs to see Judge Hefner. It was now about 4:00 p.m. I told him that the language had been agreed to and the typed agreement should be finished in about ten minutes. He said he wanted all of the women plaintiffs to sign it. He was obviously upset but was following proper procedure.

Again, on hindsight, both the judge and I made fatal blunders. The judge should have talked to the plaintiffs in chambers if he had any question about the process. I should have asked him if he wanted to do that. The circumstances were so extraordinary and the events were moving so rapidly that I didn't focus on this aspect of the procedure.

In any event, the judge and the plaintiffs did not have any official contact. We proceeded to get the order typed upstairs and to advise Ms. Sumang that all nineteen ladies had to sign. After another discussion in Palauan among Ms. Sumang, the Ibedul, and his adviser, I went back to Judge Hefner to tell him there would be no problem. The ladies, Ms. Sumang said, were all congregated and waiting, and we should have all the signatures in about half an hour. It was to take considerably longer than that. Once again, we were to come close, but not quite make it.

Ms. Sumang and the Ibedul went to collect signatures while the rest of us waited. The judge stayed in his chambers, I remained in the attorney general's office upstairs, and President Salii left as well, presumably returning to his office. An hour went by and there was still no word. The court normally adjourned at 4:30 p.m. Basse went down to Judge Hefner in his chambers and asked that he stay a bit longer. He said he would. At 5:15 p.m. we still had heard nothing. The judge sent his clerk up to say that the court was going to stand recessed until 8:30 the next morning.

The recess proved fatal to the government's hopes for a settlement. At 6:45 that evening, the signatures finally all came in. Copies were made, and I briefed the president and his cabinet at approximately 7:30 that night. My opinion was that it was now over, that Judge Hefner, while he was unhappy with what had happened, would in all likelihood sign the agreement of the parties. I was mistaken.

At 9:00 the next morning, the case was finally called. This time, both Gabriela Ngirmang and Rafaela Sumang were at the plaintiffs' table. Also at the table, surprisingly, were the Ibedul and Kaleb Udui, the Palauan lawyer, perhaps most identified with the Compact opposition. Udui had represented the plaintiffs in the *Merep* case and, after getting the words "with prejudice" removed, had signed the *Merep* settlement. The Ibedul and Udui's presence, I thought, told the Palauan world that the latest agreement was, in effect, part of the Salii-Ibedul agreement. A Palauan consensus had finally formed behind the Compact. It was too late.

Judge Hefner entered the courtroom. He quickly let us know he was not going to sign the agreement. He said there were indications that the agreement was not voluntary, that there had been intimidation. There was nothing before him, he said, except the voluntary withdrawal by the plaintiffs. This, of course, was not true. What was before him was an agreement of the parties. What he was saying was that he was treating it as a voluntary dismissal. A voluntary dismissal was of no consequence at all since another lawsuit could be filed immediately.

Judge Hefner, from the bench, orally, went on "to ponder future events." He foresaw three possibilities. First, the Compact could be approved and it would be left to academics and historians in the future to judge what had happened this day. Second, the Compact could be defeated. Judge Hefner could not do that himself. He was addressing the Congress. Then, he put forward a third possibility. There could be a new lawsuit "tomorrow, next week, or next year."

I rose to respond, but he gaveled the court to a close. I visited the judge immediately in his chambers. He was quite friendly, calling me by my first name although I had never met him. I was less willing to be friendly. I indicated that if he had problems with the settlement, he could have questioned the plaintiffs in court, since the plaintiffs and their advisers were there; or, if he wished, he could have spoken to them privately in his chambers *but on the record* rather than make a "finding" of coercion not in the record, which could not be refuted.

Judge Hefner said he had thought of questioning the plaintiffs in open court, but he didn't want to make life any harder for the women. I said I thought his opinion would only contribute to future violence, and we had had a chance to bring a halt to all of that. That went a bit far, and he called me to task on that. The conversation abruptly ended.

I believed then, and do now, that there were private discussions the day before between Judge Hefner and the plaintiffs, probably right after the judge had ordered a recess at 5:30 p.m. How else could he have found "evidence of intimidation"? Such discussions, in effect taking evidence with only one party present, normally are highly questionable. However, with plaintiffs who may have been intimidated, such discussions may be necessary. But once they have taken place, these discussions must be placed on the record. This is not a small point: democracy is dependent upon proper procedure.

There was some thought in Palauan governmental circles that Judge Hefner's opinion would pass unnoticed as a petulant outburst, especially if no press were in the room. But Judge Hefner was more purposeful than that. He had his remarks typed up immediately and sent on to Washington and the off-island press. That afternoon we received a copy.

Salii and Mirando wanted to issue a strong, written response immediately. I was reluctant to do that. Mirando looked at it as one more battle in the continuing war between the courts and the Salii administration, another battle that would eventually lead to a constitutional amendment requiring elected judges and thus reduce the court's power. I appreciated that viewpoint, but it was not a war in which I was involved or wanted to be. My role was to represent Palau to try to get the Compact ratified. Keeping on good terms with the court was critical to achieve that task. There was no sense getting into a mud-slinging match with a sitting judge, especially if, after the murder of Bedor Bins, we were associated with the forces of death and destruction. Being responsive to the client was a factor to be considered but did not always determine what to do.

My view changed when, a couple of days later, stimulated by Judge Hefner's opinion, the *Pacific Daily News* ran a series of articles analyzing Palauan society and emphasizing its history of violence. We had to respond. To let Hefner's remarks go unchallenged might be taken in Congress as an admission.

We reiterated the government's stand against violence. We agreed that the courts should not be subject to intimidation. In fact, President Salii had directed the Minister of Justice to order protection for the plaintiffs. We acknowledged that there were pressures and expressions of anger attendant upon this lawsuit, as there had been throughout the Compact approval process. The issue was whether the pressures were so great that the withdrawal was not voluntary. We then went on to what was our strongest point. The judge knew of the settlement discussions with the women in the attorney general's office; we specifically had informed him. Further, plaintiffs were in the courtroom, at the counsel table, on Wednesday with the Ibedul and counsel, Udui, when the stipulation was filed. Nevertheless, Judge Hefner did not ask them whether the dismissal was voluntary. The plaintiffs were asked nothing, either on Tuesday or on Wednesday. We concluded that we were unconvinced that any intimidation had forced the plaintiffs unwillingly to dismiss this case.

Our response was of no consequence. We were baying at the wind. Judge Hefner had returned to Saipan. The Compact was in limbo. Our case now had to be argued before the Congress in Washington.

Notes

1. Page 115. *I believed then*. In the course of writing this book, I asked Judge Hefner specifically about this text comment both orally and in writing but he did not reply.

2. Page 115. *These discussions must be placed*. Canon 3 of the ABA Code of Judicial Conduct states:

(7)   ...A judge shall not initiate, permit, or consider ex parte communications...*except* that:...

(ii) the judge makes provision promptly to notify all other parties of the substance of the ex parte communication and allows an opportunity to respond.

13

Washington Reacts; de Lugo and Farrow Mobilize Against the Compact

Judge Hefner's opinion had not only a legal impact but also a political one. The judge's suggestion that the plaintiffs had been intimidated into dropping their lawsuit carried monumental political force. It converted a debate over the formal, legal validity of the Compact ratification process into one over the acceptability of the Salii administration. The Compact opponents leaped at the opportunity to vilify Salii as a tool of U.S. militarism.

The opposition to the Compact was formidable. The speed and breadth of the response to Judge Hefner's opinion evidenced that. Within a week of Hefner's opinion, the European Parliament, various representatives from Italy, Great Britain, Greece, Belgium, Ireland, West Germany, Denmark, and France, wrote to all members of the U.S. Congress, saying, "We ask you to reject any attempt by your government to win congressional approvement for the Compact of Free Association based on terrorism and intimidation."

Jeffrey Farrow, the director of the House Territories Subcommittee, responded by sending a letter to Salii saying that the committee could not act on the Compact given the uncertainty about its legal validity and the violence in Palau. The letter, signed by the committee and subcommittee chairmen, Udall and de Lugo, and by the ranking Republican members, Young from Alaska and Lagomarsino from California, left it unclear what Palau could do to get the Committee to approve the Compact. "Action on legislation to bring the Compact into effect can be expected as soon as the right of the people of the islands and the sanctity of the institutions of their government are assured and Palau's constitutional approval of the Compact is unquestioned."

The decision of de Lugo and Farrow to delay Compact ratification was a signal to the opposition. Letters from the women plaintiffs said that they were intimidated:

Then, on September 8, 1987, Tuesday, our lawsuit was scheduled to be heard, and a van drove by, covered with a black cloth on which was written "Black September," and I heard that it was said that they were going to kill us women who were suing and would put us in the van if they lost the suit. . . .

These incidents and threatening actions mentioned above are the reasons why I withdrew my name from the lawsuit. . . . I continued that perhaps many more people will be killed.

The same day we met at Gabriela's house. The bus meant for our coffin kept passing by. . . .

Ibedul came to the house and asked us not to go to the court because it had become very dangerous. He asked us to make peace. . . .

I am still of the same opinion to pursue with the suit with anyone who would revive it. . . .

On September 8, a bus decorated in black with writings on it in a language I could not understand paraded down the street. Upon inquiry, some young kids told me the writing meant it was a coffin meant for us if we insisted on going to court.

By the time I visited Farrow, a week later, armed with legal and political arguments, the battle lines had been formed. My legal argument was that the Salii-Ibedul agreement that settled the *Merep* case was binding. The case had been decided and could not be brought again. My political argument turned on the same Salii-Ibedul agreement. A consensus had finally been reached in Palau, and the U.S. Congress should support it. Farrow gave no weight to either argument. The Hefner opinion was now before the Congress, and it could not be ignored.

I agreed with that, but the problem with the opinion was that it did not tell you anything. Hefner had detailed no allegations of intimidation. If Hefner didn't make a finding, how could the committee assume he did? "There is evidence of intimidation. There is a dead man. The U.S. has to do something about that. We are required to protect the citizens of Palau." Farrow had the high ground. Congress couldn't—indeed wouldn't—move as long as there were serious doubts concerning the welfare of the citizens of Palau and the legal validity of the ratification process. He didn't see how hearings could even be held until all of this had been settled.

It became clear in subsequent discussions with the minority side—Congressman Lagomarsino and his staff aide—that de Lugo and Farrow's strong views were their own. The Republicans had signed the letter only reluctantly. The Republicans would accept the certification from the president of Palau. Palau had amended its Constitution and ratified its Compact. As long as there were no more lawsuits and no more violence, they were willing to go forward despite the lobbying of Greenpeace and the Center for Constitutional Rights. But if there were a lawsuit, all congressional processing of the Compact would stop.

Among congressional members active on Palau, Stephen Solarz was the most powerful, in terms of both sheer intellectual strength and the stature of his committee, the Subcommittee on Asia and Pacific Affairs of the Foreign Affairs Committee. He was not one to suffer fools gladly. It was an important failing. In the "hail fellow, well met" atmosphere of the Congress, he was not one of the fellows. Nevertheless, he had risen remarkably quickly, gaining the respect, if not the friendship, of his colleagues and the public. Solarz's civil liberties credentials were much stronger than de Lugo's. In the 1970s he had taken the lead on women's rights issues. De Lugo and Farrow had never been publicly involved with civil liberties issues before. If Solarz came down with us, Congressmen on the fence would, in all likelihood, come down with us as well.

The administration wanted to complete the Palau agreement, to end the trusteeship and establish the U.S. military presence on an internationally firm footing. Solarz and Stanley Roth, his staff aide, supported these goals. They viewed Palau as a foreign policy issue. Solarz had strongly supported all of the Micronesian Compacts and was eager for ratification of this final Compact to confirm the U.S. military presence in the western Pacific. A U.S. military presence, even a nuclear presence, was far from anathema to him; Solarz viewed such a presence as necessary to protect the fragile democracies of South Asia and the South Pacific. On the other hand, the democratic actions of United States-supported countries was not something he would overlook. Solarz had taken the lead in Congress against Fernando Marcos, the Philippines military dictator, holding a series of hearings which led to Marcos's downfall.

I reviewed the legal and political situation in Palau with Solarz's aide, Stanley Roth. He asked whether people in Palau in fact could bring a lawsuit. Solarz had received a letter from the Center for Constitutional Rights saying that there would be a lawsuit "as soon as the reign of terror had ended." Was the government providing adequate protection to all of its citizens? Roth asked. I assured him that the government was. Roth pressed: Why were there no arrests? Palau is a small place. Neighbors and friends usually know what happened. "The delay doesn't help," he added.

I met with the officials of the Office of Freely Associated State Affairs (OFASA) in the State Department. Their views were critical to the situation. The administration had to certify to the Congress that the Palau government had ratified the Compact. If the administration's views were similar to Farrow's, ratification of the Palau Compact was impossible.

Once again I reviewed the key documents in the *Merep* and *Inabo* cases, presenting them to Jim Berg, the director of OFASA, as I had to Farrow and Roth. Again, I argued strongly the legal view that the combination of *Merep* and *Inabo* settled the matter and barred any further lawsuits challenging the Compact amendment process. Although that had not persuaded Farrow at all, the State Department officials accepted the argument immediately. They had felt that the *Merep* settlement alone might legally carry the day, and when that was coupled with *Inabo*, which they hadn't known about, they felt much more comfortable.

Of course, I was aware of the strong bias in the administration. OFASA had a task to perform: obtain ratification of the Palau compact. It would take a great deal for that office to be diverted from its goal.

Berg's major claim to fame in Micronesia was that he spoke Chuukese, the language of the island of Truk in the Federated States of Micronesia. In Washington, his strength was his intelligence, calm, and analytical skill. Berg felt that Farrow's warnings were not that serious. He had heard them two years before when the Marshalls and the FSM Compacts were before the Congress for ratification. De Lugo and Farrow had found themselves isolated and then overwhelmed by the pressure from the other committees. That would happen once again, he predicted. As for the Palau Compact, the State Department was clearing it with the various government agencies and would shortly send it on to the White House. From there it would go to the Congress. I felt very heartened.

Berg raised the matter of the IPSECO deal. President Reagan's statement transmitting the Compact to Congress for approval would recommend deletion of the section of federal law that insulated Compact funds from the banks. That deletion would allow Compact funds to be used to pay the banks. The administration was following the Zeder position and being helpful to the banks. De Lugo and Farrow opposed taking Compact funds away from the people of Palau to pay banks whose behavior they questioned.

All of the U.S. government officials asked about the murder of Bedor Bins. What was happening in that case? I could only say that as far as I knew Palau was actively investigating the case.

In a telex to President Salii, I reported on these discussions, with a recommendation that we report progress on the Bedor Bins investigation. Some visible development in the case was essential in order to show Washington that Palau government had respect for law. I recommended as well that the Ibedul and perhaps even the chief justice issue statements that all Palauans had access to the courts of Palau. I drafted and attached statements for the Ibedul and the chief justice, assuming that Salii wanted to proceed in this direction and that the Ibedul and chief justice would go along with this approach.

On September 25, 1987, Palau celebrated Compact Day, or a Day of National Unity, in honor of the ratification of the Compact. Salii, Koshiba (President of the Senate), and the Ibedul delivered statements supporting the Compact and asking that everyone now go forward together. The Ibedul had not used my draft. The statement was his own and a very strong one.

The Ibedul stressed the land issue: "The agreement President Salii and I signed earlier relating to land matters removed the final obstacle to implement the Compact agreement with the United States. . . . President Salii has always been cognizant of the importance of land matters in Palauan society."

Then he directly addressed Greenpeace and his change of position in support of the Compact:

Many of my friends throughout the world . . . may very well wonder what had happened to my position.

However, all my friendships with renowned world personages and organizations . . . will never replace my love and concern for the welfare of the Palauan people. My first and foremost interest is to see a strong and viable Palauan nation.

And then a final call for unity: "This is my most important request. I ask all the leaders in Palau, those who are in the government, those who head Palauan clans and families, those who lead political or social organizations, the parents, and all brothers and sisters, to come together again and to have peace among themselves."

At the festivities, the furloughed employees established a new party, the Ta Belau party, "To promote the interest of all employees of the native government" and to ratify the Compact. Mirando had mentioned to me the political potential if the government employees could be organized. Apparently he had succeeded in doing it. The chief justice was present at the celebration. Although he gave no speech, his presence gave considerable credibility to the unity message.

I distributed the Ibedul's speech and a background memorandum on Compact Day to the various congressional committees, the State Department, and the Department of the Interior, including pictures showing all of the key Palauan officials present at the ceremonies. The House Interior and Insular Affairs Committee was certain to be unaffected by Compact Day, at least publicly, but it made the committee's argument less tenable.

Of course, the congressional offices were not limited to me or to Greenpeace for their information. The Office of Territories and International Affairs in the Department of the Interior agreed to provide biweekly reports to Senator Johnston. The assistant secretary's report for early October—which I did not know about then—showed how much conditions in Palau depended on fund availability. "On 1 October the furloughed workers returned to normal duties. All of the offices were opened and operating. . . . [T]he public schools reopened. Everything appeared to be normal and without incident except for a shortage of a few teachers at Palau High School."

I talked to the Senate Energy and Natural Resources staff, Al Stayman for the majority and Jim Beirne for the minority. Beirne's tenure was even longer than Farrow's—he first worked on the Senate staff when he was beginning college—and he knew the issues in all the territories very well. Stayman was newer to the job but was regarded highly by the senators on the committee. They were very forthcoming. Their view of the *Merep* and *Inabo* cases was the same as mine—they settled the matter—and their stated view of the shooting was that it was unrelated to the broader issue of Compact ratification.   They analyzed the Compact and congressional ratification in simple terms: a ratified Compact was in the U.S. interest, and it was what the people of Palau wanted.

There was one other base to touch, and that was the Department of the Interior. Interior had a large group assembled for me. I explained to them, somewhat carefully, the legal events that had taken place. I ran through the *Merep* and *Inabo* cases and distributed the Ibedul's speech given on National Unity Day. Mark Hayward, the deputy assistant secretary of the Office of Territories and International Affairs, who was chairing the meeting, was frank. The problem, he said, was that we now have the judge's legal opinion. It may have been unwarranted. It may even be wrongly decided, but it existed. It had to be counteracted. He felt we needed an advisory opinion from the Palau Supreme Court.

Impossible, I thought. The Palau Supreme Court had never rendered an advisory opinion and it was not certain it legally was able to do so. Certainly in this case the Palau Supreme Court would not do anything that was questionable procedurally and the government of Palau couldn't ask it to.

Interior's primary concern was the murder of Bedor Bins. Many at the Office of Territories and International Affairs felt, as did Farrow, that the government of Palau was stalling and not actively seeking the killers. Privately, I shared their concerns. There were disturbing reports that the lone eye-witness and Bedor Bins's son had not even been interviewed by the police. I had been telling Salii in the strongest terms of the need to show progress in the Bedor Bins investigation.   In my next telex to Salii, I reiterated the recommendation.

Salii responded on October 19 with a long letter to Senator Johnston. (Similar letters were sent to Udall, de Lugo, and Secretary Hodel at the Department of the Interior.) The letter had not been cleared with me. Not too unusual. Salii was a very confident, impulsive leader. Clearances were not his style. This time clearance would have helped. The letter completely missed the mood in Washington.   Since Salii had a very good feel for Washington, the best of any island leader I had ever counseled, the letter troubled me. Salii's letter made three points. Palau was calm, and efforts to suggest otherwise were unfair to Palau and exaggerated by Compact opponents. Further, the Palauan people and their government were united behind the Compact. On these two points, Salii was clearly right. The press and Compact opponents were distorting the conditions in Palau. But Salii's letter dismissed too easily the shooting incidents over the Labor Day weekend, the third point of the letter.

The exaggerated reports you are hearing originate from several unfortunate incidents that took place one night last September. I am referring to the tragic and fatal shooting of the father of an attorney for the local anti-Compact group, a burning of an abandoned club house, and a small bomb explosion in a banana grove in the town of Koror which hurt no one and did no damage to property. I assure you that these were individually motivated crimes and were not part of an organized effort to topple the government.

I didn't know who suggested the letter or who drafted it. The letter was unquestionably a good idea, but it should have been sent with a detailed report or some other follow-up action on the shooting. Absent that, the letter convinced no one who was not convinced before.

Salii's next letter, of October 22, 1987, did address both the investigation of the shooting and, particularly, the charges that key witnesses had not even been interviewed. Unfortunately, it emphasized the difficulty of arresting anyone.

First of all, it is not true that the police have not interviewed Roman Bedor or the lone eye-witness who saw the get-away murder car. The police interviewed both Roman Bedor and the witness on September 16th. Records of their statements were obtained by the police and are the hinges upon which the investigation is conducted. This case is extremely difficult because except for one witness there were no other witnesses who actually saw the murderer or murderers. And the lone "eye-witness" could not and still cannot identify the hooded gun man. She was only able to give some general physical descriptions of the person who fired the shots and to assert that the get-away car was a red sedan without a license plate.

Then Salii got to the point: Let's not be diverted from ratifying the Compact.

At present there is no lawsuit in the court challenging the Compact. The only opposition we hear about comes not from the Palauan people but from foreign do-gooders who have appointed themselves without our invitation as our guardians.

It is time that the voice of the Palauan people should be heard by the people and the Government of the United States. That voice spoke most eloquently in the sanctity and secrecy of the ballot box on August 4th and again on August 21st.

The popular will was Salii's strongest point. Eventually it would persuade large sections of the Congress. But not now. The crimes were too fresh in everyone's memory.

I suggested to President Salii that we engage an academic to issue an opinion on the validity of the *Merep* case. An academic, if he were the right one and said the right things, might change the mood on the procedural issue considerably. It was as close to an advisory opinion as we could get. The president responded quite rapidly, authorizing me to go ahead.

There were two outstanding authorities in the res judicata field, Professor Geoffrey Hazard at Yale and Professor Charles Allen Wright at Texas. Hazard had been a reporter for the American Law Institute Restatement of Judgments, and Wright had authored the multi-volume authoritative text on

Federal procedure. I called them both and I reached Wright first. He said he was intrigued, but he could give no more time to outside consulting matters.

Professor Hazard and I initially chatted briefly about Yale Law School relationships—since I was a Yale Law School graduate, we had some mutual points of reference—and then I explained the issue to him. He asked to see the file. I sent him the pleading file in the *Merep* case and relevant papers in the *Ngirmang* and *Inabo* cases. He called back after a preliminary review, and we discussed fees. He wanted $5,000 for a retainer and estimated that his total bill, based on time, would be $10,000. I was pleased. That amount was not so large that Palau could not pay it nor so large that, if he were favorable to us, anyone could charge that he was influenced by the sums involved.

I telexed Salii and told him that Professor Geoffrey Hazard had agreed to do it. I hesitated before transmitting the name. My transmissions to Salii were not secure; there might be attempts by someone to influence Hazard, and that would foul matters up further. I finally decided it would be inappropriate not to tell Salii who he was hiring. I described Hazard's credentials. If Congress were seeking support for finality without looking to a court case, Hazard gave us a shot.

The Department of the Interior officials had raised the possibility that a new lawsuit might not be brought in Palau but in the United States. That possibility had occurred to me almost immediately after the shooting of Bedor Bins. I had frightened Mirando by saying that if I were the plaintiffs, I would bring a civil rights lawsuit in California or, better yet, in the District of Columbia. The law was unclear, but if a court bought the view of Palau as an island where intimidation, corruption, and violence reigned, a federal district court in the States might well hear the case and tie the Compact up for years, until it found that the civil rights of the people were protected.

Palau's isolation was critical in this regard. What was actually going on in Palau—from a Washington point of view—could not be determined by tuning in the local television or reading the local newspaper. An exaggerated opinion from a half-way credible source was likely to be determinative.

In late October 1987, Congressman Udall, the chairman of the House Committee on Interior and Insular Affairs, requested that the General Accounting Office "undertake a thorough investigation of (1) matters which would bear upon the approval of legislation to implement the Compact of Free Association with the Republic of Palau; and (2) whether the U.S. is fulfilling its responsibilities under the Trusteeship Agreement with the United Nations Security Council." I wasn't sure what all of that was supposed to mean, but it certainly would keep the GAO busy for the better part of a year. Farrow would argue, I was sure, that the subcommittee and committee could not proceed until they got the GAO report.

The Territories Subcommittee then hired Tom Dunmire as a special consultant to investigate matters in person. Dunmire, extremely conservative, had been a Republican staffer on the Territories Subcommittee who had strongly opposed the Compacts with the FSM and the Marshall Islands. It was rumored that he was forced to resign when the administration learned their own Republican staffer was arguing against their position. Not unexpectedly, de Lugo and Farrow had sought an observer who was likely to be unsympathetic to the Compact. Dunmire's other function was not publicized. He was to accompany the GAO to Palau. The GAO at first had resisted this suggestion of the subcommittee—in effect the subcommittee was sending Dunmire along as a spy—but de Lugo and Farrow were adamant.

With the tide still running strongly against us, another agency was heard from. Responding to an inquiry of the House Interior and Insular Affairs Committee, the Drug Enforcement Administration estimated a massive amount of drug use in Palau—an estimate that proved to be about ten times too large—and raised additional questions concerning counterfeiting in Palau. Palau had long been used as a point of entry into the United States for counterfeited money from the Philippines.

This was a calculated attempt to suggest that the Palau government was incapable of managing its affairs and to implicate it, albeit indirectly, in the shooting. It was also part of the larger bureaucratic fight between the House Territories Subcommittee and the Department of the Interior. Interior had supervision over Palau as long as it was a trust territory, that is, until the Compact went into effect. Under the State Department's strong policy guidance, Interior treated Palau like the Marshalls and FSM, in short, as if Palau's Compact were already ratified. Farrow and de Lugo were particularly angry at Interior for not taking a stronger monitoring and supervisory role in Palau during the trusteeship period. But Interior had remained firm.

In late October, Palau sent to Washington a five-man delegation headed by Ngiraked. Their job was to negotiate the three agreements called for under federal law before the Compact could be put into effect; the agreements on law enforcement, fiscal management, and the Civil Action Team (CAT). They were relatively standard agreements, having been used in the FSM and the Marshalls Compacts, and, therefore, they were all rapidly negotiated.

The Palau delegation did a good job. They were earnest, direct, careful in presence and style. Before returning home, Ngiraked hosted a small, modest luncheon for friends of Palau. Very few people attended—the five members of the Palau delegation, Berg and Hills from the State Department, myself, and a couple of former Interior officials who were friends of Palau and the Compact. It was a nice gesture, but it emphasized how limited Palau was both in funds and style, and how isolated and friendless in

Washington. In comparable circumstances, for any other community in the States, some congressman would have hosted an elaborate affair in the Capitol with photo opportunities and friendly news stories from local journalists.

William Butler and the International Commission of Jurists (ICJ), a relatively moribund organization, then announced a mission to Palau. Technically, the ICJ mission was private, but Farrow had called Butler and arranged for the ICJ to receive a long letter from the chairman of the Committee on Interior and Insular Affairs asking for copies of their report and asking them to look into certain areas. In sum, the committee was providing the mission's agenda.

Butler had testified in 1983 before the Trusteeship Council against the Palau Compact and at that time had charged excessive U.S. pressure. Farrow could be sure of the outcome of the ICJ mission. The House Interior Committee issued a long press release, highly laudatory of the ICJ as an objective group looking into the matter. Butler's previous testimony was not noted. No one in Palau knew about it at that time, and Butler was careful not to mention it.

The first bit of good news from our point of view occurred when the Palau government announced the arrest of three defendants in connection with the drive-by shooting at Santos Olikong's house: Joel Toribiong, a special assistant to President Salii; Paul Ueki; and Tadashi Sakuma. Ueki and Sakuma were furloughed government employees. Their trial was scheduled to start on January 26. (All three were subsequently found guilty of unlawful use and possession of a firearm and rioting.)

Hazard called me with his tentative opinion that the Ibedul-Salii agreement approved by the Court ended all legal claims challenging the Compact. Another lawsuit could not be brought. Since Hazard's opinion rested on the Ibedul's leadership role in Palau, before issuing his formal, written opinion he wanted additional information on the authority of the Ibedul. Although casual opinions on the power of the Ibedul abounded, I needed an authoritative, current view. Were there anthropologists who could provide it?

Unfortunately, Micronesia is not like Polynesia. Polynesia is a very open society, warm and friendly, quite ready to permit outsiders into their homes and allow them to become familiar with their customs. It is one reason why the anthropological literature on Polynesia is so great. Micronesia is quite different. It is a very closed society that does not readily welcome outsiders. The anthropological literature, therefore, is relatively small.

Two women, Karen Nero and Mary McCutcheon, had current information. Nero taught at the University of California at Berkeley and was completing her doctorate on the Ibedul. She had lived in Palau five years earlier and had visited the island occasionally since then. McCutcheon was at the Smithsonian Institution. She had not lived in Palau for almost a decade, but her work required her to keep up on Palau. Her academic study had been on the Reklai and on land use patterns in Palau. She was extremely knowledgeable, very pleasant, and in Washington, D.C., so communication was very easy. But the topic and the currency of the information dictated reaching Nero.

I called Nero and basically asked her to submit to me a summary of her doctorate, for which we would pay. She asked how she was to slant it. I told her I did not want her to slant it at all. I wanted the quality of the paper to be such that she could publish it in any scholarly journal. Further, there were no restrictions on her if she wanted to make available the same information to anybody else who asked for it.

Nero asked to what use the information would be put. Obviously it related to the settlement of the Compact case, I responded. If she wanted to know more than that, I would tell her, but then her freedom to talk to others would have to be restricted. It was up to her. She chose not to know.

Ms. Nero provided the information in about two weeks. I summarized it and sent it on to Hazard. Subsequently, when he rendered his final opinion, he excerpted this material. He sent me this portion in draft. I basically cleared it word for word, reading it to Nero and McCutcheon in turn. Nero viewed the Ibedul as representative of not only Koror and the Southeast Federation but of Palau as a whole, both because of his personal dominance and because of the dominance of Koror in recent times. McCutcheon gave more weight to the Reklai. The result, it seemed to me, represented a very good balance should anyone ever challenge our perception of the situation. (John Ngiraked, the minister of state, later told me he thought the discussion of the Ibedul's role in Palau was excellent and wondered how I came up with it. I confessed it was not due to any particular insights of my own into Palauan society.)

Farrow was still telling everyone that the Compact would not move at all. No hearings would be held until the problems before the committee were cleared up. These problems had expanded from the two listed in the committee's September 27, 1987, letter to a large number of others, ranging from drug traffic and fiscal mismanagement to constitutional excess.

Two different themes were involved in all of the Washington activity: Compact ratification and Palau government, or, more precisely, the Salii government mismanagement.

Farrow's publicly unyielding position brought about some countervailing pressure on him from other congressional committees. The obvious point, clearly understood by him, the Territories Subcommittee, and the larger Committee on Interior and Insular Affairs, was that the Palauan women had no incentive to file a lawsuit as long as the Territories Subcommittee would not move the Compact anyway. As the Compact moved from the Executive Branch to the Congress, the subcommittee was treated both by the administration and by the Salii government as if it were in league with the opponents of the Compact.

On November 29, 1987, the *San Jose Mercury News* reported that Lazarus Salii and the Ibedul, among others, had received payments from IPSECO totalling $450,000. Lazarus Salii had been paid $100,000. (The GAO was to show subsequently that the total amount of the IPSECO payments was $775,000 and that Lazarus Salii had received $200,000.) Mirando, speaking for President Salii, said Salii was paid for "gathering data for an airline" to be owned by British Aerospace Co. and represented by IPSECO President Mochrie. Mirando said the payment "had nothing to do with IPSECO or the IPSECO power project. . . . We sit here very confused as to why payment would come through IPSECO." The airline was never started.

The next day, November 30, 1987, President Reagan transmitted the Compact to the Congress certifying that it had been approved by Palau and that there existed no legal impediment to the ability of the United States to carry out fully its responsibilities and exercise its national defense rights under the Compact.

Suddenly, Solarz announced that his subcommittee would hold hearings on December 17. The increasingly negative publicity about Salii and the Salii administration, ironically, had helped. Solarz wanted to see for himself what was going on. It was a major breakthrough. Solarz was a giant, and the giant had decided to take the first step.

Notes

1. Page 117. *The judge's suggestion.* In addition, Judge Hefner spoke with Jeff Farrow and with the Department of the Interior. See Memorandum from Chuck Jordan, Office of the High Commissioner, to Mark Hayward, Deputy Assistant Secretary, Dept. of the Interior, Subject: Meeting with Judge Hefner (Sept. 10, 1987).

First of all, Judge Hefner stated that he believed that the only reason the plaintiffs had withdrawn their case was of intimidation through the use and threat of violence. . . . He recommends . . . some sort of independent third party review all of which has transpired with regard to the certification process so that the U.S. can, without the slightest doubt, support the process which Palau has just gone through.

2. Pages 118-119. The text reproduces the selections of the affidavits and statements sent by Farrow to the Senate staff.

3. Page 119. For a long profile on Solarz, see "The Past and Paradox of Steve Solarz," *Washington Post*, May 29, 1991.

4. Page 120. The Ibedul's speech quoted in the text and Senator Koshiba's speech supporting the Compact are found in *The Palau Gazette*, Oct. 1, 1987, pp. 2-7. They were transmitted to the U.N. Security Council by Ambassador Vernon Walters, the U.S. ambassador. Letter Dated Oct. 8, 1987 from the Permanent Representative of

the United States of America to the U.N. Addressed to the Secretary-General, U.N. Security Council, S.19200 (Oct. 13, 1987).

5. Page 121. *The furloughed employees established*. *The Palau Gazette*, Oct. 1, 1987, p. 4.

6. Page 122. *Many at the Office of Territories and International Affairs*. The OEK, four years later, investigated the government investigation at the time and charged there had been a purposeful delay. OEK, Joint Investigative Committee on Police Practices, *Report* (February 1991), p. 5. See Chapter 22.

7. Page 123. *Salii's next letter*. Letter of Lazarus Salii to Kittie Baier, Principal Deputy Assistant Secretary, OTIA, Department of the Interior, Oct. 22, 1987. Copies of the letter were sent to all of the key senators and congressmen from the committees having jurisdiction over Palau.

8. Page 126. *Butler was careful*. When, in the course of working on this book, I asked Butler about his testimony, he said he didn't remember it, but in any event, he was sure it dealt with the Compact in a general way, not with the Palau Compact specifically.

9. Page 126. *Hazard called me*. The Hazard opinion treated the *Merep v. Salii* case as a non-class representative lawsuit challenging the government. He rested his argument on the participation and involvement of the Ibedul in the settlement agreement and the Ibedul's leadership authority.

10. Page 128. *On November 29, 1987*. *San Jose Mercury News*, Nov. 29, 1987, p. 1.

14

Salii Stars at the Solarz Hearings;
The Women Testify Before the Senate

The House Foreign Affairs Committee room was enormous. It was not very deep—although deeper than the Territories Subcommittee room—but the semi-circled rows of seats seemed to stretch on endlessly to either side. The physical effect itself was suggestive of a broad inquiry. If so, the inquiry attracted few inquirers. Only Congressmen Solarz and Leach were present when the hearing opened.

Solarz set out the issues in his opening statement: Had there been intimidation? Had the intimidation prevented the judicial process from operating? These questions were never really answered. Hefner's failure to examine the issue at the time could not be overcome. What the Solarz hearings were to make clear was that the judicial process could work *now*.

The Solarz hearings were highly focused; virtually all of the oral testimony came from only three witnesses: the administration (Berg, head of the State Department's Office of Freely Associated State Affairs), Salii, and Santos Olikong (the Speaker of the House in the OEK). The Palau women who brought the lawsuit were asked to testify but none would. Gabriela Ngirmang attended the hearings, sitting beside Sebia Hawkins. Ms. Hawkins sat in her usual seat in the center of the hearing room, in the back row, observing, listening, and taking extensive notes. During a break in hearings, Stanley Roth, Solarz's aide, personally approached Ms. Ngirmang and asked her to testify, but she refused.

Salii was the key witness and, as usual, he was stunning. Salii's fluency in English, his directness, his strength and vigor always made him a good witness. Salii began by noting the almost unanimous support for the Compact in Palau. Both houses of the OEK in early September had passed unanimously a resolution supporting the constitutional amendment and the Compact vote. The Ibedul and Reklai now both supported the Compact as well. Salii linked his vision of Palau's future to the Compact.

It is still our belief that within Palau our people can together build a place where we can work, where our people can develop to the fullest their potential, where we can show we care for one another, and where we can take advantage of the natural beauty of our islands.

To begin to accomplish this vision, we need our freedom and our sovereignty. We need control over our land which we believe is very beautiful and fortunately is blessed with considerable mineral resources. We need control over our governmental institutions.

We believe this Compact of Free Association gives us that control. It permits us to carry out that vision.

There was a good deal of poetry in this, but in essence this was his belief. The Compact alone brought autonomy and sufficient funding for the people of Palau. In this, Salii was right. The opposition had not produced— indeed, would never produce—another approach combining local self-government and funding equal to the Compact.

Finally, Salii spoke to the key issue—the ability of the courts to decide fairly, and independently, constitutional questions. First, he recounted the early Compact votes and the cases challenging them. Most of these cases had been decided against the government and there had never been charges of impropriety: "There has been considerable litigation over the ballot wording and the ratification procedure. In none of these cases, most of which the courts decided against the proponents of the Compact and therefore against the Government of Palau, was there any suggestion of impropriety or of intimidation." Then, Salii addressed the women's legal challenge and their decision to withdraw: "The lawsuit was dismissed not through intimidation, but through a settlement reached between High Chief Ibedul and myself, and out of respect for the document which was signed by Ibedul, the plaintiffs in the case withdrew the . . . lawsuits."

This glossed over too much too quickly. Solarz immediately sought greater details from Salii about the withdrawal of the lawsuit by the women.

Mr. Solarz. You indicated that the litigation commenced with the support of the Ibedul and was withdrawn after an agreement was reached between yourself and the Ibedul. I gather that does appear to have been done in a completely voluntary fashion.

But serious questions have been raised about the suit involving the 29 women which was dropped. . . .

Is it your testimony today, sir, that each of the 29 women who were the original plaintiffs in this proceeding voluntarily decided to withdraw their complaint?

President Salii. Yes, sir.

Mr. Solarz. Why did they do so? What was the basis on which these 29 women were persuaded to voluntarily, without intimidation, drop their constitutional challenge?

President Salii. I believe out of respect for Ibedul and out of the accord, the agreement reached between him and myself, which was announced over the radio and television.

The doubtful likelihood of all twenty-nine simply changing their minds troubled Solarz. Solarz persisted. How did that occur?

Mr. Solarz. Did you conduct any discussions with these women or did the Ibedul? In other words, how did the process of persuasion take place? . . . . Is it your position that each of the 29 women withdrew and that this was completely voluntary?
President Salii. Yes, sir.
Mr. Solarz. Who was it who persuaded them? Was it the Ibedul, himself, or his emissary or one of his representatives?
President Salii. I know for a fact that the Ibedul in the days before was talking to the ladies, and there may be others.

Salii's answer focused on the Ibedul and his role. He and the Ibedul had made an agreement, and the Ibedul had pressured his women to agree to it. The GAO in its report was subsequently to reaffirm the Ibedul's role. The point was an important one. If the women had been intimidated to drop the case, Salii was saying he was not responsible. Compact opponents refused then or later to make the distinction between pressure from the Salii government and pressure from others such as the Ibedul. Their assumption was that all pressure and all intimidation was the responsibility of Salii and the Salii government. On the other hand, it did not seem likely that the Palau government had not been involved at all. The women were the only ones who knew and, with precision, could identify the malefactors, and they were not telling. The absence of a specific charge against Salii remained as the glaring weakness of the anti-Salii case.

Obviously the Ibedul had failed in his quest. The women had withdrawn their lawsuit, but here they were in some number stating their opposition. Had they been pressured? Of course. Physically threatened? Apparently not. They were managing to maintain their minority position in a man's world and in Palau. Intimidated? So everyone said, and so did the women. Until now. Now, the women themselves chose not to testify.

Solarz came at the issue from a different direction. Why hadn't the opposition—which was formidable—started a lawsuit once more? Were they afraid?

Mr. Solarz. . . . How do you account for he fact that there hasn't been a single Palauan citizen among the 25 to 30 percent opposed to the Compact who has been willing to lend their names to a lawsuit challenging the Constitutionality of the adoption of the Amendment?
President Salii. . . . I think that there is a deep recognition that to continue the opposition is futile and that it's been a divisive issue in Palau. The people are tired of it. We need to put it to rest and get about our livelihood on a more normal basis.

Then Solarz got to the present (December 1987).

Mr. Solarz. . . . I gather your view is that there is not a climate of fear and intimidation on Palau?

President Salii. No, sir.

Mr. Solarz. Anybody who wants to challenge this in the courts is not only free to do so, but they don't have anything to fear, and in any case, you're prepared to provide protection to them?

President Salii. Yes, sir.

I don't know if at this point Salii still felt he could stave off another lawsuit because of his agreement with the Ibedul. Certainly I did not. I thought these hearings, at best, would result in Congress finally passing the Compact legislation and getting us back in court.

Solarz examined Salii with respect to the shooting of Bedor Bins, particularly about Joel Toribiong, on Salii's personal staff, one of the three men arrested for shooting at Olikong's house.

Mr. Solarz. Did you know anything about his [Joel Toribiong's] alleged involvement in this affair prior to the time that he was arrested?

President Salii. No.

Mr. Solarz. So this was not done with your approval, or at your direction, or with your permission in any way?

President Salii. Absolutely not.

Mr. Solarz. How many others were arrested besides this fellow?

President Salii. Two others.

Mr. Solarz. And did they work for the government also?

President Salii. Yes. . . .

Mr. Solarz. . . . It is your testimony that . . . they did this . . . on their own initiative rather than as the result of any instructions directly or indirectly from you . . . ?

President Salii. There was absolutely no direction from me, no knowledge, no involvement whatsoever.

Mr. Solarz. Were they arrested by your police?

President Salii. Yes.

Mr. Solarz. Are they being tried by your prosecutors?

President Salii. I was away when the arrest was made and when I came back I ordered the police to prosecute.

No evidence has ever been produced challenging Salii's denial of involvement in the shooting.

Olikong's testimony was critical. He was the first and only anti-Compact witness to appear publicly since the Bedor Bins killing and Judge Hefner's comments. He could move the debate from rumor and public relations to firm statement. Olikong had testified before de Lugo six months previously and had not been convincing. Would he do better now? He began in what had become the traditional way for the opposition in Palau: expressing support for the Compact while, in fact, opposing it.

Mr. Olikong. . . . I urge this committee and this Congress to consider an early Congressional approval of the Compact of Free Association.

There was, of course, a condition:

Mr. Olikong. . . . The early approval of the Compact, however, by your Congress must rest upon the conclusion that the Compact was duly approved by the people of Palau in strict compliance with their constitutional processes and that the choice was freely made and given.

. . . If good reasons do exist to delay the approval of the Compact, then this committee should not hesitate to recommend to the U.S. Congress to delay and hold in abeyance the implementation of the Compact until a later date.

Then Olikong got to what the Committee was waiting for: the intimidation. What had happened?

Evidence of intimidation directed at me as a person took their form in posters all over Koror, in private telephone threats to me and my family, in personal encounters at various places and different times, and in the actual shooting at my residential house while my family and I were at home. . . .

At the outset, it appeared strange that after President Salii announced the planned layoffs of government employees that a certain element of the government work force decided to pitch tents in front of the House of Delegates of the Palau National Congress. . . .

From then on, the members of the House of Delegates *were literally held hostage to the striking government employees.* The tents in front of the Palau National Congress were manned 24 hours with financial support and contributions of food and drinks being exacted from various organizations and state governments. (Emphasis supplied)

Olikong seemed to impute to Salii the actions of the furlough committee against the OEK and the attacks upon him. No one doubted that Salii had the support of the furloughed government employees and that he supported the furlough committee as much as he could in order to keep their loyalty. Obviously Salii would show his support for their cause and, equally clearly, the furloughed employees would pressure the OEK to amend the Constitution to pass the Compact. How far had Salii gone in his support of the furlough committee? How strong was the furlough committee pressure? Were OEK members "literally held hostage" as Olikong testified? OEK members came and went freely. Had the OEK members been intimidated? That was a harder issue for me to judge. OEK members voted against the constitutional amendments pretty much in proportion to the popular support for the Compact in Palau.

On the other hand, the threats and shooting at Olikong were another matter. Whether the shooting was meant to kill or simply to send a message, that was serious business. On that point, Olikong had my attention and, I thought, the committee's as well. But Olikong let the issue slide and said no more about it. Olikong's interest was the political machinations of the island; Solarz, I thought, was interested in the personal safety of Olikong.

The issue, Olikong went on, now was not one of intimidation but rather the independence of the judicial branch and the integrity of the government. The guilty parties should be arrested and convicted. Only after that could a constitutional amendment be considered by the OEK. Olikong was wrong there. The issue was one of intimidation. Had it happened? Who had done it?

Solarz asked Olikong whether the vote on the constitutional amendment was fair: "Do you believe the general elections and the votes on the amendment to the constitution and the Compact—both of which received 73 percent—were themselves free from intimidation, chicanery, and fraud?" Olikong responded that there were threats. How widespread were they? Solarz asked. The charge seemed to break down. Olikong had only *heard* of these threats.

Mr. Olikong. There were a bus full of strikers who went around visiting people who they knew—I did not see them. But members of the House of Delegates who are majority members have told me of threats in their areas.

Mr. Solarz. We had some testimony a little bit earlier today that there was a U.N. mission in Palau that observed the August 21st vote approving the Compact and that they apparently concluded that the election was a fair one and a free one, conducted in an atmosphere conducive to an act of self-determination.

If in fact there was widespread intimidation, how do you account for this U.N. report?

Mr. Olikong. I was not in Palau, sir, at the time of the August referendum. But my sister reported to me of the violence in the neighborhoods. The United Nations people observed the polling places. They did not go to people's houses.

If there had been no intimidation, what would the result have been? About the same as the actual result on June 30: 67 percent, Olikong responded. In sum, the referendum with intimidation reflected public opinion.

Well, if that was the case—the constitutional amendment would be approved anyway—what was all the fuss about? Why should Congress wait to approve the Compact? The answer, as Solarz knew, was political. The opponents didn't want the Compact approved before the Palau election in November 1988. Solarz asked anyway.

Mr. Solarz. In your view, what would be gained by having Congress take the position that we are not going to approve the Compact unless and until there was a legal test of the constitutionality of the adoption of the amendment when . . . a new referendum would result in the same vote and the approval of the amendment in a constitutional fashion?

Mr. Olikong. . . . What would be gained is that Palau will have a constitution that is not marred by a violation.

Mr. Solarz. Why have you decided so far not to become a plaintiff?

Mr. Olikong. Because I have to think about my family, my relatives, and my responsibilities to my people. . . .

Mr. Solarz. Do you think that if, in fact, the government is prepared to provide protection to someone who initiates a suit, will someone do so?

Mr. Olikong. Yes, sir.

Olikong had not been a good witness. His style worked against him, making him appear less than candid in telling of the threats to him. He was a very heavy man, with a propensity to sweat under the lights and heat of the committee room. He patted his forehead continually with his handkerchief, contributing to an overall impression of defensiveness. Two years later I was retained by the Association of Pacific Island Legislatures (APIL), and I was to get to know Olikong much better. I was struck then by his wonderful sense of humor. The strain in 1987-88 had suppressed this wit and made him appear furtive and unforthcoming in his public appearances. But in the final analysis, what was missing from the opposition case was the testimony of the women. The intimidation charge simply had no credibility if the women sat in the committee room and refused to testify.

Solarz and Leach summarized their conclusions: police protection for Olikong and any new plaintiffs. As for the past events: a Scotch verdict, not proven.

Mr. Solarz. . . . I am personally going to take up with President Salii this question of you receiving police protection. . . . I was very pleased to hear President Salii make this offer. . . .

Mr. Leach. . . .Personal safety is something that should be guaranteed and assured and that all of us in Congress will be watching what happens in Palau with regard to yourself and others who differ with this treaty.

The report of Tom Dunmire, the consultant hired by de Lugo and Farrow, was delivered on January 9, 1988. Its primary recommendation was startling, not at all what de Lugo and Farrow had expected. "Without delay, report out favorably implementing legislation on the [C]ompact." The recommendation was not that of a starry-eyed innocent. Rather, it was the product of a man with a very jaundiced view of Palau: "Although the future of Palau is bleak and the U.S. investment is large both in dollars and good intentions, America should realize its limitations in Palau as it did in Vietnam."

On the key point, criminal violence and the role of the government, Dunmire reported, probably with considerable accuracy:

There is no doubt—even by Palauan traditional standards—that excessive intimidation, coupled with violent acts, were imposed upon some Palauans in order to obtain their approval of the compact. *Some of the intimidation was sponsored by the government; it is uncertain, however, whether officials supported the employment of violence. On the other hand, the vast majority of Palauans favor immediate approval of the compact.* (Emphasis supplied)

De Lugo and Farrow immediately suppressed the Dunmire report. The draft was restricted and not even distributed to members of the subcommittee or their staffs. Although not classified, even today the Dunmire report is not obtainable from the subcommittee.

The opposition at the Solarz hearing and internal reports of a return to normalcy in Palau affected the Senate as well. Senator Johnston announced that later that month, on January 28, 1988, the Senate Energy Committee would proceed with its hearings. This time the women agreed to testify. Perhaps Greenpeace read it the way I did. To be credible, the women had to do more than listen. Some skeptics among Palau government officials predicted the women never would testify publicly where their accusations could be challenged or answered. They proved to be accurate prophets.

Whether by fortune or shrewd maneuvering, not one of the women plaintiffs was ever to testify publicly and openly. The Congress and, indeed, the judiciary were to accept accusations from undisclosed informants in all cases. Gabriela Ngirmang agreed to testify but, unfortunately, she suffered a mild stroke and was being treated in a local hospital when the hearing began. Although the press reported that Rafaela Sumang was in Washington, Ms. Ngirmang's testimony was presented by Isabella Sumang, the daughter of Rafaela Sumang. The other witnesses were the same as before Solarz: Olikong, Salii, and Berg.

Ms. Ngirmang's statement read:

We persisted in the lawsuit until a series of violent acts, culminating in the murder of Mr. Bedor Bins on the evening before a public hearing in which our arguments were to be heard, led us to drop the lawsuit.

We feared that we, like Bedor, would be killed and that our families would be hurt. I have been insulted by a variety of recent questions about whether the intimidation was real. . . .

The same night that Bedor was murdered, a firebomb was ignited on my land, blowing up in the rear of my house sometime between 10:30 and 11:00, after the government turned the power off in all of Palau.

This was all well known. Then she added an important detail that was new and chilling: "My family and young children were sleeping in the house at the time, and one of my daughters, Ida, suffered injury to her eyes."

This written testimony concerning Ngirmang's daughter particularly upset me. I had not heard that. Had a child been hurt? Blinded? Palau government officials privately dismissed the charge as false. Who was telling the truth? Subsequently, the GAO investigators pursued the issue in their investigation, asking Ms. Ngirmang if they could see her daughter, the doctor, or the doctor's bills. All requests were denied. No oral testimony supporting it was given to the GAO. The GAO investigators subsequently never mentioned it in their report. Senator Johnston did not pursue it.

In Palau, exaggeration and fabrication are accepted as part of the normal political discourse. Support for any preconceived position was easy to obtain. Sorting out afterward what really happened in such an environment was an extremely difficult task. Senator Johnston, a former district attorney, nevertheless gave it a good try, questioning each witness very closely: "Do you know or do you not know of any threats or intimidations?"

I expected to hear specific examples of the furlough committee threatening people. However, now that the testimony was extemporaneous, not part of a prepared statement, there was nothing, even by the strictest stateside standards, that could be considered untoward.

Ms. Isabella Sumang. There was no direct intimidation at the polling places. But there was pressure on the people that was started way before the case.

And, you know, this is the whole series of things, pressuring the people, like saying, if you do not take the Compact, you will not have the money. And the Compact is money on the table and you women who are suing are keeping it from becoming a reality. . . . .

The Chairman. All right, let me see if I understand. Your position is that the election itself, the votes, there were no threats of violence or personal intimidation.

Ms. Isabella Sumang. At the polls, yes. . . .

The Chairman. Except that their campaign was based upon the fact—

Ms. Isabella Sumang. Yes . . . the campaign was . . . biased, and was not fairly given to the people to rightly have the correct information.

However this might play in Greenpeace press releases, in Washington it was not sufficient. Every presidential election in the States since George Washington has promised some group monetary benefits. Were they all to be called into question? In the States, especially in Louisiana, Johnston's home state, election campaigns were a lot rougher than that. I couldn't believe Johnston would regard such an election as unfair. Johnston pressed her.

Sen. Johnston. What was the nature of the bias?

Ms. Isabella Sumang. . . . The information that was given on the Compact lean to one side. . . .

The Chairman. . . . Was the information incorrect?

Ms. Isabella Sumang. It was in favor of the Compact. . . .

The Chairman. *Do the people of Palau, in your view, oppose this Compact?*

Ms. Isabella Sumang. *If they understood well what is in the Compact, then they would do so.*

The Chairman. What do they not understand?

Ms. Isabella Sumang. They do not understand that a third of their land will be used by the military, may be used by the United States military for 50 years or more. They do not understand that. . . . (Emphasis supplied)

What did the women want from the Committee? The answer was clear: delay.

Ms. Isabella Sumang. What our group wants is that this Committee might have an influence on keeping the Compact from being ratified by the United States Congress until we resolve our internal problems. . . .

Senator Johnston got to the lawsuit.

The Chairman. . . . When are you going to refile your case?
Ms. Isabella Sumang. As soon as the women feel safe and well-protected to go to the courts of Palau. . . .
The Chairman. Have you decided that you are going to file the case?
Ms. Isabella Sumang. Definitely, yes.
The Chairman. Well, now, if you are going to file the case, is the case ready to file now? I mean, if you have declared you are going to do something, it seems that that would be. . .
Ms. Isabella Sumang. Yes. We will do it when we are ready to do it, and let you know of it.

Then the women made a mistake. They began to jest with the Senate. The tactic backfired. To Senator Johnston this was not a laughing matter. The transcript suggests a serious interchange but, in fact, Ms. Sumang, in this interchange, treated the delay as a joke and was laughing while responding.

The Chairman. When will [the lawsuit be filed]?
Ms. Isabella Sumang. As soon as we get ourselves together and have all the security and the proper, you know, things together. What is the hurry? It is our future.
The Chairman. What is the delay?
Ms. Isabella Sumang. We have to think about that. It is our future. . . .

Olikong testified to the intimidation during the voting on the Compact. His testimony was basically the same as that given before Solarz except that Johnston pursued the intimidation charge in greater detail.

The Chairman. Now, do you concur that there was no violence or intimidation with respect to the election itself?
Mr. Olikong. In the highways and the areas adjacent to the polling places, no intimidation and violence. But in the neighborhoods, people were visited in their homes and were told that if your wife or children either campaign against or vote for the Compact, you will get it. . . .
The Chairman. What does that mean?
Mr. Olikong. Get beaten or get shot, get your house burned down, or anything

that they would like to do to you.

Olikong first talked of twelve instances of intimidation, but under pressure by the chairman, he could not identify any specific instance. He urged Johnston to charge the Salii administration with the misdeeds of the Furlough Committee.

Mr. Olikong. . . . I did not witness any violence from the police. But these furloughed people were sponsored by the administration, the executive branch.
. . . And if they do commit any act of violence, the question is who do we blame? The sponsors or only the people who committed the violent act against the citizens?
The Chairman. What would you have this Committee do? What do you think we should do?
Mr. Olikong. I would ask this Committee to investigate, and maybe the Committee has a very good knowledge of what happens.

Salii in his testimony again pledged around-the-clock police protection should anyone want to go to court. Then he focused on the requested delay and vented his frustration.

It has been five months since the election and they have not filed any lawsuit. I have written to Mrs. Ngirmang assuring her of all the reasonable protection that we can give to her. Not only before but during the trial and after.
It is very easy for opponents to claim that no matter how much assurance President Salii gives us for protection that we do not feel comfortable. I would not give very serious consideration to that claim....

Johnston summed up where he thought matters stood and seemed to agree with Solarz. He would assure security for a lawsuit, but he would not delay the Compact. Forced to testify publicly, the women had failed to persuade.

The Chairman. Well, you see, we want to allow for a legal and fair and proper administration of your government and its elections. And we certainly want the courts to be able to function.
But we cannot just say, well, we will hold it up until and if you ever decide to get around to filing the suit.
Ms. Isabella Sumang. Yes, we understand that. But, as you can see . . . the internal problems are there, whether you feel it or not. . . .
The Chairman. . . . We will follow up and try to ensure that you feel safe in exercising your legal rights. Because we would like to get this matter into court and decided there in court.

Within an hour of the Senate hearings, Farrow called Al Stayman, Senator Johnston's aide. Farrow had attended the hearings. He knew the women had failed. He explained to Stayman there was really much more. The women were frightened—frightened of Johnston, frightened of Washington, and frightened of retribution in Palau. They had not told everything they knew.

The Senate wasn't persuaded. The women didn't seem frightened at all. Given their chance, Olikong and the women simply had not produced evidence, and their testimony lacked credibility. Johnston, like Solarz, concluded that Hefner did not have the evidence.

After the House Foreign Affairs Committee and Senate Energy Committee hearings, Farrow weakened. He publicly stated to a number of people, representatives of the administration and to me, among others, that his concern now was that the litigants be free to file a lawsuit. The House Foreign Affairs Committee felt that question had been answered when Salii had offered protection to Olikong and protection had been provided him.

Both the House Foreign Affairs Committee and the Senate Energy Committee pressed ahead to pass the Compact. The Territories Subcommittee kept the public attention on the GAO report and scandals in the Salii Administration. The Salii administration seemed to be playing into the subcommittee's hands. Mirando, Salii's special assistant, was found traveling from Japan to Guam carrying with him signed Palau passport documents. The authorities seized the documents but subsequently returned them, and they were destroyed. No good explanation was given for these events.

On March 2, 1988, Udall and de Lugo sent a letter to Chairman Dante Fascell of the House Foreign Affairs Committee—really a press release—alleging the IPSECO payments, use of counterfeit currency, illegal use of counterfeit passports, and bribes in connection with a construction project. In sum, as Udall and de Lugo saw it, the issue was not limited to intimidation. From their perspective, the Salii administration was engaged in a series of questionable acts, criminal behavior that required review before the Congress approved the Compact. These questions had not been pressed by the Solarz and Johnston subcommittees because of their essential irrelevancy to the ratification of the Compact, as they saw it. Further, some of the actions charged were very recent and probably unknown to them. De Lugo and Udall could not have been certain of the truth of the anti-Salii reports constantly streaming in to the subcommittee, but they were inclined to believe them since they were consistent with their anti-Compact and anti-Salii views. Udall and de Lugo concluded their letter with an unusual phrase: "We would hope that procedures can be worked out with the Department of the Interior and other appropriate federal and insular agencies to ensure that any investigation and prosecutions which are initiated regarding this or any other matter *can continue beyond the trusteeship period*" (Emphasis supplied).

Senators Johnston and McClure read the underlined phrase "can continue beyond the trusteeship period" as suggesting partial termination, a concept inconsistent with the Compact. It confirmed their suspicion that de Lugo wanted to stall Compact approval until after the November 1988 election.

The Senate committee decided to play hardball. Its budget report recommended that if implementation of the Compact was delayed into FY 1989, then the additional $15 million needed for operation of Palau would be taken from other territories, including "construction grants from the Virgin Islands" that could be postponed. Senator Johnston, at the March 1988 appropriations hearings, rhetorically asked of de Lugo, the Virgin Islands' representative: "What Virgin Islands improvement project do you want to forego to fund Palau?"

Farrow announced a trip by Udall and de Lugo to mainland China. On the way there, or on the way back, they would be stopping in Palau. The litigation would be started, *he was certain*, between March 15 and April 2 during a visit to Palau, by either congressional staff, de Lugo, or Udall. Berg, who had brought de Lugo and Farrow watching to a high art, found out that the Air Force plane that was to fly them to China had not been reserved for them but in fact had been reserved for another committee during the recess. He questioned publicly whether any congressional trip was in the offing. He was right. The trip never took place. Even if the China trip did not occur, that did not mean the case would not be filed on the announced dates. If Farrow had made a public commitment to a case filing between March 15 and April 2, then I had no doubt that the case would be started then. I left for Tokyo on other business in mid-March, but before doing so I packed two cartons of materials to be shipped to me when the case was filed.

Farrow and the plaintiffs continued to seek some kind of media event to accompany the refiling of the lawsuit. Placing a congressman on the courthouse steps as the complaint was being filed seemed the favored approach. But getting a congressman to go along with such an obvious ploy proved too much. Other congressional staff, even those somewhat sympathetic to Farrow's point of view, questioned congressional involvement on one side of a lawsuit. Farrow himself, so it was rumored, wanted to go to Palau, but his wife feared for his safety. The best the Territories Subcommittee could come up with was Dunmire, who was already on Palau. The committee, resignedly, announced that in addition to his other responsibilities Dunmire would protect the litigants. The lawsuit was about to be refiled, with a whimper, not a bang.

Despite the Udall and de Lugo letter, the House Foreign Affairs Committee was proceeding with the Palau Compact legislation. Solarz's Foreign Affairs Committee prepared to report out the approval of the Compact after the Easter recess. Udall and de Lugo became particularly active in order to counteract the actions of the House Foreign Affairs Committee. On March 17, Udall and de Lugo wrote a letter to Salii that was almost becoming standard for them. It opened with a self-serving statement stressing their concern for the "needs and aspirations of the people of Palau" and pledging "to do everything that we can to provide the government of Palau with enough financial assistance to pay its employees, operate its power and water system, and meet its other essential obligations until the trusteeship is terminated."

Following this came the obligatory expression of support for the Compact: "This effort on our part should not be misunderstood as indicating that we do not want the Compact to be implemented as soon as possible. We do want it implemented, and we will support implementation just as soon as the problems outlined below are satisfactorily addressed." Then the litany of problems: (1) the need for a final ruling by the Palau Supreme Court in light of the Congressional Research Service legal opinion against an Article XV amendment, (2) the assurance of the prosecution of wrongdoing, and (3) the need for fiscal accounting. The committee explained the off-again, on-again trip to Palau by saying the Defense Department had failed to provide the promised plane. A visit by the committee was still planned for mid-April.

The March 2 Udall and de Lugo letter quoted John Lawn, head of the Drug Enforcement Administration, who said that more than 400 of Palau's 15,000 people may be heroin addicts, or twelve times the U.S. national average. Hills pointed out, in a rebuttal, that at a House committee hearing the previous week another DEA official testified that perhaps only 30 Palauans were addicts. Lost in the riposte and counter-riposte were the merits. De Lugo and Farrow were on to something important: not just drugs but also alcohol. Ninety-five percent of all crime in Palau was either drug or alcohol related. From 71 percent to 92 percent of all emergency hospital admissions for men over the past three years had been alcohol related. Palau officials acknowledged the problem, but the political forces seeking change had not been strong enough to do anything about it. Very modest legislation designed to strengthen Palau customs authority over drugs had been stalled in the OEK for years. In sum, if the problems of substance abuse were intended as a charge against the Salii administration, it was a cheap shot. The problem was pervasive and enduring. Excessive alcohol use was remarked upon as far back as the German period; prohibition was a condition of the League of Nations Japanese mandate. If intended to help Palau, exposure of the substance abuse issue in Washington could be helpful.

On March 24 the anger between the Territories Subcommittee and the State Department became public. The State Department charged that the Interior Committee was "cruel and paternalistic" in its dealings with Palau. Hills, in an interview, said, "If they [Udall and de Lugo] actually have evidence, it should be turned over to the government of Palau [for prosecution]. Otherwise, it is withholding evidence. And if they haven't got evidence, they shouldn't be making accusations."

On March 26, 1988, de Lugo said the agreements between Palau and the

United States on law enforcement, financial procedures, and a Palauan development plan were inadequate. The law enforcement agreement failed to ensure that "improper acts are independently investigated and, if warranted, prosecuted."

"I am very disappointed to learn it took them up to now to say the agreements are improper," said Haruo Willter, Assistant to President Salii. "I don't think it's fair."

The Senate Energy Committee reported out legislation similar to that of the House Foreign Affairs Committee on March 28, 1988. The next day, the entire Senate ratified the Compact.

The House Interior and Insular Affairs Committee continued to stall. In place of legislative activity, the committee issued its standard press release rehashing the dastardly deeds in Palau—drug running, the IPSECO corruption, financial inadequacy, and counterfeiting. By now these reasons were no longer persuasive enough to delay Compact ratification.

Notes

1. Pages 130-138. The Salii and Olikong testimony are all excerpted from: House of Representatives, *The Compact of Free Association between the United States and Palau, Hearings and Markup before the Committee on Foreign Affairs and its Subcommittee on Asian and Pacific Affairs on H.J. Res. 479*, 100th Cong., 2nd sess., Dec. 17, 1987, and March 31, 1988. Statement of Lazarus Salii, pp. 83-133; statement of Santos Olikong, pp. 133-154.

2. Page 137. Tom Dunmire, "Memorandum: Observations Pertinent to the Compact of Free Association, Trip Report, Palau, 27 November 1987" (draft, 18 December 1987). As far as I know, the Dunmire report also has never before been discussed in the literature.

3. Page 138. A profile of Senator Bennett Johnston is found in *National Journal*: Krisz, "The Power Broker," *National Journal*, Feb. 29, 1992, p. 494.

4. Page 138. *Was being treated in a local hospital.* "Palauan Suffers Stroke before Senate Hearing," *Pacific Daily News*, Jan. 29, 1988, p. 3.

5. Page 138. *Although the press reported. Ibid.*

6. Pages 138-139. The Ngirmang statement and the subsequent dialogue with Isabella Sumang and Santos Olikong are excerpted from U.S. Senate, *Compact of Free Association, Hearings before the Committee on Energy and Natural Resources on S.J. Res. 231*, 100th Cong., 2nd Sess.,January 28, 1988. The testimony and questioning of Lazarus Salii are found on pages 30-70.

7. Page 142. *The Territories Subcommittee kept.* E. Rampell, "Probe Intensifies: Investigation into a Reign of Terror," *Pacific Islands Monthly*, Feb. 1988.

8. Page 142. *Mirando, Salii's special assistant.* S. McPhetres, "Trip Report," Jan. 10-16, 1988, pp. 2-3.

9. Page 142. *On March 2, 1988.* The Udall/de Lugo letters of March 2 to Fascell, of March 17 to Salii, and March of 24 to Secretary Hodel were inserted in the *Congressional Record* of March 24, 1988, together with the *San Jose Mercury News* report on the IPSECO payments. *Congressional Record*, E821-823, March 24, 1988.

10. Page 143. *Its budget report. Washington Pacific Report*, April 1, 1988, p. 2.

11. Page 143. *If Farrow made a public commitment.* Unknown to me, Rafaela Sumang wrote to Senator Johnston: "We will be filing the suit at the end of March since we expect a federal presence on the island." Letter from Ms. Rafaela Sumang to Senator Bennett Johnston, March 4, 1988. The basis of her expectation of a federal presence is unclear.

12. Page 144. *De Lugo and Farrow were on to something.* In July 1989, the DEA flew into Palau and arrested thirteen men and flew them to Guam. The individuals were indicted and all eventually pleaded guilty.

13. Page 144. For the data on alcohol and substance abuse, I have used the conference material published under the title of *Summary of the 1988 White House Conference for a Drug Free U.S.*, held in connection with the follow-up forum held by the Salii administration in Koror, Palau, April 25-29, 1988. See also, K. Nero, "The Hidden Pain: Drunkenness and Domestic Violence in Palau," 13 *Pacific Studies* 63 (1990).

14. Page 144. *Prohibition was a condition.* Article 3 of the League of Nations Mandate.

15. Pages 144-145. *The State Department charged. Washington Pacific Report*, April 1, 1988.

16. Page 145. *"I am very disappointed." Pacific Daily News*, March 26, 1988.

15

The Case is Filed Once More; Judge Hefner Overrules the Popular Vote; Salii Reluctantly Appeals

On March 31, 1988, the Compact case was filed once more. The women plaintiffs asked the court to reopen the original case rather than start a new one. This tactic permitted the plaintiffs to append a series of affidavits alleging intimidation as the reason for the withdrawal of the original lawsuit. The affidavits repeated the charges made in the letters to Farrow. Since the lawsuit had begun again, the affidavits should have been irrelevant, but they would tend to give sympathy to the plaintiffs and cast doubt on the government. Insofar as the lawsuit was a political statement—indeed at essence a political dispute—and the documents were being read by Congress, the plaintiffs were getting into the record a series of statements about the deeds and misdeeds of August 1987. The tactic also ensured that none of the women would ever be questioned about what they said.

Plaintiffs filed the papers by fax from New York, in itself somewhat unusual and probably a violation of the rules of procedure. It was not something we, the government of Palau, could complain about at this stage. This case could be begun from anywhere by almost anyone and the judge would accept it, and, by now, so would the government of Palau. Salii called me in Tokyo to tell me that the lawsuit had begun and to ask that I come to Palau right away.

Immediately after the filing of the lawsuit, again operating by fax, the plaintiffs moved to amend the complaint. They dropped some women and added others. The purpose was to give the case a new name. With different plaintiffs, there was a better argument that the case was not barred by the Ibedul-Salii settlement in *Merep v. Salii*.

On the legal issue in the case—whether Article XV could be used and, if so, how—we were strong, not obviously overwhelming, but very strong. If there had been no violence, I thought we would win. Nobody in the Palau government thought that, either before the violence or now. In the government there was a sense of doom. The Palauans around Salii saw an element of the last days of the British raj in all of this: white judges holding on to power by judging natives and faulting them for not following the ever-changing rules.

The reason for my original optimism about the legal result was the simple doctrine that the will of the people should prevail in constitutional amendment cases. We had a host of cases and the rules were uniform: very liberal in permitting the people to vote on a constitutional amendment, very strict in deciding whether the Amendment had actually passed. In fact, I had not been able to find a single example—and the plaintiffs never found one, either—where a court had prevented the people of a state from voting to amend its Constitution on the ground that the procedure to permit the vote was not followed. The courts bent over backwards to permit people to vote on any amendment, no matter how flawed the procedure. Again and again, courts reasoned the same way: the people are sovereign, the greatest latitude must be accorded to the people's ability to amend their constitution. Unless the constitution explicitly states that the amendment procedures were the exclusive means to amend the constitution, the courts will not limit the plenary right of the people. Somehow courts always found a way to say that the constitution had not set out the exclusive amendment procedures.

Even making allowance for local judicial self-confidence, even local judicial arrogance, this principle of popular will, in normal circumstances, should have permitted us to win and win easily. The murder of Bedor Bins and the corruption charges against Salii had damaged the Salii government, it is true, but if the Palau people were still strong, the argument would hold.

The opponents understood that as well. Their public relations effort, in short, was designed not only to undercut the Salii government but to undercut the Palau people, by arguing that the people themselves were unworthy. Their argument was that the Palau people were violent, their interest was solely financial, and their government was totally corrupt, a reflection of themselves. It was brutal and painful to watch, and yet in the last analysis it was almost totally successful. The Palau people would not only be damaged in the eyes of the United States and in the eyes of their own court, but in their own eyes as well.

I got to know Dunmire much better during this period. Dunmire had been adamantly opposed to the Compact, and I had felt he was not sympathetic to the territories. His view was more subtle than that. It was true that he was against the Compact. He felt it was simply not in the U.S. national interest. He adhered to Congressman Burton's view of Micronesian governments: they would be corrupt or excessively oppressive, and the people in Micronesia would be prey to these governments, governments they could not control. Now that the Palau Compact had already been negotiated, he felt the subcommittee was being foolish, looking into social and political issues that were well known. Better to approve the Compact, get out quickly, and not look back.

On Sunday, April 10, the weekend before the oral argument before Judge Hefner, the International Commission of Jurists (ICJ) issued its report. It was hand carried to Palau by Anne Simon, the lawyer for the plaintiffs from the Center for Constitutional Rights in New York City. In some way the plaintiffs would bring it to the court's attention. There was no way to prevent that. Simon introduced it in a documentary appendix that she submitted to the court.

The report was terribly biased, sloppy in preparation, and almost cavalier in its use of facts. Distortions were rampant. The timing alone indicated its view. The ICJ report was intended to create an atmosphere hostile to the Salii administration in Palau and in the States and to influence the court to "prove" its independence by voting for the plaintiffs. It was, in short, a crude attempt to influence the court.

At issue were, supposedly, two questions: whether the plaintiffs had been intimidated eight months back and whether the courts were independent and capable of rendering independent decisions now. Few people really doubted by now that plaintiffs had been subjected to enormous pressure and many had been intimidated. The ICJ weighed in heavily on that point.

The ICJ report reviewed the fact that in August 1987 a Furlough Committee was formed, composed of employees released from the government because of the inability of the government to pay their salaries. The furloughed government employees were very angry and they became a strong political force. But this didn't tell us much.

How much responsibility for the activities of the furlough committee should be placed on the government? Were they an independent group, or were they acting after consultation with the government? The answer to that was—and still is—very unclear. Their goal and the goal of the government were the same, and one knew what the other was doing. But was this like the poor people's march and the Kennedy administration, where both wanted civil rights legislation and the march bore witness to the force of the people? That was the Palau government's point of view. On the other hand, was this a simulation, a group of employees forced unnecessarily to be unemployed by governmental action and then at governmental urging engaging in coercive behavior? This was the Territories Subcommittee's view and that of the women plaintiffs.

If the question had been argued at that level and, indeed, responded to at that level, the ICJ would have been making a serious contribution to a complex question. But that was not the level at which the ICJ wished to act.

The ICJ instead at key points retreated into broad statements that were in essence meaningless. Thus, the ICJ found "evidence of government complicity in many of the matters cited in this report," a finding that left the report open to be read almost any way one would want to read it. And just to throw in a general blast at the government, the report said, "Sadly *there are also serious allegations of corruption against prominent Palauans, which we consider it proper to mention* but not elaborate. There were also many allegations of *incompetence and waste*" (Emphasis supplied).

Allegations of "incompetence" and "waste" and "allegations of corruption against prominent [nationals]" can be made about any country in the world. It was a cheap shot, in a document that only pretended to find facts. Presumably one did not have to ask why it was "proper to mention" the allegations.

On the issue of the courts' independence—supposedly the burning question--there was little to debate. The courts had ruled against the government consistently in the past. You can't get more independent than that. The ICJ knew that and even mentioned that in passing. But, of course, the ICJ purpose was to get the courts to rule against the government in the *future*.

In a blatant effort to influence the decision, the ICJ pulled out all the stops, even highlighting the racial difference among the judges.

It would be a misfortune if it were considered necessary or even desirable in such sensitive situations, always to resort to off island judges of non Palauan origin. For the survival of the Rule of Law in Palau in the long term, it is essential that such independence be demonstrated, repeatedly, by indigenous judges.

Not only was this paragraph untrue, it was unfair to the one judge who had shown the greatest integrity and courage during the entire Compact ordeal: Chief Justice Nakamura. Nakamura had sat on the *Gibbons v. Salii* case and ruled against the government. He had maintained a position of dignity, ensuring that the courts were functioning well and independently—although ICJ didn't want to say that. What was necessary was for the Palau judges to demonstrate their independence one more time, "repeatedly."

The press greeted the ICJ report as a beacon shining the light of truth on the corrupt Salii government. It sparked news stories in the press, both in Micronesia and in the States, repeating the old charges against the Salii administration.

I gave some thought as to how best to respond to the report. I found a page where there were at least three factual inaccuracies, and since both Hefner and I would be present and knew the facts, this would allow me to quickly undercut the report. I spent a lot of time figuring out a way to do it in thirty seconds. More than that would give the ICJ report too much prominence. But the chance never came. Anne Simon had gotten it in the record and did not mention it further.

On Monday, April 11, Simon arrived. She and her associate, Susan Quass, were very intense and made a point not to talk to me. Rafaela Sumang had been in the attorney general's office with me when she signed the settlement agreement. She was an older, pleasant woman. Whenever we were to meet, as we did when she entered the Palau Pacific Resort, she rather naturally said "hello." Her daughter, who was younger and whom I did not know, adopted the Simon view. The enemy was evil and I was the enemy.

The oral argument rapidly developed in the direction we originally thought it would take: a discussion of inconsistency and whether the OEK was required to follow procedures of Article XIV. But to get there the judge had to wrestle with the settlement agreement between Salii and the Ibedul. Did it bar the women from bringing the case once more?

The modern view is to interpret broadly these settlement agreements and bind "foreseeable" litigation. If ever litigation was foreseeable, it was in this case, which was exactly the same case started by different parties. The Ibedul had by his position in Palauan society and in previous cases established his role as one with sufficient representative capacity to bind all parties.

Although I thought we were unlikely to win with this argument, Prof. Hazard's opinion, which we appended to our brief, was forceful and clear. He relied on the Ibedul's stature in Palauan society.

Judge Hefner got around the settlement by suggesting that the agreement between Salii and the Ibedul was not a judgment at all, just a memorandum that decided nothing. This was simply wrong. A consent judgment is one entered into by the parties and agreed to by the court. That's what the Ibedul-Salii agreement was. As for Hazard's opinion, Judge Hefner was dismissive of it.

Inconsistency was the heart of the substantive issue. We had to have an inconsistency between the Palau Constitution and the Compact so we could use Article XV of the Palau Constitution rather then Article XIV, with all of its limitations. In *Gibbons v. Salii*, the case that initiated me in Palau Compact politics, the Supreme Court of Palau had specifically held, there was an inconsistency between the Compact and the Palau Constitution. I didn't see how the women plaintiffs could get around that. Ms. Simon argued that *Gibbons v. Salii* found an inconsistency only in that it required a 75 percent majority but not otherwise. I was scornful of this reasoning in my argument, both before Hefner and later on during the appeal before the Palau Supreme Court. My derision was not a debater's ploy. I truly never comprehended this argument. Apparently Judge Hefner did: he held on this reasoning that there was no inconsistency between the Constitution and the Compact despite the ruling of *Gibbons v. Salii*.

We had cited a number of cases to indicate that where there was constitutional ambiguity, as there certainly was here, the will of the people should prevail. But to this court the argument rang false.

Judge Hefner appended an extraordinary epilogue to his opinion expressing his view of the people of Palau as being interested only in money:

Approval of the Compact is a prerequisite for substantial funding which, it is presumed, will bring almost immediate gratification to a large majority of the citizens of the Republic. But tomorrow's lucre pales in the face of today's recognition of the integrity and stability of the Constitution of the Republic.

Hefner's opinion questioned whether the United States should accord any validity to the actions of the Salii government or to the actions of *any elected* Palau President:

Apparently, some members of the United States government recognize the [presidential] certification *simply because it is by the duly elected president of the country*. . . . [T]he unquestioned reliance upon the certification of the President of Palau does not comport with the reputation of the United States for fostering and supporting democracies for emerging countries under its political wing. (Emphasis supplied)

To my shock, after the Hefner opinion Salii did not want to appeal. Salii believed the courts of Palau were totally biased and would never rule in favor of the government. I had assessed the chances of victory as very poor before Judge Hefner. These were his women; he had protected them and he cared about them. He was not likely to say all of his efforts had been for no purpose. But I thought our chances much better on appeal, perhaps as good as even money. Salii always smiled at these odds and mocked my optimism: "Arnold, I'm glad that you believe that." I thought the Hefner opinion sufficiently weak that it was of little consequence. Salii pressed me on that. Salii argued, with some justice, to the opposite conclusion. Didn't that indicate that no matter how strong our legal position, the court would rule against the Palau government? Further, wouldn't the appellate court go along with its colleague, Judge Hefner? Salii had a point. It's always better to be the appellee, and the Hefner decision, no matter how weak, gained some credibility by virtue of it being the decision of the trial court.

Unstated was the public relations campaign. It not only damaged Salii personally but it also gave the Hefner opinion considerable respectability. People wanted to believe that Hefner was interpreting the law properly. The isolation of Palau also was a factor. In this highly visible case, the judges of Palau had to feel beleaguered: beleaguered by the Salii government with its allies and the Furlough Committee, and beleaguered as well by the press and scholars, who now were suggesting that any independent court would rule in only one way, against the government. In a situation like that, the judges would tend to band together.

Nevertheless, I thought we had to play it out, to give ourselves a chance. We owed it to the people of Palau. Salii owed it to himself. It was the first time I saw the toll the battle had taken. Salii gave a deep sigh. "We'll see."

The next evening, Salii called a small meeting at his office with Isaac, now promoted to attorney general; Basse, the assistant attorney general; and myself. Salii worked all the time; early morning and late evening meetings were not uncommon. This time we met around 6:00 p.m. Salii had with him three people I had never met before who spoke—and understood—only Palauan. Isaac thought they were governors of three of the sixteen states of the Republic of Palau, but he wasn't sure. The Palauans at the table had to have the comments of each of us translated, and the give and take was therefore limited and stilted. Their presence, I thought, was cosmetic. This was Salii's decision alone to make. Salii structured the meeting very carefully: Basse was to speak first Isaac next, me last. That was unusual. Meetings with Salii tended to be unstructured. He enjoyed informal interchanges.

We lawyers all agreed: we should appeal. But the assessment of success varied. Isaac thought the issue hopeless based on his view of the merits of our case and his view of the courts; Basse was only a bit more optimistic, relying, like Isaac, heavily on the personalities of the Court. I was the most optimistic of all. I could not judge the personalities of the court, but I had read all of the reported opinions of the Court in order to judge the quality of the Court. I judged it as fairly high: not willing to defer or be supportive of the legislature or to the executive—even when legal doctrine required it—but still a solid court.

I had thought the appellate court would be moved by the legal argument. No case anywhere had ever interpreted a Constitution as preventing the people from being permitted to consider an amendment. If the Palau Supreme Court upheld Hefner, Palau would be unique in American jurisprudence. I conceded the special character of this case: the Bedor Bins killing, the charges of intimidation against the women, and the political importance of the Compact. All of that worked against us; there was no question about that. Still, the legal argument was extremely strong. I did not persuade Salii. I had the uncomfortable feeling that this meeting was pro forma, held as a courtesy to me.

The meeting broke up without a decision by the president. No decision meant no appeal. I was sure of that. As I reflected on the discussion, the one argument that seemed to move Salii was my comment that he owed this to his U.S. supporters in the States and in Guam. That night I called Berg and Hills and told them of Salii's inclination not to appeal. I urged them to call him.

Hills is a very emotional man. The same passion that was quick to anger against Farrow and de Lugo now was quick to support Salii. Hills felt passionately about Salii, perhaps more than anyone else in the U.S. government. The next day, Hills telephoned Salii and, apparently, moved him. Two days later, I met with Salii in his office. He agreed to an appeal. He joked, with sardonic humor, about the likely outcome. His pain was visible. I wished I knew him well enough to embrace him.

Notes

1. Page 147. I had thought the case would be started with new plaintiffs so that we could not argue their case was barred by the settlement of the previous case, the *Merep* case.

2. Page 147. *Affidavits alleging intimidation.* If there was intimidation, one would have expected the aye votes to increase and the nay votes to decrease—in sum, for nay voters to change their minds. This did not happen. In 1983, total registered voters totalled 8,338, with a remarkably high number—7,246—actually casting ballots. The aye votes totalled 4,452 (61 percent). After Salii's election and a strong press for Compact approval, the total registered voters increased substantially and the number of aye voters increased with it. In December 1986, the total votes cast were 8,824, with 5,789 (66 percent) aye votes. What prevented the December 1986, aye votes from carrying the day with 75% was a sudden increase in nay voters. The nay votes had been almost consistently around 2,000: 2,103 in 1984 and 1,957 in February 1986, for example. In December 1986, they increased substantially to 2,986, an all-time record.

3. Page 148. *The courts bent over backwards.* For example, the Kentucky Court of Appeals considered whether, under that state's constitution, two specific provisions relating to amendment procedure were the "exclusive modes of amending or of revising their constitution." In fact, the people had chosen a third method nowhere mentioned in the Kentucky Constitution. The court took a broad view, finding it "inconceivable to assume the people might be divested of the power to reform their government by the procedures established in [these] sections . . . of the Constitution. Nowhere is that power limited either expressly or by necessary implication." *Gatewood v. Matthews*, 403 S.W.2d 1716 (Ct. App. Ky. 1966).

4. Page 149. *The Palau people would not only.* E.g.: "Naturally, Palau wishes to proceed toward self government as contemplated by the trusteeship agreement. But, as things presently stand, Palau will never survive on its own because of corruption and inefficiency in government." Letter from Senator Joshua Koshiba to Thomas Richardson, President, U.N. Trusteeship Council, March 20, 1992.

5. Page 149. The text reviews the ICJ report as delivered. While writing this book, I spoke to William Butler a number of times and asked for the back-up interviews and data. I also asked for a face-to-face interview. Butler promised to find the files and permit me to review them but, finally, my calls went unanswered. He never agreed to an interview.

6. Page 150. *I had found a page where.* For the curious reader, the three errors appeared in the original mimeograph version of the ICJ report on page 42. In the printed version, which appeared subsequently, the material appeared on pages 35-36. The three errors were:

1. "Only Rafaela Sumang appeared *in court*." In fact, nothing happened *in court*. It was announced by the attorney general, as indicated in the text, that the women were coming down for the purpose of discussing the lawsuit.

2. "file a petition for an adjournment to obtain counsel. She was given a Stipulation of Dismissal to Sign. She thought it was for a postponement." In fact, the petition for adjournment to obtain counsel was filed the week before. She brought no court documents with her.

3. "Judge Hefner became concerned. He said *in court* that he would not

allow the dismissal to be filed unless it was personally signed by all plaintiffs in person." In fact, Judge Hefner said nothing in court on this issue. As indicated in the text, he told Eric Basse *in chambers* he wanted all plaintiffs to sign. (Emphasis supplied)

7. Page 151. *As for Hazard's opinion.*

Professor Hazard . . . opined that the plaintiffs are barred from bringing this action. . . .The court need not tarry long on this proposition. Suffice to say . . . the Ibedul did not purport to represent or deal away the rights of the voters of the Republic in the Memorandum of Understanding, and even if the Ibedul attempted to relinquish or extinguish the plaintiffs' right to sue in this matter, there is simply no basis, either by applying "analogous" United States law or any provisions of Palau law, for supporting such a result. Op. of Judge Hefner, *Merep v. Salii*, Civ. A. 139-87 (ROP Supt. Ct. Tr. Div., 1987).

16

Farrow Tries Secret Diplomacy; de Lugo Introduces His Compact Bill and Hoodwinks the GAO

In Washington, outside of public view, de Lugo and Farrow were battling over the GAO report which, in draft, had been delivered to them in March ready for release. With the case being argued on appeal later that month, the GAO report, which did *not* substantiate the voter intimidation charges against the Salii administration, would be an unexpected bonus for Salii in the public relations war.

The GAO team took the position that the report should be issued as soon as possible because it was highly relevant to the ongoing congressional debate about Compact approval. Farrow disagreed. He told GAO the subcommittee was not happy with the product. It failed to address some significant issues. The GAO challenged that. What other issues? The GAO offered to conduct any additional work as a separate, follow-on effort, but what they had completed should be issued right away. Farrow rejected that possibility. The negotiations turned nasty.

In early June 1988, Milton Socolar, Special Assistant to the Comptroller General in addition to the GAO investigating staff, met with Congressman de Lugo to resolve the impasse. About five minutes after the start of the meeting, de Lugo brought up the drug problem in Palau. He noted that the committee had held a hearing earlier that week at which important new evidence had surfaced about Palau's drug problem. The GAO needed to conduct additional work on law enforcement issues affecting Palau. A return visit to Palau was required.

The GAO staffers were outraged. They were being manipulated for the subcommittee's political purposes. They wanted to release what they had. Socolar overruled his staff and surrendered to the subcommittee's wishes. No part of the GAO report would be released until the entire report was completed. When would that be? Probably not until after the Palauan and

U.S. elections in November. Although the draft report was barred from the scrutiny of others, de Lugo was to refer to the findings of the draft GAO report in subsequent correspondence and in public hearings.

The Senate Energy Committee and the House Foreign Affairs Committee viewed the Compact issue as primarily one of U.S. foreign policy. They wanted to put the Palau Compact behind them and approve it as it was negotiated. The other Micronesian island chains—the Federated States of Micronesia and the Marshalls—had received the same basic deal; no special treatment for Palau was warranted.

They viewed the U.S. trusteeship as basically positive. The U.S. health and education policies had been successful. Throughout Japanese rule, the Palauan population had fluctuated between 4,000 and 6,000 people. Under U.S. governance, the population almost tripled, from the 1946 population of 5,634 to 15,122 in 1991. Beginning with the sending of the Peace Corps volunteers to Palau and elsewhere in Micronesia, the United States rapidly expanded the educational opportunities from the limited three-year schooling under the Japanese to a high school program, a college-level teacher training program, and finally, the creation of the College of Micronesia.

De Lugo and Farrow understood these accomplishments, but they saw what had yet to be done. In the Territories Subcommittee's view, the forty-one year trusteeship had been a failure. Palau was bankrupt and had debts of nearly $100 million. Its jail and hospital were primitive and dilapidated. Heroin addiction was rampant. Marijuana was the largest cash crop. Many of the islands still had no electricity. These remaining problems in Palau had to be addressed before the Compact could be approved. They pledged not to budge until then.

To the other committees, such an effort to "solve all the problems of Palau before the Compact can be approved," as a Senate committee aide put it, would keep the Compact before the Congress forever. They saw the U.S. role as completed: the time had come to turn over government to the islanders themselves.

The strain between the Senate and House over the Palau Compact began to show. On the Senate floor, Senator McClure, the ranking Republican on the Energy Committee, commented.

Last Congress the Palau compact was approved, not conceptually, not in principle, not theoretically, but approved. . . . [T]here are undoubtedly those unwilling to release what they perceive as the reins of empire, or who would, in Kipling's phrase, wish to "Take up the White Man's burden," but it is now 1988, not 1899.

Playing to the political minority in Palau to foster some ulterior motive is simply not supportable. An agreement was reached with the House, the administration, and Palau last year to end the trusteeship and permit the peoples of Micronesia to regain the sovereignty which is theirs by right.

On April 27, 1988, the House Foreign Affairs Committee reported out legislation ratifying the Palau Compact. The House Interior Committee, the only committee which had not taken any action, went public to explain its delay. De Lugo and Udall released GAO's preliminary findings that IPSECO paid over $1 million to Palauan leaders "for which no justification can be found." De Lugo and Farrow called upon Hodel to open a criminal investigation. Hodel refused. On April 30, 1988, Udall and de Lugo invited Salii, Koshiba (president of the Senate), Olikong (Speaker of the House), and Chief Justice Nakamura to fly to Honolulu and meet secretly with them. The meeting was a disaster. No Palauan high-level leaders attended. Only Koshiba went from among the Palau invitees, and only Committee staff attended from Washington.

Then the fact of the meeting leaked. The Republicans on the committee who had not been invited were furious. "No one even asked me about it" said Representative Robert Lagomarsino of California, the Territories Subcommittee's ranking Republican. "It seems to me they're doing some back door negotiating. I'm not very pleased."

Hills relished Farrow's embarrassment. "It is almost amateurish to think that something like this could be done and everyone wouldn't know about it," he scoffed. The committee had rebuffed repeated executive branch efforts to have a meeting of all parties involved, Hills asserted.

In early May, 1988, I met with Berg and Hills and their staff at the State Department. By now, Berg felt, as did Al Stayman, Senator Johnston's aide, that we would not win the lawsuit on appeal. Hefner's decision had affected them as it had affected Salii. They knew, of course, of Salii's reluctance to appeal, and they respected Salii's judgment. Further, the opinion was so strongly against us that it had to say something about how the Palau judges were going to decide. Hills wanted to write a public statement to Chief Justice Nakamura or Salii pointing out the importance of the rule of law in Palau and the faith the United States held in the appellate process. I was strongly opposed. Any attempt to influence the decision would be resented and make matters worse. The long Compact negotiations with Palau, the continual failure to get the Compact ratified, and the intense congressional in-fighting had given birth to a new consensus: Palau was jinxed; its politics too uncompromising and too convoluted to untangle. Berg was still optimistic about congressional action. He felt Farrow had hurt his position by the secret meeting in Honolulu and was losing bipartisan support on the committee by his tactics.

Critics charged that Farrow was playing politics with Palau, delaying until a Democratic administration could be credited for ratifying the long-awaited Compact. Hills openly accused the Interior Committee of "stalling . . . in hopes of negotiating a better compact after Reagan leaves office." Farrow felt the pressure. He responded: "Never for a minute have I considered putting this off until a Democrat got into office."

On Sunday, May 29, 1988, a second meeting in Honolulu took place. This second one was publicly announced rather than secret. The attendees were: de Lugo and staffers Farrow, Ken Jones, and Gail Mukaihata from the House Territories Subcommittee, Salii, and Haruo Willter, Palau's Washington representative and a long-time aide to Salii.

In Honolulu, de Lugo and Farrow softened their public posture. They spoke of the Compact being approved in the current session of Congress and committed themselves to reporting the Compact legislation out of the committee by July 4. De Lugo offered not a spoonful of sugar but a bucketful in exchange for the bitter pill. The sugar took the form of a good deal of extra funding: (1) a $9 million grant for a new hospital in Palau, (2) a U.S. loan of $25,000,000 at 7 percent to pay off the IPSECO debt, (3) continuation of grants for postsecondary education, and (4) additional technical assistance to control drug imports. Then the bitter pill: a special federal appropriation to fund a Palau special prosecutor and public auditor, with the power in the Department of the Interior to name interim nominees.

Then de Lugo and Farrow got tough. Unless the Salii government supported their legislation, the House Interior Committee would amend the Compact to remove the full faith and credit provisions. Each year Palau would have to come to the Committee for Appropriations, and the committee would then decide how best to continue to assist Palau. The fight for continued imperial control was joined.

The stories differ on precisely what was agreed to in Honolulu. After an initial meeting among all of them, de Lugo suggested staff work out the details. After two days of staff meetings, there was to be one more meeting with Salii and de Lugo present. Salii had postponed this final session more than once. De Lugo doubted Salii would show up. But finally, Salii did come. He appeared nervous, Farrow remembered, but in all other respects the meetings were normal, very cordial.

De Lugo subsequently claimed that at the final meeting there had been an agreement on his bill and even a handshake on it. Willter insisted that de Lugo's characterization of a Salii-de Lugo agreement on the contents and wording of the de Lugo bill was "simply not true." There was no text of the bill at the meeting. Their oral agreement only covered the general framework of a bill. Farrow agreed there was no text, but he said there were agreed-upon concepts that were set down in writing. Willter denied they were ever shown to Salii or him.

De Lugo's bill became public on July 7, 1988. It was a careful balance of carrot, stick, and bureaucratic self-interest. The carrot was the provision of additional funds—close to $88 million—to fund both the hospital, the IPSECO settlement, drug enforcement, and the offices of the special prosecutor and public auditor. The stick was the requirement not only to staff the special prosecutor and public auditor offices but to submit to additional federal control over the internal affairs of Palau through the Office of Inspector General in the Department of the Interior.

As a matter of principle, the Senate and the administration opposed giving Palau more money. Additional funds amounted to another renegotiation of the Compact. Negotiations had to end. Further, from their point of view, the special prosecutor requirement amounted to an intrusion into Palauan affairs at the very time the United States was supposedly granting the island nation independence. Practically, it would mean endless wrangling with local Palau politicians charging corruption against their opponents. It was not a direction the Senate or Administration wanted to pursue.

Willter sent a stiff letter to de Lugo objecting to the insular affairs chairman "forcing Palau by an Act of the U.S. Congress to hire a Public Auditor and a Special Prosecutor" as a means to solve financial and law enforcement problems in Palau. "I feel that the Committee has gone too far into local matters involving local policies with which the Committee is not familiar."

In July 1988, de Lugo called for hearings before his subcommittee. Salii did not attend. The hearings were unusually combative, with de Lugo openly charging Salii with cowardice for not appearing and insinuating wrongdoing against a number of Palauans who were at best marginal players in the drama. "The motives of anyone who opposes a thorough investigation at this time are suspect," de Lugo said.

Berg and Hayward, the administration witnesses, got a strong going over from de Lugo. De Lugo labeled Interior "know nothing" and "do nothing" and criticized State for trying to ram the Compact through Congress before corruption, drug problems, and local constitutional approval procedures were resolved. De Lugo ended by saying, "I've got the votes," and adamantly insisting, "No bill will be approved by the Subcommittee without these [auditor and prosecutor] provisions."

Willter wrote de Lugo afterward: "The manner in which the hearing was conducted has alienated . . . Palauan leaders." Willter charged that the committee "is creating more reasons to delay the Compact implementation." De Lugo and Farrow were equally angry. There had been a deal in Honolulu, and Salii and Willter had reneged on it.

Regardless of the cause, the hearings were so unusual that the *Washington Pacific Report*, in an extraordinary reaction, dubbed the hearings "a star chamber proceeding." The hearings were never printed, and today, even in transcript form, are unavailable.

Right before the hearing, de Lugo announced that the GAO was returning to Palau. Salii responded angrily to the prospect of a GAO return: "Tell them they're not coming to Palau. . . . I don't even want to hear their schedule."

Interpretations of Salii's reaction varied. Compact opponents and de Lugo and Farrow viewed it as the natural reaction of a man who had something to hide. That, coupled with the opposition Salii had to the special prosecutor and public auditor, reinforced this impression. The special prosecutor and public auditor positions had been established under Palau law, but the OEK had rejected Salii's nominees as his political cronies.

Salii set out his position as one based on principle. As Salii saw it, the new special prosecutor and public auditor positions, as they were now evolving, would be responding to the federal government, specifically the Subcommittee on Territories, who were funding their positions. They would no longer be individuals weeding out corruption but rather an extension of the Territories Subcommittee seeking an imperial role likely to permit it to determine local elections and provide the justification for continued delay of the Compact.

One's reaction, my own included, depended upon how much corruption and strong-arm tactics you really thought there were. What was really going on in Palau? Exaggeration and overstatement by local Palau politicians, who saw a chance to bring down Salii, permeated the anti-Compact forces. There was also a clear bureaucratic self-interest on the part of the Territories Subcommittee to justify its failure to ratify the Compact.

Further, the receipt of the IPSECO payment, if that were all that was involved, could be viewed as typical Third World politics. Even the furloughing of the employees could be viewed as a variant of the government employee strikes, a time-honored tactic in Palau. Finally, every time there was an open hearing where one expected to hear major disclosures (the Solarz hearings or the Johnston hearings), the opponents had done terribly. The women wheedled their way out of them. The other witnesses produced almost nothing.

But still, Salii's supporters had to be troubled. The Pacific-based journalists were unanimously hostile. Not all of them were simply being politically correct. They could only prove IPSECO. They mentioned the Babeldaob road project and they seemed to sense something more. Judge Hefner's ire had gone beyond what I considered appropriate in judicial behavior. But nobody questioned Hefner's integrity. He had been based in Palau some years before, so he had a feel for the islands. What did he know? The seizure of a briefcase full of Palau identification documents being carried to Guam by Mirando, Palau's special assistant, was very disturbing. The government's discussions with the corrupt Matthews and Wright underwriting firm to finance a $400 million bond issue were unexplained.

Something more than IPSECO was involved. How much more remained uncertain.

Notes

1. Pages 157-158. *The Committee had held a hearing.* House of Representatives, Subcommittee on Insular & Interior Affairs of the Committee on Interior and Insular

Affairs, *Implementation and Amendments to the Insular Areas Drug Abuse Act, Oversight Hearings*, 100th Cong., 2nd sess., June 16, 1988.

2. Page 158. *They viewed the U.S. trusteeship.* On the trusteeship, see K. Kmedsen, (ed.), *Proceedings of the Pacific Islands Studies Conference, History of the U.S. Trust Territory of the Pacific Islands*, (1985).

3. Page 158. *Under U.S. governance, the population.* The 1946 population figure is found in J. Useem, *Report on Yap and Palau*, (1946), p. 70. The 1991 data is found in Department of State, *Annual Report to the United Nations on the Administration of the Trust Territory* (1991).

4. Page 159. *On April 30, 1988, Udall and de Lugo.* The text follows the press reports and public commentary at the time. Farrow feels the secrecy reports were unfair and designed to embarrass the Territories Subcommittee.

5. Page 159. *He felt Farrow had.* N. Brewer, "De Lugo: Staffer Sowing Discord," *Pacific Daily News*, July 17, 1988, p. 3.

6. Page 159. *Hills openly accused; Farrow felt.* D. Cloud, "End-of-Session Leaves Palau Twisting," *Congressional Quarterly*, November 26, 1988, p. 3400.

7. Page 160. *The fight continued.* H. Graves, "U.S. Aid Offered, Not Control," *Pacific Daily News*, June 26, 1988, P. 3A.

8. Page 160. *Was "simply not true."* *Washington Pacific Report*, Aug. 1, 1988, p. 5.

9. Page 161. *"The motives of anyone who opposes."* N. Brewer, "Palau Compact OK Unlikely This Year," *Pacific Daily News*, July 9, 1988, p. 3.

10. Page 161. *De Lugo ended by saying.* "De Lugo to Feds: `I've Got the Votes'," *Washington Pacific Report*, Vol. 6, no. 20, July 15, 1988, pp. 1-2.

11. Page 161. *The hearings were so unusual.* The hearings were never printed and are not available from the committee even in typed manuscript. The text reflects my written notes from the hearing supplemented by newspaper accounts.

12. Page 161. *Washington Pacific Report in an extraordinary reaction.* *Washington Pacific Report*, July 15, 1988, p. 2.

13. Pages 161-162. *Salii responded angrily.* N. Brewer, "Salii Tells GAO Not to Return," *Pacific Daily News*, July 17, 1988, p. 3A; H. Graves, "Feds to Reinvestigate Palau," *Pacific Daily News*, July 11, 1988, p. 1.

17

The Appellate Court Argument;
The Changed Mood in Palau

I felt we should keep our appeal simple, while at the same time arguing a comprehensive theory of constitutional interpretation relying on Article XV.

I emphasized the will of the people.

> The Constitution must be interpreted broadly to permit the people to amend their own fundamental governing instrument. . . .
>
> This court has an historic opportunity to . . . reaffirm its faith in the people of Palau, in the democratic processes in Palau and in the Constitutional government in Palau.

A philosophical aside may be in order here. Judge Hefner's stated approach—and it was one widely articulated by the judges sitting in Micronesia—was that the law was an objective body of doctrine to which a judge looked and detachedly applied to the case before him. The judge was engaged solely in a mechanical act, applying the Constitution and measuring the Compact up against it. That classic vision of the law was one widely held by judges and treatise authors in the eighteenth century. In the twentieth century, Justices Oliver Wendell Holmes and Benjamin Cardozo devastated that position as they showed that the law was fashioned and created by judges when they decided particular cases.

I hoped my emphasis on the role of the people would force a recognition by the judiciary of the broad discretion it had and the important role it was playing in Palauan nation building.

Ms. Simon's brief was different, both in style and in the nature of her position. The brief was a series of tactical forays putting forth various procedural improprieties, any one of which might strike the court's fancy. She offered no overarching view of the constitutional amendment process but suggested a series of reasons why at various points the constitutional amendment process was improper and this Compact vote invalid.

A few days before the oral argument, Salii surprised me by showing me Attorney General Phil Isaac's criminal contempt citation arising out of the Remeliik assassination case. A hearing on the criminal contempt charge was scheduled two days before the oral argument. I had not known there had been a criminal contempt charge. The relations between the courts and the executive branch were worse that I thought, and went beyond Salii personally and those Palauan officials close to him. A judicial finding that the Palau attorney general, the leading legal official for the island, was in criminal contempt would ruin us politically in Washington. To avoid that, Isaac had suggested that Salii grant him a pardon. I told Salii privately, during our discussion, that this was totally unacceptable. It only would reaffirm the argument that Salii was contemptuous of the courts and their judicial decrees. If we hoped to win the Compact case and build credibility with the Congress, we had to get off the collision course with the courts.

Salii called a meeting that afternoon with the vice president, the attorney general, and me. Salii opened the meeting by asking for my opinion of the idea of a pardon. I said a pardon was inappropriate at this time, leaving aside for the moment whether a pardon would be acceptable at any time. Salii responded shrewdly. He said he had no problem with a pardon now or in the future. What was Phil's reaction? Isaac realized he had gone too far. He backtracked. An apology on his part would probably settle it, he said. The meeting ended with Salii suggesting that I try to negotiate a settlement, basically an apology, with Kevin Kirk, the special prosecutor on the case, and Judge Sutton. Salii had chaired the meeting masterfully, moving the attorney general in the direction he wanted him to go without ever confronting him.

Kirk and I had lunch that day, and we worked out the language of the apology rather easily. Isaac, however, proved to be much tougher. The precise language concerned him. I didn't understand that and told him so bluntly. "No one cares now and no one will care in the future what the language was. Apologize and get the criminal contempt citation out of the way. The key thing is to get the Palau government, including the attorney general's office, back on track with the judges, with both recognizing and respecting their roles in enforcing the laws of Palau."

After an afternoon's negotiation with Isaac over the language of the apology, Kirk and I went to see Judge Loren Sutton. Judge Sutton, whom I had never met before, greeted me warmly and talked to me in his chambers while we waited for Kirk. Somehow, I mentioned that my daughter was in law school. He asked about her courses and gave me a book for her. He had an ease of manner and graciousness that I could only envy.

After Kirk came in, Judge Sutton was given the apology. Pointedly, without looking at the language, Sutton said the apology was acceptable to him if it was acceptable to Kirk. However, on the public acknowledgement of the apology, Sutton was very specific: it was to be read on the radio and printed in the *Gazette*, since Isaac's charges had originally appeared in those media.

After this was all worked out, I brought the letter upstairs to Isaac for his signature. Isaac had second thoughts. He reviewed the language once again, nitpicking each word. He would not say he "respected" the judges because he did not. I have a boiling point, and during this interchange I reached it. I left the letter with him and said it was now up to him.

I thought he would sign the apology and this would settle it. But he didn't sign it. Instead, he went to Kirk himself, and the next day he boasted to me that they now had new language that had been worked out where he didn't have to say he respected the court. The Remeliik case remained with him still.

Two days before the oral argument, Ms. Simon and I were called to Judge Sutton's chambers. Judge Sutton, together with Judges O'Brien and Ngiraklsong, comprised the three judges who would hear the Compact case. Sutton, as chief justice of the panel, wanted to know how we felt about security. Obviously, the question was addressed to Ms. Simon. Her response was thoughtful and honest. She said the mood was quite different than last time. However, at least one uniformed policeman should be present to, "in effect, show the flag." (Of course, that meant that later on the press would state that police were required to keep order.) Sutton said he had decided on three. I said nothing. The public relations impact of three police on duty to keep order would hurt us, but there was nothing I could say.

We both asked about logistics: the seating arrangements and the time to be permitted each of us. Sutton said he would give us what time we wanted, but the judges had read the briefs and 20 minutes for each side might be adequate. Since both Ms. Simon and myself had come 9,000 miles for the argument, 20 minutes seemed a dishearteningly short period of time. After some bargaining—Ms. Simon and I were on the same side on this one—Sutton effectively dropped all time limits, while setting nominal limits of 45 minutes each with 10 minutes for each side in rebuttal.

Oral arguments are usually not critical to a court's decision. Judge Sutton's statement that the judges had read the briefs and, therefore, a short oral argument was all that was necessary reflects the view of appellate judges everywhere. In this case, as in most, the briefs would determine the decision. But I felt the oral argument here might be of greater importance because of the amount of publicity that had gone on before and clearly had influenced the trial court. I thought that to win, we had to have the appellate court hear the reasonableness of what we were saying.

The three judges had reputations of being not very active questioners, and during the appellate argument they lived up to their reputation. However, although they were not talkative, there was—it seemed to me—a palpable change of mood from the trial court. The tone was more balanced and, therefore, more sympathetic to the government.

There were few Palauans in the courtroom. They had been told by the government to stay away. After the argument, the few who were there came up to me to ask what happened. Had we won? Could we win? To me, it was a poignant moment. White counsel, from Washington and New York, arguing to primarily white judges in a language the community did not fully understand. I wished I could be reassuring. It had gone well, very well, but I really couldn't tell about the final outcome. They wanted more. I tried to explain the details of the case. That was the wrong approach. They wanted comfort, not legal analysis. Even their questioning was inarticulate. They questioned with their eyes. I tried to be more reassuring. They had been through so much. Whatever excesses there were had been committed by the government officials and by a few individuals. By and large, these people had done nothing but vote. They voted their views again and again and then found their votes were for naught. Now they were helpless. They sought comfort from their lawyer. Maybe he possessed the talisman to ratify the Compact and, if not, at least to restore their dignity. I could not lie to them. I left before the dialogue was really over. It hurt too much to go on.

I recounted to Salii my estimate of the oral argument. The court seemed receptive; we had a good shot. Salii had already had reports that generally agreed with my own view. Unfortunately, Salii was now where the Palauan people were. He no longer dared to hope.

Notes

1. Page 164. *Comprehensive theory of constitutional interpretation*. The argument was this. Inconsistency existed because that's what *Gibbons v. Salii* held. Therefore, Article XV applied and could be used. In fact, Article XV was intended to be used for just this situation, where there was an inconsistency. Article XV was a self-contained whole. There was no need or reason to impose requirements from elsewhere in the Palau Constitution, namely from Article XIV, the general amendments article.

2. Pages 164. *A philosophical aside*. See M. Horwitz, *The Transformation of American Law: 1870-1960* (1992).

18

The Unthinkable Occurs

The political sniping in Palau intensified. Salii's opponents in the OEK accused Salii of covering up his corruption and denying Palau precious U.S. aid in the process. In late July 1988, political opponents of Salii formed a coalition to defeat him. Although off-island commentators made much of the coalition, Salii was dismissive of it. He felt the coalition would soon disintegrate. The coming election would be a contest between him and Roman Tmetuchl.

For Salii, the news got worse. In the middle of August, Vice President Remengesau broke with Salii and publicly endorsed de Lugo's legislation. Remengesau added pointedly that he couldn't understand why anybody would not support having a special prosecutor in Palau unless they had something to hide. The following week, Ngiraked, Salii's Minister of State, also broke ranks and came out in favor of the de Lugo legislation. In state elections on the island of Koror, Salii's opponents won 14 of 16 seats. Was Salii so vulnerable he would lose the presidential election in November? Most people did not think so. Not yet, at least. The charges of corruption had weakened him, but it was his inability to deliver the Compact that was hurting him the most. The Compact was his strength.

Salii began with a very weak political base. By family and by birthplace, he had little traditional power. He had patched together a powerful coalition led by the Reklai and Polycarp Basilius (the Reklai's brother) in northeast Palau. This, coupled with Salii's own intelligence, strength, vigor, and a very small political base in the Southwest, in Anguar, had mustered enough votes for Salii to win. But the battering over the last year had had an effect. Salii's strength and vigor had been drained from him. He faced a tough fight in November. Salii was not a particularly adept political campaigner. His vigorous sense of command, which awed Washington was not as impressive in Palau. In Palau, traditional forms of discourse and clan relationships dictated and limited the political dialogue. He didn't look forward to the campaign.

Salii liked to get away from Palau. The islands were never a comfort for him. Intellectually, he was distant from most Palauans, even from his strongest supporters. Normally, he flew to Hawaii or the States. Now the United States was cut off from him. He had to stay in Palau, isolated and alone. Visitors were warmly greeted, almost effusively so. Asterio Takesy, the Deputy Foreign Minister of the FSM, and, like Salii, one of Micronesia's politician-intellectuals, remembers visiting Palau during these months and being greeted eagerly at the airport by Salii. Palau was no longer an island that would lead Salii, as its president, to a world where his intellectual and political skills would flower. Palau was now an island that would limit him to ritual politics and ritual combat. Nothing remained but dodging OEK political daggers, rebutting an unending series of press stories about his corruption, and drafting futile petitions to a hostile judiciary.

By mid-July, Salii became more distant. I visited Palau in late July to report on the IPSECO negotiations. I had been meeting with the bank representatives and I thought an agreement was in sight. I was on island for a week. Salii didn't see me. We only talked a few times on the telephone. On August 8, in New York, in the IPSECO case, Judge Robert Sweet ruled that Palau owed the banks $45 million. Around August 14, Salii learned informally that the Palau Supreme Court would rule against the government on the Compact case. He had expected to lose. If the decision confirmed his judgment, it also closed one more door on his hopes for Compact ratification.

On August 18, Salii received by fax the GAO letter announcing GAO's return to Palau for further investigation. The new scope of work included direct attacks on Salii: investigation of the renovations to Salii's home, Palauan law enforcement activities; and the IPSECO power plant contract. The approach envisioned a public airing of complaints. The GAO would "meet with Palauan officials . . . and Palauan citizens whose views are relevant to addressing these issues. Willfully or not, the GAO became a party to the effort by de Lugo and Farrow to remove Salii from the presidency. The GAO letter ended almost sarcastically. "If the proposed timing for our trip is inconvenient for you and the other Palauan officials and citizens affected by our work, we will be happy to discuss an adjustment to the schedule."

In the president's office on August 18 and 19, Thursday and Friday, business continued normally. Wilhelm Rengiil had flown back from the States and saw Salii on Thursday. Ngiraked, while campaigning with Rengiil in the States, continually mentioned that if for any reason Salii could not run, he, Ngiraked, would run in his stead. Rengiil had been offended by Ngiraked's statements and had flown home to tell Salii about them. Salii made light of Ngiraked's ambition and seemed unconcerned. Rengiil noted no change in Salii. (Rengiil to this day believes Salii was murdered.) What was Ngiraked talking about? Confronted with the statements much later, Ngiraked said he was concerned that Salii, after his nomination, might be indicted and unable to run. In that eventuality, he wanted to be sure that the people looked to him as someone close to Salii who shared his views on the Compact. Did Ngiraked know of anything specific? No, he did not. Federal enforcement officials, admittedly very guarded in this area, did not lead me to believe there was any indictment coming out at that time.

On Sunday, August 21, the Ta Belau party, the party established by the furloughed workers, was scheduled to nominate Salii. This would kick off his presidential campaign. Salii flew to Peleliu on Thursday to tell his followers there informally of his candidacy. It was his practice; he had done so in 1985 as well. Friday morning, Salii breakfasted with Charles Matsutaro, Palau's liaison officer on Guam. According to Matsutaro, during the breakfast meeting Salii was in extremely good spirits. Yoichi Singeo and Bonifacio Basilius, Salii's special assistants, also saw him many times during these last two days of his life, and say they could detect no cause for concern.

On Friday, he briefed a Palauan delegation from Guam on his upcoming presidential nomination. Salii left the office Friday afternoon at his normal hour. On Friday night, August 19, Joyce Isechal, Salii's secretary, went to Salii's home and delivered the nominating petitions and letters to be answered. He looked them over, took action on some, deferred action on others. She thought it all normal. Looking back, like Willter, she is dumbfounded.

About 7:00 a.m., Willter, Salii's longtime friend and political aide, called from the airport. He had just returned from Washington. Salii asked him to come over at once. Willter dropped his bags at home and drove over to Salii's house. They spent the next two hours driving around the island together, in Willter's new Subaru, talking. At Salii's request, Willter had asked Farrow what was really going on. Was the committee's unrelenting opposition to the Compact in fact a statement about Salii? Did the committee want Salii out of office? Farrow said no. Willter didn't believe him. Salii had asked the same question of Farrow some months before when he was in Washington. Farrow had said no then as well. Salii also didn't believe him. It was conventional wisdom that Farrow and de Lugo wanted Salii out of office. Willter told Salii of Farrow's response. Then Willter's gloss came: the committee would oppose him, now and during the election.

Willter dropped Salii off two hours later. Willter has maintained to everyone, and he has been asked hundreds of times, that there was no indication during his long conversation that Salii was going to kill himself. He has replayed in his mind and aloud that long conversation and can find nothing suggestive of a farewell. Willter does not believe Salii was murdered but suicide makes no sense to him either.

Once home, Salii greeted his wife, Tina, his Filipino housekeeper, and his driver, Hernando Iyar. They were preparing lunch in the backyard of their home. Salii said he would join them shortly. He asked Tina if Iyar could be sent to get some mangos. He asked Iyar to destroy some papers he had taken home with him. That in itself was not unusual. Salii frequently took papers home with him from the office and, after completing work on them, asked them to be destroyed. Iyar burned them on the hill beside the house. That night it rained; the ashes were gone.

Inside his home, Salii put on a Japanese dressing gown. He went to a locked cabinet and took out a .357-caliber magnum revolver he had borrowed from his security guard four months before. He sat down before his desk in a large chair, put the gun to his temple, and killed himself. He was fifty-one years old.

Tina Salii, the housekeeper, and Iyar heard the noise of the shot. Iyar walked around the house, found nothing unusual and returned to lunch with the two women at the rear of the home. About twenty minutes later, Tina Salii went inside the house and found her husband sitting in his chair with a gunshot wound through the head, the revolver on the floor by his chair. There was only one bullet wound. The single bullet had entered his head about one inch above his left ear and exited on the other side. Tina fainted.

Salii's security guards called the hospital. An ambulance came and took him to the hospital, where there were desperate efforts to revive him. But it was hopeless.

In Palau, the overwhelming reaction was the thought that he must have been murdered. But even before the coroner's report was issued, murder seemed a strange hypothesis. It would envision an intimate of Salii who could shoot the president at extremely close range. Further, the murderer would have to have planned to kill the president of Palau at noon, in broad daylight, entering the house through the one door that was unlocked, the side door, a door that could be seen by Tina and her servants as they prepared food in the backyard.

The coroner concluded that Salii's death was suicide. The coroner directly confronted the raging rumors of homicide. His reasoning was that unless the shot was self-inflicted or the victim was asleep, the bullet could not travel so evenly. If it were homicide, the victim would instinctively move his head and the trajectory would change.

The official press release and even the coroner's report, somewhat surprisingly, emphasized that the gun was found by Salii's chair. In fact, when the police came, the gun was missing. The gun had been picked up by Salii's security guard from the floor near the body, wrapped in a cloth, and given to Carlos Salii. Several hours later, the gun was recovered from him in his home.

Salii's desk in his presidential office had been cleaned out. If Salii had cleaned out his desk, when did he do it? The night before? Early Saturday morning? Had he gone out alone before he met Willter? Had Salii been planning to kill himself for many hours? Or had he suddenly, after his conversation with Willter, driven to the presidential office? Why? Did Willter know more than he was telling?

Some say Salii left a single cancelled check on the desk, the check he had written a month before to the government of Palau paying for the repairs to his home. Stapled to the check was the invoice for the repairs from the Palau Department of Public Works. I have not been able to confirm whether there was such a check and I tend to doubt it.

Most saw the suicide as Salii's response to his desperate, losing struggle with Farrow and de Lugo, his growing recognition that he could not bring about the Compact. He had always hoped that the scenario for Palau would be the same as that for the Marshalls and FSM. Senator Johnston and the administration would eventually overwhelm de Lugo. The GAO investigation demeaned Salii, undermining his dignity and pride. He could put up with that. Salii's view was that the GAO investigation would prove little. But the GAO investigation totally changed the dynamics of the situation—Salii could see that—and would permit de Lugo and Farrow to hold back Palau's self-determination effort.

Some said more was involved than Compact ratification. Perhaps an indictment or an arrest was imminent. On what grounds? The obvious suspect was the IPSECO power plant deal. Salii had admitted receiving $100,000 from IPSECO, and there were rumors there might have been more money involved. But this was not new. If he had done wrong, so had other leaders in Palau. Salii had argued that the money was received when he was in the private sector to assist in establishing a private airline owned by Mochrie of IPSECO. The defense may have be weak and the embarrassment strong, but this was enough to convert a man eager to announce his candidacy to one who would commit suicide?

Worsening matters for Salii was the questioning of Mirando by federal officials. Mirando had initiated discussions with the DEA in Ohio implicating the special assistant to Salii. Perhaps Mirando was implicating others as well. Was Salii's suicide committed not so much to shield himself but to shield others in Palau?

I don't believe that corruption was the critical issue to Salii, however that was played in Washington circles. Salii, like other Micronesian island leaders, saw himself in relation to his island. He may have felt constrained by Palau and its people, but it was their favorable view of him, in the last analysis, that he needed. To be seen as a failure may have brought unbearable pain.

Even today, discussion of the cause of Salii's death rouses strong and very different, reactions. Five years after the death, alone in his office with me, Hills shouted: "Farrow killed him. He may want to deny it, but he did. Just as sure as he pulled the trigger himself."

Over lunch years after Salii's death, Farrow was detached as he analyzed Salii's suicide in political terms. Salii was losing his presidency. The GAO had just informed him that they were returning to Palau to look into his criminal behavior. Farrow's conclusion: Salii was cornered by his own wrongdoing.

Notes

1. Page 169. *In late July 1988, political opponents*. B. Perry, "Anti-Salii Coalition Formed," *Pacific Daily News*, July 24, 1988.

2. Page 169. *Remengesau broke with Salii*. D. Cloud, "End-of-Session Tempest Leaves Palau Twisting," *Congressional Quarterly*, Nov. 26, 1988, p. 3400.

3. Page 170. Letter, Nancy Kingsbury, Associate Director of the GAO, to President Lazarus Salii, Aug. 18, 1988.

4. Page 171. *At Salii's request*. D. Cloud, *Congressional Quarterly*, Nov. 26, 1988, p. 3400.

5. Page 172. *He was fifty-one years old*. Press reports continually referred to Salii's age as fifty-four. Salii was born on November 17, 1936.

6. Page 172. *The coroner concluded*. Autopsy Report by Medical Examiner Hee Yong Park of President Lazarus Salii, Aug. 22, 1988.

7. Page 172. *The gun had been picked up*. GAO, *Record of Discussion with Bill Stinnett, DOI Law Enforcement Coordinator for Palau and the Freely Associated States of Micronesia*, Sept. 13, 1988, p. 6; Republic of Palau, *Official Statement on the Death of President Lazarus E. Salii*:

The revolver had been handled by others immediately after the shooting and before the police arrived at the scene. The revolver was taken from the scene and was wrapped in cloth by a relative. It was not obtained by the Police until several hours after the shooting had occurred. As a result, accurate fingerprint identification was and still is inconclusive at this point.

See also, H. Graves, "Gun Handling Hinders Salii Probe," *Pacific Daily News*, Sept. 6, 1988, p. 3.

19

The Case is Finally Decided;
I Am Disappointed, Palau is Not;
Greenpeace is Bitter

Almost no one in Palau in the days after Salii's death remained untouched. For the majority of the people, Salii's death stunned them and, further, beat down their political spirit. They were sure that once again their president had been murdered: first Remeliik, and now Salii. The primary danger was civil unrest, if Salii supporters felt their leader had been assassinated. President Remengesau, with this threat preeminently in mind, quickly announced that Salii's death was a suicide. Amidst the political uncertainty, Tina Salii arranged the details of her husband's funeral. Salii's funeral was Friday, August 25, a week after his death. After that funeral weekend, Palau returned to an apparent normalcy.

The Supreme Court opinion that Salii had learned of before his death was issued officially on Monday. Since I had flown in to attend the funeral, I was on island when the appellate division issued its opinion. We lost in a very careful opinion. The Supreme Court of Palau ruled in our favor on three points: There was an inconsistency and, therefore, Article XV could be used. Finally, Article XV could be used at any time. We did not have to wait for a general election.

Article XV did not mention any procedure required to present the amendment to the people. Not only did Article XIV require a three-fourths vote of the OEK before the amendment could be voted on by the various Palauan dates, but the rules of the OEK specifically mandated a three-fourths vote of the OEK on a constitutional amendment whether the amendment was under Article XIV or Article XV.

Here was where the strength of the people of Palau had to be called upon. The people had an overriding ability to amend their own Constitution; the Constitution should be interpreted to permit them to do that. We argued that since Article XV did not list any requirement, any reasonable method was appropriate. Passage by the OEK, by any margin, of a constitutional amendment to be presented to the people for their vote should be sufficient.

The appellate court would not go that far. An Article XV amendment was still governed by the Article XIV requirement that required a three-fourths vote of the OEK. Since we had not gotten a three-fourths OEK vote, the constitutional amendment was invalid. I remembered Judge Ngiraklsong's comment on the tennis court. "The court is not going to do anything that could be regarded as stretching the letter of the law." All of the i's and t's would have to be dotted and crossed in this case. Strict constitutionalism was the order of the day.

I was terribly disappointed. I went over to the Senate and told Koshiba, the President of the Senate, of the decision. Koshiba gathered as many of the senators as he could, and I reviewed the holding of the appellate tribunal at considerable length. I then expressed my deep regret. On the contrary, they said, they were very pleased. If the constitutional amendment could be voted on at any time, Palau was in control once more. At a time of their choosing, they would proceed with a constitutional amendment and approve the Compact. They congratulated me and thanked me.

As I left the OEK, I saw Olikong. He did not know of the decision. I explained it to him. He was very disappointed and angry, saying he thought it made no sense to permit amendments under Article XV.

In Washington, Greenpeace put out a bitter press release.

20

Congress Fails to Approve the Compact; An Unexpected Successor to Salii Wins Office

Ta Belau, which had planned to nominate Salii, had a decision to make the day after Salii's suicide. What to do now? Ta Belau decided to delay its nominating convention only two days: from Sunday to Tuesday. Ta Belau's strategy in proceeding with the nomination so soon after Salii's death was to foreclose others from declaring as Salii's successor and thus dilute the importance of its selection. Ta Belau then turned to Ngiratkel Etpison, the governor of a small state on Babeldaob and a close associate of Salii. At the funeral, Etpison would be anointed as Salii's successor.

Could Salii's party, Ta Belau, transfer power to its candidate, Etpison, a man quite different from Salii? Salii was not rich, had never held Palau political office, was fluent in English, and was well known to U.S. officials. Etpison was a wealthy businessman and governor of Ngatpang State, but had little political experience and was unknown to U.S. officials. He did not speak English at all.

Ngiraked was especially bitter at Ta Belau's nomination of Etpison. He was a Compact supporter and claimed that Salii had promised the succession to him: "As his Campaign manager, I had an understanding with the late President Salii about being his replacement candidate." He announced his own candidacy for President. Having failed to persuade the Ta Belau to nominate him, Ngiraked would probably not get the Palau citizenry to elect him. Ngiraked, more than any of the other candidates, was relying on off-island support. He knew the off-island vote well. He had headed Salii's campaign and, in fact, had begun to campaign in the States and in Guam for Salii. In his campaign literature, Ngiraked had himself photographed in a business suit sitting on the edge of a desk similar to that of a successful business executive, an open appeal to the off-island constituency.

It was clear who in the field were heirs to the Salii mantle. What was unclear was whether there was any mantle to inherit. Outside Palau, the rumored corruption of the Salii administration had damaged Salii's popularity; on the other hand, support for the Compact was very high outside Palau.

The other candidates were all former Compact opponents who had opposed Salii. Tmetuchl, the elder statesman of Palau, the runner-up to Remeliik in both 1980 and 1984, had long been the heir apparent to the presidency. Many Palauans, however, still believed that his son and nephew, despite their acquittal, had killed Remeliik. Tmetuchl tried to make a virtue of what had been his vice in the past. He was presented as a strong, decisive leader, the type necessary to take charge in Palau at this time. Tmetuchl, like Etpison, favored the earliest possible implementation of the Compact of Free Association without further negotiation.

Remengesau was regarded as the compromise candidate. Even his accession to the vice presidency had been the result of a compromise. After the strong Salii, the people might want a softer figure. Remengesau's strongest asset was the Palau desire for stability and continuity. Had Remengesau, in the brief period since Salii's death—2 1/2 months—been able to establish his own distinct identity and gain sufficient Palauan stateside support? To do this, Remengesau distanced himself from the Compact disputes. The IPSECO debt negotiations were halted. He supported the legislative proposals of Congressman de Lugo, but with considerable ambivalence.

Although it was a large field, including the Ibedul, Moses Uludong, Santos Olikong, and Ngiraked, conventional wisdom held that Remengesau, Etpison, and Tmetuchl were the leading contenders.

After Salii's death, the Compact political dynamics on Palau totally changed. The Palauan political leadership, including Remengesau, Senate President Koshiba, and House Speaker Olikong, united behind de Lugo and his legislative solution. They wrote to Senator Johnston: "Only an enhanced package of compact benefits, such as represented by [the de Lugo bill], would stand a good probability of approval by the Palauan electorate."

The Palauan leaders came to Washington to plead their cause. But their arguments didn't persuade the Senate. Administration officials were also opposed. "We told them there were two things we would never agree to do," said a Senate aide involved in the talks. "We would never guarantee more money for Palau. And we would never increase U.S. taxpayer liability for the IPSECO debt." All talks broke off on September 18.

A compromise on IPSECO emerged in early October. Palau agreed to settle the IPSECO debt for $32 million, payable in the first year of the Compact. To make this payment to the banks, both the House committees and the administration agreed to disburse $37 million in Compact funds in the first year of the Compact, rather than over fifteen years, as originally provided.

De Lugo, accommodating to the administration, agreed to reduce the additional funds for Palau in his legislation from $30 million to $9.3 million. On October 6, the House passed H.J.R. 597 with these changes. Suddenly the goal of all this legislative maneuvering—getting the United States to approve the Palau Compact—once again seemed within reach. The day after the House action, the Senate passed its own version of the de Lugo bill with all the additional money taken out and no change in the original Senate position on IPSECO which precluded using Compact funds to settle the IPSECO debt. The stalemate was alive and well.

In a letter to de Lugo, Johnston said this was the Senate's final offer. Senate aides looked forward to the conference where agreement had to be reached between the House and Senate passed bills. As the Senate saw it, the House Interior bill, the de Lugo legislation, would simply lose in conference to the Senate and House Foreign Affairs Committee members. De Lugo and Farrow had anticipated that possibility, however, and, as the session came to a close, avoided a conference. The Senate Energy Committee blinked first, agreeing to $28 million in the first year of the Compact for IPSECO.

On October 21, the last day of the session, in mid-afternoon, a dozen House members met, including de Lugo. The House members agreed to accept the Senate and administration's IPSECO solution and the Senate stripped-down bill if, in return, the Senate and the administration would support the special prosecutor and public auditor provisions in the next congressional session. At midnight, with a congressional adjournment nearing, de Lugo assented warily. He wanted concrete assurances from Senator Johnston and the State Department that they would, indeed, follow through next year on their commitments. Right there, Berg and Hills wrote out in longhand the letters binding the State Department. All sides, including Farrow, seemed to agree. Then the staffs dashed to the floor of the House of Representatives.

Suddenly, de Lugo hesitated. His demands seemed to have been met, yet he refused to proceed. Farrow was at his side on the floor and de Lugo repeatedly asked Farrow what to do. Time was running out. Bills had to be at the Speaker's table in five minutes if they were to be considered at all in this congressional session. Leach ran over to de Lugo and urged him—actually, screamed at him—to introduce the bill. De Lugo seemed paralyzed. Time ran out.

In Palau, Congress's failure to act on the Compact seemed to still all talk of the Compact in the presidential campaign. All candidates favored the Compact except Uludong, who wanted commonwealth status.

The last thing Palau needed was a closely contested election would prevent any side from having a mandate. Even worse would be an election clouded by charges of impropriety. Palau got both. As election returns came in from Palau, Etpison and Tmetuchl had commanding leads, 500 to 600 votes over Remengesau. The Ibedul and Ngiraked were considerably behind. Uludong and Olikong brought up the rear. In Palau alone the vote was very close, but it looked like Etpison would win there. Off-island, Ta Belau's organization and the Salii legacy did not seem to hold, or perhaps Etpison was the least known outside Palau. In the Marianas, Remengesau was the overwhelming victor, Tmetuchl a strong second, and Etpison a much weaker third. In Guam, the pattern was repeated, although there the three candidates were closely bunched. But Remengesau's strength off island could not overcome his weakness in Palau. He was out of it.

The off-island vote made the election between Etpison and Tmetuchl extremely close. Finally, all the votes were in. Etpison won by 39 votes. Tmetuchl charged fraud. The Palau Election Commission held up certifying the election results.

The most serious of the Tmetuchl allegations involved a box of votes from Babeldaob, an area of Etpison strength. The box was locked and the Election Commission key could not open the lock. Finally, when the box was broken open, all the votes in it were for Etpison: 70 votes in all. The allegation was that the previous lock had been broken, the votes tampered with, and a new lock put on.

The Election Commission rejected all of the challenges: "It cannot be humanly possible for anyone to tamper with the cast ballots because the inside lock was securely locked, and there was no evidence that tampering occurred." Tmetuchl went to court but his case collapsed.

Etpison won. Ta Belau had succeeded in passing the mantle to its nominee.

Notes

1. Page 177. The quotation is excerpted from Ngiraked's political advertisement.

2. Page 178. *Tmetuchl, like Etpison favored. Washington Pacific Report*, Nov. 15, 1988, p. 1.

3. Page 179. The drama of the compromise and then failure to reach agreement on the Palau Compact legislation was reviewed in D. Cloud, "End-of-Session Tempest Leaves Palau Twisting," *Congressional Quarterly*, Nov. 26, 1988, p. 3398. Walter Surrey, a senior Washington attorney who represented the banks in the IPSECO project, was present in the House gallery and confirmed various details.

4. Page 180. *Etpison won by 39 votes*. K. Ola, "Etpison President by 39 Votes," *Pacific Daily News*, Nov. 11, 1988, p. 1.

5. Page 180. *Tmetuchl went to court*. K. Ola, "Vote Count Protected," *Pacific Daily News*, Nov. 13, 1988, p. 1. "Tmetuchl Challenges Etpison Election in Court," *Washington Pacific Report*, Dec. 1, 1988, p. 4.

21

The GAO Report; The Evaluation of Salii; Political Paralysis in Palau

Ta Belau's triumph—Etpison's succession to the Presidency in January 1989—was a Pyrrhic victory. The power of the presidency was gone. The OEK, with de Lugo's encouragement, had become the strongest branch of government in Palau and exercised its power by bringing the executive branch to a halt. The OEK refused to ratify any of President Etpison's cabinet selections and, by restricting Etpison's budget, refused to permit the president, who was in desperate need of skilled assistance, particularly in English, to hire anyone from outside Palau.

The vice president, Kuniwo Nakamura, rapidly distanced himself from Etpison, positioning himself for his own run for the presidency three years later. He formed a close working relationship with Congressman de Lugo, continuing the anti-Compact stance that had marked his career.

With the Palau executive now divided and weak, the direction unclear, President Etpison appointed a Commission on Future Palau-United States Relations, chaired by Vice President Nakamura, to recommend what to do. The members of the commission were openly anti-Compact and also strongly anti-Salii. Many, such as Governor Uludong and former Speaker Olikong who had testified in the Congress against the Compact and against Salii, had run for president against Etpison as well. Others, such as Roman Bedor, whose father had been killed over the Labor Day holiday in 1987, and Johnson Toribiong, the nephew and counsel to Roman Tmetuchl, Salii's long-time rival, were also identified as opposed to Salii and Compact ratification.

The Palau-United States Future Relations Commission's recommendations, if followed, would have assured that no Compact would ever be approved. First, it rejected any constitutional amendment. Palau would be stuck with the 75 percent requirement. Only the Compact would be changed. The commission then stated that a referendum should be held in 1989. What should be done if 75 percent were not obtained, the almost certain eventuality? The commission's answer: "Nothing. . . . No more referenda." Etpison and Palau were paralyzed.

That is not the way de Lugo told it to all who would listen. He argued that H.R. 175, his legislation, would bring about a 75 percent super-majority at the next referendum. De Lugo misunderstood—intentionally or not—the dynamics of the situation. Two years before, in 1987, with Palau unified under a strong leader and the United States strongly supportive, the pro-Compact forces had obtained 72 percent aye votes. Since Salii's death, the Compact had been hit so hard so many times it was no longer capable of 72 percent in Palau. The people of Palau were beaten. They did not believe a Compact would ever be put into effect no matter how they voted. The weak, divided leadership in Palau—and a more disinterested administration (Berg and Hills, the key figures in the Office of Freely Associated State Affairs in the State Department, were leaving)—could not rouse the Palau electorate for another effort. A hospital, which was basically all that was left in the de Lugo legislation, together with a public auditor and a special prosecutor, was not sufficient to excite the Palau voter. Unsurprisingly, the plebiscite on the Compact in early 1990 resulted in the lowest pro-Compact percentage ever: slightly less than 60 percent in favor of the Compact.

The GAO finally released its report in August 1989. The report, held up for six to eight months after de Lugo indicated he had seen a draft of it, turned out not to be the condemnation of the Salii administration that people had expected. Links between the Salii administration and the killing and intimidation, long assumed by the opposition, were not there. Farrow, de Lugo, and the GAO staff had fought over the language of the report. Farrow and de Lugo had insisted that the conclusion of the International Commission of Jurists' report, that "there has been a breakdown of the rule of law in Palau," should be reaffirmed. The GAO refused.

The GAO examined first the referenda of August 4 and August 21, the referenda on the constitutional amendment and the ratification of the Compact. Were these fair? The GAO concluded that they were. The GAO then investigated the actions of the furloughed workers in July 1987. Were the courts intimidated? Farrow and de Lugo insisted that the GAO reaffirm the ICJ report conclusion. Again, the GAO refused. They arrived at an awkward compromise. GAO would state its own conclusions and then would include, in a rather unusual paragraph, the ICJ conclusion. The GAO stated: "The Chief Justice . . . reluctantly concluded that public confidence in the integrity and impartiality of the judiciary could be maintained only by assigning the case to another judge. . . . [H]is action was motivated by a desire to maintain the court's integrity and not by intimidation, as some compact opponents had alleged." Were the women intimidated? The GAO concluded that they were and for that reason dropped their lawsuit; indeed, they had been pressured into withdrawing their lawsuit. "All 12 women stated that pressure from the furloughed workers and concerns about violence precluded them from continuing the lawsuit."

Interpreting Salii's relationship to the furloughed workers is crucial to any judgment of the man and his presidency. It is not without controversy, and the GAO's review of the activities of the furloughed workers does not totally settle the issue. Based on the evidence, it seems to me that his furloughing of the workers was mandated by a legitimate financial crunch. However, Salii knew, as did all of the political leadership in Palau, that the workers, once furloughed, would be a powerful political force. That was the record of striking general workers in the past. Salii's initial focus was on the OEK, and insofar as the furloughed workers were to become a political force, I believe he expected pressure to be brought on the OEK and the OEK to respond by passing the constitutional Amendment.

Compact opponents and some Palauan politicians argued that the Salii government manipulated the furloughed employees. And there is little doubt that to some degree it did. In August 1987, executive branch officials permitted the furloughed workers committee to attach a notice to the August 7 paycheck of all government employees asking them to participate in the furloughed workers' demonstration at the OEK. Then the notice stated, "Your failure to comply may consequently result in an adverse action against you." In addition to the threats, there were bribes. The chairman of the furloughed workers committee had received checks totaling over $10,000 during August and September 1987 from a Compact-related account administered by President Salii's office. Although Salii denied it, the GAO found that Salii had provided funds and food to other furloughed workers. Salii also had permitted furloughed workers to use government vehicles, including cars, trucks, and a bus, from July through September 1987. And about 20 percent of the furloughed employees continued to receive salaries from U.S. program grants.

Farrow, in discussions with me, made a point of these salary payments. His information was that they were paid to Salii's closest supporters and no one else. There is little doubt that Salii did not just furlough the government workers and then look away. The furloughed workers did take on a structure, and that was encouraged by Salii, who expected, after the strike, to continue to utilize the strikers as the basis of a political party.

Salii kept in close touch with the furloughed workers. He knew what they were doing. On the night of the Bedor Bins killing, Salii was immediately notified by the committee, permitting him to visit Bedor Bins at the hospital and to disperse the Furlough Committee members at the police station. But were these actions of the Furlough Committee ordered by Salii? Had he channelled the pressure of the striking governmental workers in that fashion? There is no evidence that he went that far. Some Palauans feel that initially Salii did orchestrate events but later on the workers splintered, and different leaders urged groups of them this way and that.

The GAO investigators, examining the situation many months later, said in private discussions with me that they felt he never had control; he just thought he did. GAO noted in its report that "program directors or boards decided not to honor the President's request that all nonessential employees be placed on furlough for morale purposes." The GAO found no direct link between Salii and the violence.

With respect to a number of questionable financial transactions by the Salii administration and by Salii himself, no matter how one reads the GAO report, the conclusion is inescapable that many in the Salii government, including, in all likelihood, Salii himself, appeared bent on making a lot of money as a result of their official positions.

Salii signed a number of contracts that were questionable under Palau law, either because they avoided OEK notification or because they avoided required competitive bidding. Salii might well have wanted to avoid the OEK simply in order to get things done. The OEK was rife with backdoor relationships and alliances within Palau to stymie the Salii administration, all destructive of any forward motion by Palau. The bypassing of the competitive bidding requirements is another matter. Avoiding competitive bidding is more efficient. But when combined with paying higher prices than available elsewhere and with informal understandings unrelated to the project, then it is simply corrupt.

Let us review the contracts GAO questioned. The $26 million contract to construct a twenty-two-mile road on Babeldaob Island, signed in August 1987 and subsequently terminated in September 1988 after Salii's death, was questioned by GAO and the Department of the Interior's Office of the Inspector General. Although the project followed competitive bidding procedures, the winners in all likelihood were preselected by including financial provisions in the bid documents that favored the final contractor. The winning bids were substantially higher than those for other road construction on Palau: $1.2 million per mile on this Babeldaob road compared to $800,000 per mile for other projects. Salii himself seemed to have been deeply involved in this project, personally replacing the Minister of Natural Resources as the contracting officer for the road and disregarding the law that required the National Director of Program, Budget and Management to certify the availability of funds. In an unusual action, Palau's Office of the Attorney General reviewed the contract for legal form but did not determine whether the requirement for the certification of funds had been met.

Hard to explain as well was the very large bond deal in the amount of $398 million to finance capital improvement projects in Palau. The Palau bond deal was one of a number of very large Micronesian bond underwritings put together by Matthews and Wright, a small New York investment house. These underwriting agreements paid exorbitant fees to

Matthews and Wright even if the bond proceeds were never used to build anything. In Saipan, the first of these Micronesian Matthews and Wright financings, the promised homes were never built. In Guam, to put the underwriting agreement in place, Matthews and Wright bribed the governor. Was corruption involved in Palau as well? The answers are not certain, but the deal is suspicious. The size of the bond issue was far beyond Palau's needs and the Palau Development Bank Board members were asked to approve the bond issue on extremely short notice.

The key contact point in Palau for the Matthews and Wright deal was Mirando, the stateside adviser and legal counsel to Salii whose power flowed directly from Salii. In the weeks immediately following Judge Hefner's opinion, Mirando had been especially active. Mirando had organized a corporation, Pacific Ventures, on September 11, 1987. On October 16, 1987, in the name of Pacific Ventures, he signed two agreements with Salii. Under the first agreement, Pacific Ventures was given the exclusive right to prepare a "plan for the construction and leaseback of the national capitol of the Republic of Palau." Under the second agreement, Pacific Ventures would produce and distribute Palau coins." (Both contracts were cancelled shortly after Salii's death, before any payments were made.)

At about the same time, on September 30, 1987, Mirando signed a consulting agreement with Salii on matters relating to the Compact while retaining the right to "do business, as a lawyer . . . *without* hinderance or *conflict of interest being at issue*, including providing his service to persons doing business with the Republic of Palau" (emphasis supplied). The fees appear small, $250.00 a month, but the in-kind contributions were substantial: free housing and utilities, automobile transportation, and government per diem for travel outside Palau. Most important, the access to Salii envisioned by the contract was total. Why would Salii enter into agreements like that? What was envisioned for Salii himself by Mirando's contracts?

Standing out in the GAO review, and embarrassing to Salii, was the private housing subsidy. In November 1985, Salii leased a new house where he lived until his death in August 1988. The government of Palau spent over $90,000 renovating the property, of which Salii contributed $20,000. The renovations consisted primarily of changing the interior layout and extending the front of the house. The renovations were for Salii's convenience; they were not for security purposes. It is not clear whether President Salii was entitled to housing under that executive order. But a $70,000 expenditure for personal renovations was improper. Salii seemed to be personally more troubled by this payment. Among island public officials, as in many Third World countries, payments made by foreign contractors in connection with projects that the government wanted anyway are not viewed with the same opprobrium as in the States. But private payments of government funds are unacceptable by any standard.

De Lugo and Farrow used the GAO report not only to examine the Salii administration's actions but to challenge the basic rationale of the Compact itself: its presumed financial benefit. The GAO, at de Lugo's request, included an important financial analysis comparing free association (Compact ratification) with continued trusteeship (Compact rejection). The GAO conclusion: about the same. The Compact was a lot better in the first few years, but the trusteeship would provide greater financial benefits in the later years. It seemed to make little difference whether the Compact was approved or not.

But the GAO analysis was limited. The GAO report discussed U.S. public funds only. Unmentioned was the very favorable effect on private investment, particularly Japanese investment, if the Compact were ratified and Palau's political future settled. Unmentioned as well was the role of the U.S. Congress and the Palau political structure. Continued trusteeship meant funding was dependent on annual Congressional appropriations, and continued trusteeship meant continued Interior Department review of Palau governmental activity. Self-government as a value was lost in the welter of numbers.

Reactions to the GAO report were immediate, strong, and quite varied. De Lugo rushed to give his own spin on the GAO report in a subcommittee press release. First, a partisan attack: "The Reagan Administration abdicated its responsibilities in Palau. . . . It did not know of many problems it should have and it did not act or act effectively when it did know of problems." Then a blow to Salii. "The late President Lazarus Salii of Palau and a group of associates (often secretly) negotiated a number of other questionable, ill-advised, and, possibly, illegal deals." And finally, self-congratulations on the de Lugo legislation, which "GAO's independent findings fully justify." Pointedly, the subcommittee set out a continuing task for itself and the Department of the Interior: to help "Palau to tackle problems or by combatting problems itself where Palau cannot do so alone for so long as Palau's transition to self-government continues."

The Senate committee was furious at the GAO report. The testimony before Senator Johnston, and indeed, the testimony before Solarz's committee in the House, was never once mentioned in the GAO report. At these hearings, in public view, the charges of the anti-Salii and anti-Compact forces were aired and the witnesses cross-examined. Surely, that testimony should have been brought to bear on the investigation.

The Palau government responded to the GAO report in a joint statement by President Etpison and the OEK leaders, Senate President Koshiba and Speaker Kyota. The statement followed the de Lugo party line, attacking not only the Salii administration but U.S. officials who had kept their distance: "It is clear from the report that the uncertainty of our democracy and the pending Compact process allowed some in Palau to abuse the public trust for their own personal gain and some United States officials to adopt an ill-conceived policy of ignoring problems and tolerating abuses in Palau." They, too, congratulated themselves on what they had done so far: "We have already undertaken actions to begin to meet some of these problems. For example, the public auditor, federal programs coordinator and tax advisor have been appointed; services have been made subject to competitive bidding; a new procurement manual will be completed by October." But they were Palauan. Even now there was some pride. They argued for rapid passage of the Compact: "One fundamental lesson from this report is that the political status of Palau cannot be allowed to remain perpetually in limbo."

They had to say that. It was hopeless, of course. They knew that. They knew where they wanted to go. It was just that they no longer could see a way to get there.

Notes

1. Page 182. *Only the Compact would be changed*. Committee on Future Palau-United States Relations, *Report*, June 1989, Position Statement, p. 2.

2. Page 182. *"No more referenda." Ibid*, p. 40.

3. Page 182. On the de Lugo legislation generally, see J. Davidoff, "Islands' Quest for Autonomy Making Headway on Hill," *Congressional Quarterly*, Aug. 19, 1989, p. 2184.

4. Page 182. *"The plebiscite on the Compact in early 1990."* "Palau Compact Vote Falls Short for the Seventh Time," *Washington Pacific Report*, no. 10, Feb. 15, 1990, p. 1.

5. Page 184. The quotes are from GAO, *U.S. Trust Territory: Issues Associated with Palau's Transition to Self-Government, A Report to Congressional Requesters* (1989) and GAO, *U.S. Trust Territory: Issues Associated with Palau's Transition to Self-Government, a Supplemental Report to Congressional Requesters* (1989).

6. Page 184. *Salii himself seemed to have been*. Office of the Inspector General, *Audit Report: Babelthuap Road Projects, Republic of Palau*, (Washington, D.C.: Department of the Interior, May 1989), p. 10.

7. Page 184. *Hard to explain*. In addition to the GAO, a number of newspapers examined the Matthews and Wright actions in great detail. See, e.g., Goodman and Demick, "Suspect Bond Issues Put Communities in a Bind," *The Philadelphia Inquirer*, June 29, 1987, p. 1.; D. J. Shea, "Palau Calls a Mammoth Bond Issue, But its Not Likely to Get an Answer" *The Bond Buyer*, Nov. 5, 1987.

Bedor Bins's Murderers Named; Remeliik Assassins Revealed

In 1989, with Palau helpless and the new Bush administration uncertain how to proceed, all initiative shifted to the U.S. Congress. Solarz and Johnston effectively withdrew from the playing field. Without a Palau or administration initiative on the Compact, they could do nothing. Only de Lugo and Farrow had a vision for Palau which did not include Compact ratification.

They rapidly resurrected the de Lugo bill that had failed in the last Congress. The bill became law on December 12, 1989. De Lugo and Farrow had worn down the administration, Senator Johnston, and Congressman Solarz, but at a price paid by Palau. To get the special prosecutor and special public auditor, de Lugo and Farrow agreed to the elimination of almost all of the money promised Palau in the bill as originally introduced. A straitened budget stripped the benefits from that legislation as the Bush administration proved no more generous than the Reagan administration before it. What remained in the de Lugo bill was $9 million for a hospital and permission to use Compact funds to pay the IPSECO debt. Johnston and Solarz, on the other hand, had finally gotten Congress to approve the Palau Compact "subject to . . . a referendum . . . free from any legal challenge." In sum, the Compact had finally been approved by the U.S. Congress. Now Palau only had to agree to it.

De Lugo and Farrow were betting heavily on the special prosecutor to get Palau's house once more in order. It was a view shared by the newly elected OEK leadership. That leadership was not ready to give the laurels of Compact ratification to the new Palau administration, headed by Etpison, an ally of Salii. Those who had opposed Salii looked for public approbation, appointing a Joint Investigative Committee on Police Practices in September 1989 to prepare a report. Others sought more: to heal the open wounds in

Palauan society as a result of the Bedor Bins killing by a full investigation of what happened.

That report, which was not published until February 1991, examined the furlough period, reemphasizing the findings of the GAO report. It linked, as did Judge Hefner, the police assistance in settling the lawsuit of the women to police intimidation.

Charges were made by numerous witnesses that a police officer, in uniform, accompanied a group of furloughed workers door-to-door, *intimidating and threatening anti-Compact citizens*, and that policemen ran errands in police vehicles for the Furlough Committee, which was at the time camped outside the OEK building.

More seriously, law enforcement officers were accused of "turning a blind eye" to criminal acts, if not actually participating in them. . . . No police protection was provided to anti-Compact people in spite of numerous death threats. (Emphasis supplied)

By focusing on more than just the police role in the women's lawsuit but on police misconduct in general, the OEK was going beyond the actions of the Salii administration to the Police Department as an institution and making a valuable contribution to the restoration of public confidence in its own police. The report faulted the investigation of the Bedor Bins murder, the firebombing of Gabriela Ngirmang's home, and the Olikong drive-by shooting. "Critical evidence in these cases was not gathered or was treated in a casual manner. Neither the Bureau of Public Safety nor the Attorney General's Office has aggressively pursued these cases in over three years because of politics."

Finally, after a year and a half, on May 23, 1991, the Assistant Secretary of the Interior for Territorial and International Affairs appointed David Webster as the interim special prosecutor for Palau. Webster had some Micronesian experience, having served as assistant attorney general in the Federated States of Micronesia the year before. To come into a society of political intrigue and clan loyalties going back generations without previous exposure and without a knowledge of Palauan seemed a very long shot. Despite the odds and the skeptics, within a year his appointment brought results.

On March 4, 1992, Webster announced the arrest of four men for the murder of Bedor Bins. Paul Ueki, the alleged gunman, had been convicted in the Olikong drive-by shooting. His accomplices were furloughed government employees. If they were convicted, the open wounds from the furlough period might heal and the de Lugo and Farrow insistence on the special prosecutor would be justified.

But there was to be more. The Remeliik assassination was no longer an issue in Washington—if it ever had been. Washington bureaucracy focused on the Compact and, to a lesser extent, on immediate Palauan social service needs. It accepted the Remeliik assassination as one more example—albeit extreme—of Palauan political machinations. The Remeliik assassination case bemused officials in Washington without engaging them. In Palau, the issue was regarded differently. Most saw it as a political embarrassment that the people of Palau should put behind them. In the Salii and Remengesau administrations the official position was that the culprits had been discovered, arrested, tried, convicted, and then let go by the appellate court. As far as I could tell, most people in Palau agreed with that view. The seamy record of those tried gave credence to that theory. Further, now that the Remeliik assassination case and Compact ratification were separate issues, the ACLU and their liberal allies no longer were interested. Only Tmetuchl did not relent, continuing to argue the innocence of the three who had been tried and convicted of the crime. His views were generally discounted. After all, he was fighting for his son.

Less than a month after the arrest of the suspects in the murder of Bedor Bins, Webster, the special prosecutor, announced his solution to the mystery of who killed President Remeliik. The solution evolved accidently and very slowly. Heinrick Ngewakl was a brutal man, terrorizing his children and wife, regularly administering terrible beatings to them. Bearing the greatest brunt of this man's brutality was his step-son, the mentally disturbed Sulial Heinrick. After a particularly bad beating of his mother and brother, Sulial couldn't take it any more. He took a rifle and shot and killed his step-father, Ngewakl. In prison, Sulial became increasingly angry. He was all but forgotten. He had been told that his family would bring him toilet articles, a radio, and a tape recorder, but nobody ever came. Angry, Sulial asked to see the head of the Criminal Investigation Division in Palau, Besure Kanai. "I want to talk to him about the killing of the president. I was there when he was killed."

"Who did it?"

"Patrick Ramarii."

Kanai was not sure he believed it. Prisoners are all too ready with stories about someone else's misdeeds. It was the only leverage they had. Sulial had been certified as mentally ill. Ramarii was constantly in need of money, but was that sufficient to cause him to kill the President? He seemed a contented enough young man who spent his time hunting and fishing. Ramarii was now living in Saipan. Kanai had no money to travel to Saipan to interview him. Kanai decided that when Ramarii returned to Palau, he would question him. It could wait. Probably nothing to Sulial's story. Sulial was returned to prison.

A few weeks later, an owner of a general trade store approached Kanai. Patrick Ramarii had bought an amazing amount of goods and charged them to John O. Ngiraked, including a boat, a truck, and a motorcycle. Why should Ngiraked buy such expensive things for Ramarii? "You should look into that." Kanai agreed. He would talk to Ramarii as soon as he returned from Saipan. There was still no urgency about the investigation.

A bit later, Ramarii and his pregnant wife attended a party. A young man approached her, jested about her and her baby, touched her hand and left. It was a harmless flirtation, perhaps not even that. Ramarii viewed it differently. He was immediately suspicious. "What was that about?" he asked her on the way home. She said it was nothing. Ramarii, half-drunk, exploded. He beat her unmercifully with bamboo canes. When he was through, she was in the hospital. He was in prison in Palau. Ramarii could be questioned at last.

Kanai repeated to Ramarii what Sulial had told him. Ramarii denied everything. The purchases and gifts by Ngiraked he explained as family obligations. (Ramarii was Ngiraked's cousin through adoption.) Ramarii was returned to prison. But Ramarii, after the questioning, was less sure of his stance, less confident of what was going on. Suddenly, Ramarii's bond was increased. Ramarii's suspicions grew. Why had Ngiraked allowed the bond increase? Ramarii needed Ngiraked, but he distrusted him. Perhaps Ngiraked would lay the blame on him alone. He felt unsafe in jail guarded by policemen loyal to Ngiraked. Ramarii brooded, fearful of the unknown going on outside the prison. How much had Sulial told? Why? Finally, he acted. Ramarii asked to talk to the special prosecutor or investigators once more. There, after an initial hesitation, Ramarii confessed. He was the gunman. He had killed President Remeliik.

Ramarii fingered, as the man behind the Remeliik assassination conspiracy, John O. Ngiraked, the Minister of State in the Salii administration and a prominent politician who had run for president in the last Palau election. In exchange, Ramarii was allowed to plead down to a ten-year sentence. Ramarii implicated not only Ngiraked but also Emerita Kerradel, Ngiraked's second wife, a forty-year-old mother of four and a Koror businesswoman; the late Heinrick Ngewakl; and Ngewakl's twenty-eight-year-old step-son, Sulial Heinrick. Sulial, like Ramarii, was already in prison charged with the killing of his stepfather, Ngewakl.

The weakness in the Ramarii/Ngewakl/Ngiraked thesis was the absence of a motive. The case was built upon Ngiraked's ambition to become president of Palau. But that seemed unlikely. Vice President Oiterong was the popular heir apparent to Remeliik. And, as it turned out, Ngiraked did not even run in the election to succeed Remeliik. Ngiraked—who denied any involvement in the Remeliik assassination—charged that Ramarii was offered $100,000 to say that Ngiraked plotted the death of Remeliik as part of a scheme to clear the Tmetuchl name. In Palau, Webster's announcement of Ngiraked's role in Remeliik's assassination was greeted with skepticism. Ngiraked was not well-liked, and many of his deals were questioned. But a murder based on presidential ambition was a bit hard to swallow. People waited for the evidence.

The Bedor Bins murder case proceeded to trial first. The story, as the prosecution told it, was that on September 3, 1987, the Furlough Committee rented from Noboru King's Rental Car Company a 1982 Mitsubishi Colt hatchback four-door red sedan. Furlough Committee members boasted of what they were going to do. The police were told that a little before twelve o'clock they were going to shut off the power, kill Roman Bedor, set off a bomb at Ngirmang's house, and make a fire somewhere. The lieutenant in charge responded, "Never mind, these guys cannot do this; they are scared."

The special prosecutor's case was based on piecing together the testimony of several witnesses to prove the identity of the murderers. Thus, one witness saw Paul Ueki wearing Levi jeans, shirtless but holding a white shirt. His comrades wore army-type camouflage uniforms, which had become the uniform of the Furlough Committee. Others saw the foursome in a red Mitsubishi sedan parked near the OEK building shortly before the power shut off in Koror. Still another witness said that shortly after the power shut off, he saw a red Mitsubishi sedan in front of Bedor's law office. He also saw a shirtless person wearing Levi-type jeans and with a white shirt wrapped around his head. That person shot Bins twice.

Bedor Bins's younger son, Masao, ran from the house to help his staggering father. He saw the red Mitsubishi Colt sedan speeding away from the scene. Peter Sugiyama was standing outside in the front driveway near his store as the red car left the Bedor Bins driveway and entered the main highway going toward Koror. A shot was fired at Sugiyama that went over his head. The car had no license plate. Sugiyama drove after it and found the car, the hood still hot to the touch, parked at the OEK building, which served as the informal headquarters for the Furlough Committee.

Two police officers saw the suspects' red Mitsubishi sedan speeding away from the Bedor Bins home while they were on their way there after the shooting. The police officers made a U-turn and chased the car, but it got away. They identified Radis Modelchel as the driver, with Ueki, Elias Ngiratkakl, and a fourth person as passengers. At the OEK, another witness saw Gandhi Baules, the fourth person, leave the car and talk to the Furlough Committee leaders. A little while later the red car left with the accused foursome inside. One headlight was out. The car was stopped for the headlight violation. The detective saw the license plate 1588 on the front seat.

The story was cohesive, but at key points the identification was not certain. After over six weeks and more than forty witnesses, Justice Sutton directed an acquittal of all four defendants on the murder charge on the grounds that the identification was too vague and legally insufficient.

Although technically the murder of Bedor Bins remained open, the indictment and trial seemed to satisfy the Palauan populace and heal the sore in Palau society. Nevertheless, Judge Sutton's decision to acquit the defendants of the murder charge in the Bedor Bins killing emphasized once more the distance between the popular will of the people of Palau and the views of the off-island judiciary. The local newspaper, in a thoughtful editorial, stated: "Without passing judgment on the sincerity and dedication of judicial and law enforcement officers in upholding the rule of law, we believe that the exoneration of the suspects in the [Bedor Bins] killing sadly bespeaks the failure of our criminal justice system. For to say the least, the acquittal of the suspects drives home the message that one can commit a dastardly crime and still go free."

Inside Palau many felt that the Bedor Bins case had been badly prepared. The acquittal was somewhat academic; some of the defendants would be convicted of lesser offenses related to the Olikong drive-by shooting. But it was an ominous foreshadowing. The Remeliik assassination was a murder case, which would be even more difficult for the prosecution to win.

Webster, unbeknownst to the public, may have already critically damaged the Remeliik assassination case. Statements by witnesses to policemen and other investigators—prior to trial—must be preserved and made available to the defense. The purpose is to assure that the key witnesses do not doctor their testimony later on. So important are these preliminary statements that if the police do not provide them on demand, the witnesses' testimony may be stricken.

The key witness was, of course, Ramarii, the self-confessed murderer. His taped confession was the basis of the prosecution. The taped confession would have to be given to the defense, otherwise Ramarii's testimony, perhaps, could not be used at all. Without Ramarii's testimony, the prosecution had no case.

Webster had been off-island during the initial, key questioning of Ramarii. On his return, his key staff—Robert Canfield, a former Nevada State policeman, and two officers from the Palau Criminal Investigation Division, Augustino Blailes and Valentine Tirso—played him the tape. Webster couldn't make it out. The tape was scratchy; much of the talk was in Palauan. "You can throw it away. I'm going to depose Ramarii anyway," he told them. They knew better. Canfield hid the tape in his drawer. It would still be available.

Evidence of this character in the most significant case in Palau history couldn't be kept secret. Inevitably, police security broke down. Information about the tape was leaked. At a preliminary hearing, Webster learned of it. He returned to his office in fury. He had told the staff to destroy the tape. Why had it not been destroyed? "Do it now," he ordered. The tape was destroyed. Ramarii's testimony, the critical testimony in the case, was now at risk.

With the Bedor Bins case dismissed and the Ngiraked trial for the Remeliik assassination about to begin, the Department of Interior suddenly fired Webster, the interim special prosecutor. Webster had concealed the fact that in December 1988 the state of Florida had disciplined him and suspended him from the bar for 18 months.

Thrashing about for a substitute, Palau got lucky. The Department of Justice sent a powerhouse, an exceptionally experienced hand, Jerry Massie, from its Terrorism and Violent Crime Section. The Remeliik assassination case would be prepared carefully, without press leaks or congressional interference.

Massie is black. For the first time in Palauan history, the U.S. government would be represented on island by a man of color. Still, Palau had to be shown. Was Ngiraked, indeed, the master conspirator behind the Remeliik assassination?

The trial lasted four months, the longest trial in Micronesian history. The government alone submitted approximately one hundred exhibits and called seventy-five witnesses. The evidence began to take shape and to persuade. The key witness was Patrick Ramarii, the self-confessed killer of Remeliik and a cousin by adoption of John O. Ngiraked. Since Ramarii had made a deal to reduce his sentence, his credibility was suspect. However, his knowledge of the details of the murder bolstered his stature.

As Ramarii and prosecution witnesses told it, some weeks before the assassination, Heinrick told Ramarii: "Big Brother will be asking something of you." A few weeks later, Ngiraked and Emerita (Ngiraked's second wife-to-be) called Ramarii to meet with them in Heinrick's house. Ngiraked explained his need in financial terms. "The government has taken the Loveboat from me."

The Loveboat, anchored in Malakal, was to be a pleasure yacht. Although the yacht was owned by Hong Kong businessmen, Ngiraked had an important stake in the vessel. He had sold his partners on his ability to ensure that the Loveboat could operate freely in Palau, so that in 1985 it would provide extended tourist voyages throughout the islands of Palau. But Remeliik had embarrassed him. Remeliik had rejected Ngiraked's personal plea and then seized the Loveboat when it continued to harbor in Babeldaob without permission. More than presidential ambition was involved. Ngiraked had just lost the governorship of Ngaraard State. Ngiraked's financial life rested on the Loveboat. The rejection by Remeliik of Ngiraked's plea added a bitter personal aspect to the Ngiraked-Remeliik relationship. Ngiraked and Emerita agreed to pay Ramarii $10,000 after the murder was committed and $1 million if Ngiraked, as a result, became president of Palau. Some political motivation was there as well.

"Patrick, if you do this for us you will be out of hunting and fishing. Once you do it you can come to our house forever," Emerita said.

"Who will do this with me?" Ramarii asked.

"Heinrick Ngewakl," responded Ngiraked.

Ramarii did not like that. "I want to pick the assistant. How about Sulial?"

Heinrick was dangerous. He didn't trust Heinrick.

Heinrick called Sulial into the meeting and Heinrick asked Sulial if he would do this thing.

"What thing?"

"Kill the president." Sulial's head dropped. Sulial was terrified of Heinrick. He had no choice. He said, "Yes."

"The president comes and goes at night," Ngiraked told them. "Heinrick has a boat that can take you away."

They all clasped hands. "We are all brothers. We are all seeds from the same mother."

As they departed, Ramarii said to Heinrick, "You must tell me when the time is right."

On Friday, the 28th, Heinrick told Ramarii that the time was right. That night they would kill the president. The murderers took the boat to T-dock. Heinrick and his younger son, Oscar, stayed with the boat. From there Ngiraked, Sulial, and Ramarii went to Remeliik's home at Topside. But they were too late when they reached Topside. Remeliik was already home. The plan was put off until the next day, Saturday. The next day, in the late afternoon, the scenario was replayed. Ngiraked and his wife had an engagement elsewhere, so Heinrick drove the assassins, Ramarii and Sulial, from the boat dock to Topside.

Sulial and Ramarii took up their positions, crouching behind the large bushes that bordered the driveway. They waited.

Remeliik arrived early Sunday morning. When he opened the car door, he heard the click of a rifle trigger. Remeliik raced around the front of the car to the entrance of the house. Ramarii leaped over the car and cut him off. They wrestled. Ramarii was too strong for the president. He forced Remeliik away from him. The president could not keep his balance. Ramarii quickly raised his carbine and fired. The bullet struck the president in the upper leg. He tumbled down the slope. Ramarii fired three more shots and killed him. Sulial was astonished at what had occurred. He had not envisioned this. He was paralyzed, uncertain what to do. Ramarii dragged Sulial by his belt back to the boat. Heinrick ferried them back to Babeldaob, where Ramarii, at Heinrick's house, disassembled the carbine and later disposed of it.

The defense challenged Ramarii's story. They asked to hear the tape, to hear the story as it was told the first time, before Ramarii had thought about it and before the prosecution had discussed it with him. Of course, the prosecution did not have the tape. It had been destroyed. The defense moved to strike all of the Ramarii testimony. Without that testimony, the prosecution case would collapse.

Judge Sutton was presiding over the case. His rulings in other major cases all had been against the Palau government: the first Remeliik assassination case, the Compact case of *Fritz v. Salii* that I had argued, and, just recently, the Bedor Bins murder case. The defense felt that Judge

Sutton was feeling the pressure. After dismissing the Bedor Bins murder case, it would be extremely difficult for him to throw out this case too. Judge Sutton ruled that Ramarii's testimony could be admitted but he would allow broad cross-examination focusing on the missing testimony.

At the trial, Oscar confirmed key parts of Ramarii's story. Oscar testified that he had seen a .30-caliber carbine at his house with a clip of ammunition. He had, indeed, been in the boat, and saw Ramarii and Sulial come into the boat and throw the carbine on the bottom of the boat. Other witnesses also confirmed the story. An old fisherman saw two figures that night wading into the water. And a prison convict told the court that Heinrick had approached him about killing Remeliik. Oscar said Heinrick told him to say they were home that night.

Despite all of this testimony, the most damaging evidence against Ngiraked and his wife was the fact that for over a year following the murder of Remeliik, Ngiraked paid Ramarii thousands of dollars in cash and gave him large gifts. Defendants claimed that the gifts carried out Palauan custom required by the relationship between Ngiraked and Ramarii, and were not payment for the killing of President Remeliik. After all, Ramarii had lived with Ngiraked. The defense showed that Ngiraked gave many gifts to Ramarii even before the murder.

In Palau, popular sentiment had changed. The testimony had been persuasive. At the end of the trial, many, perhaps most, Palauans believed Ngiraked had done it. Yet what of the burgundy pickup truck seen by Remeliik's daughter, Patricia, outside their home? What was it doing there? How did it fit in with the Ngiraked conspiracy?

Ngiraked had threatened Ramarii and told him that if he failed he would have people there to punish him. Perhaps Ngiraked was not bluffing. Another theory has it that there were two sets of conspirators and would-be assassins that night. Ngiraked's group attacked first. Massie believed that. And then there was a third possibility: perhaps, Patricia was mistaken.

Ngiraked was found guilty. He and his wife were sentenced to life in prison. Even those convinced of Ngiraked's guilt were shocked at the life sentence given to Emerita. She was a mother with two young children, and her involvement was marginal. To the defense, the sentence demonstrated the pressure Judge Sutton was feeling.

Ngiraked continued to protest his innocence: "We are victims of political maneuvering."

Notes

1. Page 189. *The bill became law on December 12, 1989.* Public Law 101-219, *Implementation of Compact of Free Association with Palau,* 103 Stat. 1870, Dec. 12, 1989.

2. Page 190. *That report, which was not published until February.* OEK Joint

Investigative Committee on Police Practices, *Report to the OEK*, Feb. 1991, p. 5.

3. Page 190. *By focussing on more than just the police role.* Joint Investigative Committee on Police Practices, *Report to the OEK*. Feb. 1991, pp. 5-6.

4. Page 192. *Ramarii fingered as the man behind.* "Alleged Assassin Talks," *Pacific Daily News*, April 21, 1992.

5. Page 192. *Ngiraked—who denied any involvement.* "Alleged Assassin Says Cousin Lied," *Pacific Daily News*, April 3, 1992.

6. Page 193. *Thus, one witness saw Paul Ueki wearing.* "Bedor Murder Suspects Acquitted," *Tia Belau*, June 28, 1992, pp. 1,7.

7. Page 193. *Justice Sutton directed. Republic of Palau v. Ueki et al.*, Criminal Case #97-92 (June 9, 1992), dismissed the suit against Ueki. Subsequently, on similar grounds, the suit was dismissed against the other defendants. F. Whaley, "Bedor Murder Suspects Acquitted," *Pacific Daily News*, June 29, 1992, p. 3.

8. Page 193. *Judge Sutton's decision to acquit.* Commentary, *Tia Belau*, June 28, 1992, p. 6. The Remeliik assassination case was linked in the public mind to the Bedor Bins killing. Ibid.

9. Page 194. *Department of the Interior suddenly fired Webster.* "Palau Fires Special Prosecutor," *Pacific Daily News*, Sept. 20, 1992, p. 1.

10. Page 195. For a profile of Jerome Massie, see "Prosecutor Conviction of Ngiraked Was a Sound One," *Pacific Daily News*, May 2, 1993, p. 3.

11. Page 195. *The government has taken the Loveboat.* W. Higuchi, "Love Boat Docks in Palau Harbor," *Pacific Daily News*, Nov. 25, 1984, p. 1. The boat's official name was the Aesarea. The Loveboat was what Palauans called it.

12. Page 195-196. At various points in this chapter there is quoted dialogue. I was unable to talk to Webster and, therefore, quotes attributed to him about the tapes are based on second-hand comments. They may be overdramatic. Further, since the transcript for the trial was unavailable at the time of the writing of this book, I have relied on conversations about the testimony with Jerome Massie, the public prosecutor, and Kevin Kirk, defense counsel for Ngiraked, and then reconstructed the dialogue.

13. Page 197. *Ngiraked was found guilty. Palau v. Ramarii, Heinrick, Ngiraked and Kerradel*, Criminal Case No. 114-92, Findings of Fact and Decisions After Trial (Palau Sup. Ct., April 29, 1993); F. Whaley, "Milestone in Long Assassination Story," *Pacific Daily News*, April 30, 1993, p. 4.

14. Page 197. *Were sentenced to life in prison.* "Assassin and Wife Sent to Prison for Life," *Pacific Daily News*, June 15, 1993, p. 1.

15. Page 197. *Ngiraked continued to protest.* F. Whaley, "Ngiraked Found Guilty," *Pacific Daily News*, April 30, 1993.

23

At Last: Ratification of the Compact; New Lawsuits are Filed

The arrest and trial of the killers of Bedor Bins and President Remeliik initially had no impact on Compact ratification. The OEK continued to seek out and investigate the wrongdoing of the Salii administration. Until that was done, the Compact had to wait. Etpison was too weak to overcome this OEK opposition. In Washington, the Administration, without pressure from Palau, could do little.

At the end of 1990, the United States requested that the Security Council terminate its trusteeship responsibilities with respect to the Northern Marianas, the Federated States of Micronesia, and the Marshall Islands. The termination resolution, almost universally praised in the Pacific and in Micronesia, passed the Security Council 14-1, with only Cuba in opposition. Palau remained the last trusteeship in the world.

The administration's attitude toward Palau had changed. After twenty-five years, the U.S. government was tired of negotiating with Palau. Palau's military value after the collapse of the Soviet Union and the Communist empire, even as part of a strategy of denial, was very small. Impatient, the State Department leaked a cable suggesting the United States should unilaterally terminate the trusteeship and simply declare Palau independent. De Lugo and Farrow assured the Palauans that they would not permit this. But the Palauans worried; unilateral termination terrified them. The U.S. offer of the Compact might not stay out there forever. It was the ever-present, dangerous U.S. hole card. One could debate refinements of the Compact forever, but there was no debate that $400 million under the Compact was better than nothing.

On May 2, 1991, the House Interior and Insular Affairs Committee held hearings to see how things were going in Palau. President Etpison and the OEK leadership testified that the islands were now unified and needed only modest changes in the Compact to finally get it ratified. Congressman de Lugo and Farrow said nothing. Neither Senator Johnston, Congressman Solarz, nor their aides would even meet with the Palauans.

A constitutional amendment could be presented to the people to be voted upon either by OEK legislation or by the people directly, by a petition. Salii had tried the OEK route. It failed because the Supreme Court held that the amendment needed a three-fourths vote of the OEK, and it did not get that. One could get around that requirement by using a popular initiative, a petition signed by 25 percent of the voters. That would do as well. Before his indictment, Ngiraked circulated a petition to amend the Constitution so that the Compact might be approved by a majority vote. By fax, he consulted with me on the precise language.

The Ibedul reverted to his anti-Compact stance and in April 1992 sued to delay the vote on the constitutional amendment. His argument was that the OEK had not passed legislation to set forth how the petition method would work. If the Ibedul's position was correct, it meant the OEK could prevent the people from amending the Constitution by doing nothing. That couldn't be right.

Yet the question remained. How did a constitutional amendment initiated by popular initiative really work? Some OEK action was desirable. The trial court, Chief Justice Arthur Ngiraklsong, engaged in the wisdom of Solomon. He delayed the vote until the general election in November 1992, as the Ibedul asked, to give the OEK time to legislate. But if the OEK did not legislate, he would set the ground rules.

The Ngiraklsong decision created a problem for the OEK members. They were ambivalent on the Compact. They had long opposed the Compact's ratification because of their fear of the power to be gained by the president, who would preside over the Compact's inauguration. But was this alone what delayed the OEK ratification? If so, those dangers were less now. Salii and Tmetuchl, the strong men of the past, were outside the political fray. Etpison and Nakamura were healers who sought reconciliation, not political control. (Etpison's close association with Salii, perhaps, prevented him from playing a healing role as much as he would have wished.)

In August, the OEK developed its own compromise constitutional amendment legislation. First, delay the vote until the general election in November 1992. Unless Etpison won—which very doubtful—he would not benefit from the constitutional amendment. Second, the OEK added a catch-22. The plebiscite on final ratification of the Compact by majority vote should not be held "until after the Republic of Palau has received a favorable response from the United States on the requested modifications to the Compact of Free Association."

At the general election, the constitutional amendment was approved. Only a majority vote now would be required for Compact ratification. But the Compact would not be approved if the United States did not approve

Palau's "requested modifications." Thus, even after the constitutional amendment, business would go on pretty much as usual. More, perhaps endless, negotiations would follow.

And then a sudden favorable turn. The 1992 November elections, both in Palau and the United States, brought to the fore new faces detached from the Remeliik and Salii administrations. In Palau, Etpison and Vice President Nakamura announced their candidacy for the presidency quite early. After long reflection, Tmetuchl chose not to run for the presidency. Johnson Toribiong, his nephew and counsel, ran instead. Toribiong's nationalist message and his own intellectual brilliance excited the young. His closeness to Tmetuchl may have damaged him. Etpison lost in the primary and then swung his support to Nakamura. Toribiong lost a very close election to Nakamura. Etpison finished well back.

The new president, Kuniwo Nakamura, one of the younger brothers of the former chief justice, came from a remarkable family. After World War II, his Japanese father had been required to leave the island, but unlike many Japanese men, he had taken his wife and eight children back to Japan with him. Five years later, in 1951, he arranged to operate a shipping line in Palau and gained permission from the U.S. authorities to relocate to Palau with his family once more. When Kuniwo Nakamura returned to Palau, he was eight years old, without any knowledge of English. He learned English, so he now speaks it fluently. Nakamura had opposed the Compact from the beginning. His older brother was the author of the nuclear ban at the Palau Constitutional Convention. The Compact could now be approved by a majority vote if "modifications" were obtained. What would Nakamura do?

The U.S. Congress changed as well. Congressman Morris Udall, chairman of the House Interior and Insular Affairs Committee, had pretty much given de Lugo and Farrow free rein. Udall retired at the end of 1992, drained by his struggle with Parkinson's disease. Congressman George Miller, former head of the House Education and Labor Committee, was appointed in his place. Miller brought enormous energy and a strikingly different vision of the U.S. role in the territories. De Lugo and Farrow viewed the territories as struggling, developmental governments constantly needing U.S. assistance. Miller made no such allowance. He made the same demands on island governments as he would on state governments.

Miller's first exposure to the territories was to a series of territorial governmental scandals: Samoa (padding of payrolls), the Virgin Islands (questionable procurement practices), and the Northern Mariana Islands (abuse of foreign workers). De Lugo and Farrow had tried to protect the island politicians and their infant governments, explaining away the improprieties as the natural result of new governments. Miller was appalled. Miller viewed de Lugo's softer approach not as sympathetic to the islands' developing institutions but as a cover-up. Miller's displeasure with de Lugo and Farrow was open. There were rumors Miller was going to abolish the subcommittee altogether.

Miller's attitude was reflected in a different view of the Compact. De Lugo and Farrow had taken strong positions challenging an international role for the Freely Associated States of the Federated States of Micronesia and the Marshalls. De Lugo and Farrow sought a strong review role for the United States over the FSM and the Marshalls. Miller was less interested in holding on. As far as he was concerned, the Compact of Free Association meant independence with as much international stature as other countries were willing to accord them. Our State Department and the international community readily accepted these Freely Associated States, according them independent status in almost all respects. Miller had no problems with that.

In short, the OEK could no longer rely on de Lugo and Farrow to help them in the OEK's continual fight with Palau's president. Power was returning to the Palau presidency. The opportunity might be there to ratify the Compact if Nakamura were to act, and if Palau ratified the Compact, it would mean independence.

Shortly after Nakamura took office on January 28, 1993, he appointed an Advisory Review Committee to recommend action on the Compact to meet the OEK request for modifications. The seven-member committee was young. A new generation would decide what to do about the Compact. Two members of the committee, like the president himself, were linked to the past opposition to the Compact: Roman Bedor, whose father, Bedor Bins, had been killed on Labor Day in 1987, and Kaleb Udui, Jr., whose father had insisted on removal of the words "with prejudice" in the settlement agreement with Salii. Bedor was related to President Nakamura by marriage. Perhaps that had helped. Nakamura thought it did. In any event, the Committee's report was unanimous and positive on the Compact. The Advisory Review Committee recommended ratification subject to a number of changes: (1) the United States should agree to pay the costs of cleaning up any nuclear damage by the United States to Palau's environment, (2) limit land for U.S. military purposes to the Malakal and Airai sites, (3) reduction of the fifty-year term in the Compact to fifteen years, and (4) continuation of Palau's eligibility for U.S. federal programs under the Compact. Nakamura reversed his stand. He proposed approval of the Compact with the modifications. The State Department decided to give it one more chance. As long as it did not mean a return of the Compact to the Congress, State would see what it could do.

For the first time, the United States agreed in writing to take no land other than the Malakal and Airai airports. The United States would treat a nuclear accident as if it had occurred in U.S. territorial waters. In short, the United States would be responsible for clean-up and damages. The United States would not go back to fifteen years after it had, at Palau's initiative and with congressional approval, extended it to fifty. As for the federal program, it would give Palau what the FSM and the Marshalls got